OTHER MEN'S
SONS

MICHAEL ROWE

OTHER MEN'S SONS

Cormorant Books

Canada Council   Conseil des Arts
for the Arts   du Canada

The publisher gratefully acknowledges the support of the
Canada Council for the Arts and the Ontario Arts Council
for its publishing program. We acknowledge the financial support
of the Government of Canada through the Book Publishing
Industry Development Program (BPIDP) for our publishing activities.

Printed and bound in Canada

LIBRARY AND ARCHIVES CANADA CATALOGUING IN PUBLICATION

Rowe, Michael, 1962–
Other men's sons / Michael Rowe.

ISBN 978-1-897151-01-3

1. Gay men. 1. Title.

HQ76.R684 2007   306.76'62   C2006-901863-4

Cover design: Angel Guerra/Archetype
Interior design: Tannice Goddard, Soul Oasis Networking
Cover image: "The Eyes of a Child", 2000, acrylic on canvas,
36" x 48" © Steve Walker. Used by permission of the artist.
Printer: Marquis

CORMORANT BOOKS INC.
215 SPADINA AVENUE, STUDIO 230, TORONTO, ON CANADA M5T 2C7
WWW.CORMORANTBOOKS.COM

For David Anderson

To live is to battle with trolls in the vaults of the heart and mind;
to write, that is to sit in judgement over oneself.

— IBSEN

Contents

*M*irrors

Introduction

GOING ON THE WELL-PROMULGATED theory that most readers justifiably don't bother to read long-winded and largely self-serving author introductions, I'm going to be as brief as I possibly can in introducing this second collection of my essays and journalism.

The essays in my first collection, *Looking For Brothers*, spanned a nine-year period, between 1989 and 1998. *Other Men's Sons*, this second collection, covers a much shorter period — roughly 2000 to 2005. They are arranged in three sections — "Mosaics," primarily culture criticism and journalism that explores the tone of the times and the nuances that inform gay culture; "Portraits," profiles of individuals; and "Mirrors," essays that are autobiographical in nature. There is some overlap in all three sections, just as there is in life.

The noted French essayist, playwright and philosopher Eugène Ionesco once said: "Why do people always expect authors to answer questions? I am an author because I want to ask questions."

This is doubly true for journalists. Asking questions is the air we breathe. Scratch any journalist and you find someone to whom asking questions comes as naturally as eating, sleeping, or having sex. Our role usually has less to do with telling our own truth than it does with allowing people to tell their own truths through us, the writer as intercessor. Filtering the real truth from the ersatz is an acquired skill and one that most journalists spend their careers refining. There is never a shortage of people willing to use journalists to advance their own agenda, be it in Hollywood, or in politics. This explains the dance of death between celebrities trying to protect some private part of themselves, and journalists who need to get them to open up, to trust their interlocutors, with the full confidence that they won't be exploited in the process.

Essays, on the other hand (at least autobiographical ones) require a different sort of dance of death, a private *tarantella* that involves making yourself naked and vulnerable and as honest as you can possibly be, trusting yourself to tell the truth about *you*. Morally this is a very tough gig. The writer May Sarton frequently said that the goal of autobiographical writing was to go as deep as possible, on the assumption that the deeper one went the more universal one became, and that something very deep could be very clear, like clean well-water. Later explorations of Sarton's life and work indicate that she was not always completely honest, but it is clear that she *tried* to be, even at her own expense, and she rarely let herself off her own autobiographical hook. I admire that. By exposing her own raw nerves, she connected viscerally with her readers. By not setting out to be a role model, she inadvertently became one.

My own goals are much less lofty. There are both essays and journalism in this collection, and I would like to think that my stories, and the stories of the men I've written about, illuminate at least some small part of the mosaic that is twenty-first century gay life. The older I get, the more reluctant I become to making sweeping statements about gay life and gay writing. But one exception to this reluctance is the observation that media representations of gay life occasionally illuminate, influence, and codify gay life — even to gay people. As we have become more and more out and open, we have also become less marginalized in our art, our literature, and our filmed representations. Many of the most visible gay people work in the arts, often as writers and actors, so in this cultural context, it is possible, in some cases, for the "personality profile" to be lifted above the level of mere titillation for the masses and into the realm of genuine social commentary. When members of a particular subculture number somewhere between five and ten per cent of the general population, an articulate sharing of common experiences tends to attract some attention.

Two of the pieces in this book — "The Full Paige" and "Gale Force" — were written as cover stories for *The Advocate*, and deal with the Showtime television series *Queer As Folk*. Of the two actors they showcase, Peter Paige is gay, while Gale Harold is straight. Paige's story falls under the rubric of gay men's lives, while Harold's story showcases the effect a sensitive and gifted straight man playing a gay man has on the way gay people see themselves. Between its inception in 2000 and its final episode in 2005, *Queer As Folk* was a purveyor of archetypes. The show's detractors see this as one of its failings, and accuse the producers and actors of perpetuating stereotypes of shallow, flighty gay men whom they insist bear no relation to people anyone seems to know. A rather careless glance up and down Church St., or Santa Monica Blvd. in West Hollywood, or the Chelsea neighbourhood of New York City suggests that this claim of misrepresentation is, at best, dubious. If critics want to see the characters on *Queer As Folk* as huge, acid-pink caricatures, they would have to begin by taking a long, hard critical look at their community and honestly ask themselves if anything on *Queer As Folk* could not be found on a Saturday night in any large city, anywhere. Furthermore, they might be missing the point entirely, as the show's devotees would tell you in no uncertain terms. If interpersonal relations are the currency of the human realm — let alone the queer realm — then *Queer As Folk* is rich in them. The show has explored nearly every relationship combination extant: there are relationships between tricks, lovers, husbands, wives, parents, and siblings. It has included intergenerational relationships,

platonic and otherwise. It has explored HIV-positive/negative relationships, and tentatively explored the consequences. Love it or hate
it (and many gay men do hate it) the show has had a profound
impact on how the straight world sees queer society, and how queer
society sees itself. It's fine to sneer, but the show's cultural impact
in this first decade of the twenty-first century is undeniable. In my
opinion, an examination of the lives and fortunes of the actors playing these characters can only add to the dialogue. The view of other
well-placed openly gay personalities like Clive Barker is offset in this
collection by the stories of less-well known gay men, such as *Playgirl's*
thirtieth-anniversary centrefold, Scott Merritt, who came out in the
pages of *The Advocate* in 2003, or Phillip Ing, the creative force
behind MAC's AIDS fundraising supernova, Fashion Cares. Ing's story
of growing up gay in a conservative Chinese-Canadian milieu, which
first appeared in *fab* magazine, sheds some light on the true nature
of ethnic diversity; it also speaks one of the truths of gay culture: we
are tributaries that eventually flow into a larger, more homogenous
river. Whether that is ultimately enriching appears to depend on the
individual, and his private path.

There are also stories in *Other Men's Sons* that have straight
men and women as their focus: "Drew Harris and the Oracle of
Colour," is a meditation on the work and vision of the painter Drew
Harris, an artist of international standing whose searing paintings
speak volumes in a language of colour and wrestled chaos; "The
Carpenter's Hands" was originally written as an introduction to
The Highway: Recollections of a 21st Century Heretic by Mark
Braun, a liberal Christian writer whose take on fundamentalist
Christianity and its dangers dovetails perfectly with mine and whose
awareness of — and concern for — the naked ill will that conservative fundamentalists bear for gays and lesbians resonated with me
on a deep level. Still another is a portrait of Angie Moneva, a young
woman I have known since she was a twelve-year-old girl growing
up in her parents' Church St. restaurant, Café California, in the heart
of Toronto's gay ghetto. Her story is the story of how a child raised

in a world populated daily by a loving gay community of "big brothers" (or "big sisters," depending on the chosen perspective) can be forever touched, shaped and blessed by the experience.

In 1999, a young soldier was murdered in his bed at Fort Campbell, Kentucky. What first appeared to be a routine example of gay bashing, coddled and spun by the profoundly homophobic U.S. military, evolved into a story that challenged the very foundations of sexual orientation and gender identity. Pfc. Barry Winchell, a soldier with the most macho infantry unit in the U.S. military, was involved with a pre-operative male-to-female transsexual nightclub performer in nearby Nashville, Tennessee, named Calpernia Addams. While both Winchell and Addams considered themselves to be heterosexual (Winchell had no interest in men, and saw Addams as female) it has been suggested by many involved that it was Winchell's relationship with Addams that brought about his death when it was discovered, and Winchell was branded gay. Addams's relationship with Winchell formed the basis of the Ron Nyswaner-scripted film, *Soldier's Girl*. I first became aware of the Winchell murder while reading *Vanity Fair* in 2000. I was on a plane to Vancouver, and I wept openly when I read Pulitzer Prize-winner Buzz Bissinger's brilliant account, "Don't Ask, Don't Kill." It was the first time a piece of journalism had ever affected me in that way, and I confess that although profoundly shaken, my response was leavened with a measure of envy for Bissinger's skill. Although I put the magazine away, Barry Winchell's story stayed with me, refusing to rest. In 2002, I found myself on assignment for *The Advocate* at Canadian Forces Base Borden, approximately sixty kilometres north-north-west of Toronto, one of the locations of the *Soldier's Girl* film set. I spent several weeks on the set, interviewing the actors and the producers who were bringing Barry's last days to life through the medium of Ron Nyswaner's powerful screenplay. I ate with the cast and crew, watched the filming at various locations, and absorbed the producers' commitment to the story by osmosis. I met and spoke with Calpernia Addams, by now a gracious and elegant woman. Still, I wasn't satisfied that

I had the heart of the story, so in early 2003 I flew to Kansas City to interview Barry Winchell's parents, Pat and Wally Kutteles. I found the heart of his story in his parents' courage and honesty, and in their willingness to open themselves to me.

After writing that story, I will never *not* measure the petulant, paranoid, neurotic demands for control by every minor-league celebrity I've ever interviewed — or will interview in future — against the cauterized yet open heart of Barry Winchell's mother as she recounted the emotional cost of her son's murder.

I include Winchell's story among the stories of straight men in this instance. The amorphous sexuality of men who love transsexual women is open to interpretation and definition, but if Barry Winchell had the courage to love and honour Calpernia Addams's femaleness, to be a man to her woman, then I take my cue from him out of respect. It would have been a privilege to know him. The lesson for me in writing "Walking With the Ghost of Barry Winchell" is that the sharp, cruel blade of homophobia hacks apart a variety of lives, gay and straight alike, old and young, parents and children, and as long as anyone can be murdered on the mere *rumour* of being gay, we have a long way to go as a society. Part of the process for healing any wound is cleansing it and exposing it to open air, so it is more essential than ever in these times of torrential social upheaval and change that gay people be visible and out. Telling our stories and having them heard is a precondition to that healing.

Many of the pieces in this collection were originally written for magazines and consequently appeared in slightly different versions when they were first published, owing largely to the editorial "house style" of each periodical and the limitations of space. They appear in this volume in the form in which I initially envisaged them, so any fault the reader might find in my presentation of these stories rests firmly with me, not my original editors.

As for the personal essays, I'd rather let them speak for themselves and allow the reader to judge them and the personal truths I've tried to tell on their own merits.

In the end, to be a working gay writer at the dawn of the twenty-first century is a wondrous privilege. Part of the duty accompanying that privilege is the documentation of our stories: to continue to move beyond oral history; to leave a written account of these times of momentous change, in the hopes that somewhere, beyond the protective reach of their gay elders, gay or lesbian adolescents may read something we've written and know that they aren't alone.

The title essay, "Other Men's Sons," deals with the notion of chosen family. It also deals with the multiplicity of ways we as gay people can love, and what a gift it is to be who and what we are, without apology.

As gay men, we are all the sons of other men before we become men ourselves. In telling these stories, my hope is that the personal has some chance of becoming at least part of the universal.

MOSAICS

Walking With the Ghost of Barry Winchell

2003

PAT KUTTELES, THE MOTHER of murdered army private Barry Winchell, sits at the head of a long wooden dining room table, sipping coffee from a mug held lightly in her strong, capable hands. She works nights as a psychiatric nurse and, like all night-shift workers, she comes home in the early morning and sleeps a good part of the day. She graciously curtailed her rest this afternoon in order to be an accommodating hostess to a journalist from Canada, but insists she doesn't mind. Her husband, Wally, protective of his wife's time and solicitous of her well-being, refills her coffee cup before sitting down with us. In Kansas City, dusk comes early in mid-winter, and the late-afternoon light is growing chilled and obscure. Inside the house, though, there is warmth and yellow light. The pine panelled walls are decorated with family portraits painted by Wally in a charming American *naif* style. The mementos, books, and photographs lining the other walls would not be out of place in any family home anywhere in the heartland. The air is redolent with the comforting, familial aroma of freshly brewed coffee, and the dusty, faded fragrance of old cigarettes.

There's something impalpable here as well. If memories are imperceptible, they still form a powerful base-note to the homey all-American potpourri of the house. Although there are only three of us sitting around the table, there appears to be an invisible fourth who never seems to stray too far from his mother's side.

It runs against the natural movement of life when parents bury their children, but in an oddly comforting rejection of this perversion of the natural order, Barry Winchell lives on in his mother's face. From the one photograph of him that was flashed around the world in the days, months, and years since his murder — his official army portrait, in fatigues and cap, standing in front of an American flag — it's clear where he got his good looks. Barry and his mother share the same high cheekbones, the same light-coloured near-almond eyes, and the same serene, direct gaze which, though not masking pain, certainly frames it in a dignity that doesn't invite pity. It's not difficult to imagine that same limitless gaze in Barry's eyes during the four months of harassment and psychological torture he endured before his cruel death. He didn't complain to his parents about it, nor did he complain to his girlfriend, Calpernia Addams. He appears to have cleaved to his unit's code of sinewy endurance. Barry was part of the 101st Airborne Infantry, the "Screaming Eagles," whose tougher-than-thou machismo is legendary, even by U.S. Army standards. The 101st led the way on D-Day and held the line at the Battle of the Bulge. In the mid-sixties, the 1st Brigade and support troops were deployed to Vietnam, followed by the rest of the division in 1967. In almost seven years of combat in Vietnam, the 101st participated in fifteen campaigns. It has subsequently been instrumental in both of the wars against Iraq, as well as in peacekeeping missions in Rwanda and Somalia. Barry believed in the army and was proud to be an American soldier.

He was murdered in his bed in the pre-dawn hours of July 5, 1999, beaten to death by a near-alcoholic fellow private named Calvin Glover, who was enraged at having lost a fight to someone he thought of as "a faggot." Glover had been goaded for several hours by Barry's roommate, Justin Fisher. Months earlier, Fisher had discovered Barry's relationship with Calpernia Addams, a transgendered nightclub performer in nearby Nashville, and it seemed to drive him into something resembling a jealous frenzy. Fisher's obsession with Barry Winchell continues to strike many involved with the investigation as excessive, as did his zealous persecution of his roommate once Fisher became aware of Addams. Given his own familiarity with Nashville's gay nightlife, he appears to fit the classic, self-loathing gay-basher profile perfectly: a straight-identified man with confused desires, who develops a twisted love for a man who not only doesn't return that love, but shares it with someone the basher sees as an unworthy rival, in this case a pre-operative transsexual. The resulting rage would leave him with no choice but annihilation of the object of his thwarted love. This may have been on Fisher's mind when he finally convinced Calvin Glover that there was only one way for a real man to handle the disgrace of losing the fight with "a faggot" earlier that day. At that point, Fisher put a Louisville Slugger baseball bat in Glover's hands and aimed him in the direction of Barry Winchell's sleeping form.

In the three and a half years since Winchell's death, the army has consistently refused to take any responsibility for the atmosphere of homophobia and anti-gay violence at Fort Campbell, and has even gone as far as to say that no such atmosphere existed there, at least not to an "unacceptable degree." Furthermore, they have dismissed Pat and Wally Kutteles's wrongful death suit, effectively stating that it is beneath their notice that an American soldier's head was smashed open by another American soldier for no other reason than *suspicion* of homosexuality, on a U.S. Army base operating under the suffocating "don't ask, don't tell" policy, or that one had anything to do with the other.

"All I could think of in the months following his murder was that recruiting slogan, 'Be All You Can Be,'" says Pat Kutteles. "My son tried to be all he could be and he was murdered."

In March of 2003, I flew from Toronto to Kansas City to try to walk with the ghost of Barry Winchell. I'd spent the summer of 2002 as a journalist on the set of the Ron Nyswaner-scripted film,

Soldier's Girl, in exclusive attendance on behalf of *The Advocate,* for whom I was writing about the filming. Nyswaner's powerful film explores a version of Barry's last months, seen primarily from the perspective of Calpernia Addams. The film was praised when it was shown at the Sundance Film Festival, receiving critical garlands for the strong performances by Troy Garity as Barry Winchell, Lee Pace as Calpernia Addams, and Shawn Hatosy as Justin Fisher. Nyswaner's script was hailed as a major achievement, not only as a screenplay but as a damning vision of the hell the U.S. Army visits on gays and lesbians, or anyone they suspect of being gay or lesbian.

Because of the film, and previous articles about the murder in *Rolling Stone, Vanity Fair,* and *The New York Times,* "Barry Winchell" now belongs to history. In the minds of the public, he has become as much a byword for martyrdom, or the symbol of what happens to good American soldiers who are victims of prejudice and finger-pointing as he ever was a living, breathing *person,* let alone *someone's son.* At the end of the day, the journalists have their stories, the actors have their performances, and the filmmakers have *Soldier's Girl.*

Pat and Wally Kutteles, on the other hand, have empty arms, and a house full of echoes.

There is a special hell reserved for parents of murdered children who feel the need to fight for changes in the system that led to their child's death, or for justice, but whose only method of achieving those goals is to regularly open up afresh wounds that are literally unimaginable to most people. Not the least of these wounds for the Kutteles family is the cognitive disconnect of occasionally hearing their son's name bandied about by strangers as though he were some sort of celebrity.

"It's surreal," says Pat. "Sometimes it hurts, because there is absolutely no closure. You're jerked back and forth. We go to Washington to fight against General Clark getting his third star," she says, naming the U.S. Army general who was the top officer at Fort Campbell when Barry was murdered. Clark was cleared of any responsibility for tolerating the rabidly homophobic atmosphere at Fort Campbell, and never intervening to stop the harassment. He was subsequently relocated and promoted, a gesture which seemed to add insult to injury, and struck many as profane. It angered Barry's family, gay rights advocates, and even some members of Congress. "We come back home, and I go to work," Pat continues, "and we do day-to-day things. Then a reporter calls. Then we're off to Sundance to see the movie. And then we're on CNN or *60 Minutes*. And then we come back to the world where you're trying to get over your child's death. The world where, with every holiday and birthday that goes by, your child is on your mind. Constantly, as you're trying to deal with his death, you're jerked back and forth. It's indescribable. Sometimes, I just want to scream."

Not surprisingly, given their relationship to the subject matter, they have mixed feelings about *Soldier's Girl*, though while acknowledging the limitations of dramatic storytelling, they admire the film.

"I wanted to see it at Sundance, because I wanted to see audience reaction," says Pat. "Wally and I are too close to it. All we can see it what's missing. On its own, it's a good story and a good movie. I think it will impact people."

Wally concurs. "We watched it the first time very critically, and it kind of bothered me for a while. Then we watched it the second time at Sundance and we just enjoyed it."

"What Wally and I discussed with Showtime was that we need to get the message out," Pat explains. "And if the movie does that a little bit, then it's good. If it tells a story, and shows some of what happens in the military, and what *can* happen — the McCarthyism that goes on, and how you can point the finger at someone and 'label' them — then it helps. I shook the whole time watching the film the first time."

"She broke into tears," Wally clarifies.

"It was very difficult," Pat says steadily.

Wally shows me an unpublished picture of a much younger Barry Winchell, with longer hair and a dazzling, mischievous smile.

It's a far cry from the young man's battle-hardened soldier's affect in the official army photograph. In this photo, Barry's face is alive with curiosity and possibilities. "He was no angel!" Wally laughs. "He was a tough kid. He wouldn't take too much lip from anybody." While he gives Troy Garity high marks for his performance in *Soldier's Girl*, he feels that his son's onscreen representation was still a little "softer" than Barry was in person. "He was a scrapper," Wally says, with no small measure of pride.

Pat and Wally have been married for twenty years. When Barry was four, Pat fled her son's abusive father. They lived for a time in their car. When she married Wally Kutteles, he became Barry Winchell's only father and Barry is never referred to as anything but his son. The early privations, however, shaped Barry in very specific ways.

"He used to bring home kids that got kicked out of their houses," Pat remembers. "Barry was big into the homeless. When we lived in a car, Barry used to find quarters and give them to me. He was big into taking care of people who didn't have a home, and were rejected." Later, when Pat was married to Wally, and working with teenagers as a psychiatric nurse, she and Barry would sit up late and talk about the people she encountered. "He'd listen to me when I'd come home and tell him about the kids I worked with. I did ten years with adolescents. I had regular kids who were kicked out of their homes and kids with A.D.H.D."

And she'd tell him about the gay kids. "There was one kid who was sixteen years old and he was gay. When his parents brought him in, they dropped off everything he owned. They didn't want him back. When they went to court, they wouldn't even talk to him, or look at him. They didn't want him because he was gay." The tradition of those late night talks continued all through Barry's adolescence. "Barry would come home from his dates, or I'd come home from work, and we'd sit up at two or three o'clock in the morning and talk and smoke. He was such a sensitive kid. Very caring about other people, a very loving child."

Barry was learning disabled, and this was perhaps his first awareness of the pernicious nature of labels. "Kids with learning disabilities are treated as though they were stupid," says Pat softly, the memory of it stirring the embers of a long-smouldering fire. "They often become defenders of the wronged, because that's how they've been treated. Barry couldn't read until the second grade, which is when he learned his ABCs. Once he learned to read, he was reading at a high school level within a couple of years. His abstract IQ was 147 and his overall was 128. He could look at a blueprint and tell you how to put it together, even though he couldn't read the instructions. You go through life being called 'stupid,' and you become very sensitized to the feelings of other people, very empathic. And that's the way Barry was. He wanted to take care of the world."

When Barry entered the military, his aptitude for its structure and life was such that he felt he had come home. "He told me that he felt he finally fit in," says Wally. "He wanted to make a career of it." Barry proved to be a skilled marksman and he loved the technical manuals. "The army had challenges that he could easily meet."

The nature of loss and unhealed wounds is such that even grieving parents can get caught up in the joy of re-telling favourite anecdotes. Although their hearts are breaking even as they relate the stories, the ever-present pain takes a back seat, momentarily, to the joy of bringing back the loved one for the duration of the telling. Pat and Wally have humorous stories about Barry's adventures on the firing range, and fond ones of him helping other soldiers climb the rope on the training course, and of medals won. Barry wanted to be a helicopter pilot. He was working towards that goal with his familiar joy and excitement at conquering yet another challenge.

"He wanted to fly helicopters," says Pat. "He went up in a Blackhawk and people were getting sick next to him [because of the speed and the altitude]. He was in love," she laughs. "He was *absolutely in love*." Then, the shadows move in. Her face darkens, and she sighs. "He had one more month to go before helicopter school," she says quietly. "And then he would have been away from Fisher."

∞∞∞∞

IN THE AFTERMATH OF Barry's murder, Pat and Wally received thousands of letters from around the world expressing sympathy for their loss. Only three of them were ugly, and they were postmarked nearby: Topeka, home of the Rev. Fred Phelps and his Westboro Baptist Church organization. Wally shudders at the memory of the filth and venom contained in the letters sent by Phelps to the grieving couple. "They were obscene," he says in revulsion. "He's supposed to be a 'Reverend?' He's the work of the devil." Among other things, the letters assured Pat and Wally that their murdered son was burning in hell and waiting for them to join him in his torment. In the years since Barry's death, Phelps has sent out rambling, incoherent "press releases" about the family, larded with misspellings and grammatical errors, in which he calls Barry a "dead Army fag" and his parents "antichrist [sic] fools now recruiting for a fag Army," and "two old idiots so dirt-dumb they can't see that the American sodomite media is making dupes of them." The time and place of Barry Winchell's funeral was kept out of the press, which spared the Kutteles family the monstrous invasion of Westboro picketers shouting obscenities that descended on the funerals of Matthew Sheppard, and others.

"We got a call from Vice-President Gore, with condolences from him and Tipper," Wally remembers. "I started asking him about General Clark and he didn't want to hear it. He couldn't wait to hang up." He laughs mirthlessly. "I wish that Clinton had the guts that Truman had. Truman said, 'I declare as commander-in-chief that there will be integration in the armed services and if you generals don't like it, leave.'"

The circumstances of Barry's death — the discovery of his relationship with Calpernia Addams by Fisher, his murder at the hands of Calvin Glover in what could only be described as a savage gay bashing — have placed Pat and Wally in an unusual quandary. Although there is no real evidence that their son was gay (the jury being out on the sexual orientation of men who date transsexuals), Barry was the victim of a gay hate crime, and, consequently, Pat and Wally have become de facto heterosexual gay rights activists. Nothing in their lives could have prepared them for this bizarre turn of events.

"Pat worked with gay people in the hospital and Barry knew that," says Wally. "Barry had gay friends, too." He was even the object of their unrequited love at least once. "He had a sixteen- or seventeen-year-old gay friend who was being picked on and Barry stuck up for him," Wally says, adding that Barry was "a big kid," and when he intervened protectively on someone's behalf, they were left alone. "The kid took a liking to Barry," Wally sighs. "Every-where Barry would go, the kid would follow him." Barry's *inamorato* would repeatedly telephone the house late at night and leave love letters tacked to the front door. "Barry said, 'I can understand him feeling that way, but I have a girlfriend and I just want to be left alone.'" Calpernia Addams has said that Barry related to her as female and treated her like a lady. There is no evidence that even in a cloistered, sweaty, macho world like Fort Campbell was Barry tempted to explore homosexuality. To Pat and Wally Kutteles, however, their son's sexual orientation couldn't have mattered less. Whatever it was, or wasn't, paled before the terrible circumstances of his death.

"When I found out what happened to Barry, and why — that it was a hate crime — I started to go after the military," Pat says fervently. "Barry was pointed out and labelled gay. He was harassed daily for four months. What about the safety of the other men and women in the military, the gays and lesbians who are just trying to serve their country? What about their safety? They have parents, they have families, and no one is protecting them. If we don't fight against hate crimes, and for those people who are targeted, I feel as though we're letting Barry down. Because that's what Barry would have fought for. He would have fought for the rights of *everybody*. I have to fight for what Barry would have wanted. No matter how hard it is, no matter how long it takes. I have to fight for my son's ideals. And that's what we're doing."

"It doesn't reflect the promise of America to have a military that is prejudiced," says Wally, a veteran of the war in Korea. "They're supposed to be fighting for our rights. You're supposed to be proud to be in the military. I was proud to be in the military. Both my brothers were proud to be in the military. Pat has two brothers who were in the Marine Corps. Not one of them liked what happened. It's embarrassing that the military which they, and I, were in, would act like that, then scramble, lie, and cover up to justify it."

Wally remembers the army's initial shuffle-and-dance in the months following the murder, when the facts began to surface regarding the way Barry's initial complaint about Fisher's harassment had been handled. It became clear that the tragedy might have been averted had the officialdom at Fort Campbell taken the events leading to Barry's death more seriously.

"Fisher used this gay thing to get Barry," Wally says furiously. "He pumped Glover with this crap. Fisher is the one who started spreading the rumours around. A lot of the soldiers took it seriously, but some of them just kidded around about it, they weren't serious. Some *were* serious and this hurt Barry. This was going on for several months. Barry and his sergeant went to the inspector general's office to complain. They sent them *back* and told them, 'You should talk to your officers about this first.' So they went back and talked to the officers and got nothing." During the inquest, Lt. General Ackerman, the army's inspector general visited Pat and Wally at home. "He sat at this table — *in that chair*," Wally says, jabbing his finger accusingly at the place where I'm sitting. "I asked him, 'Why was Barry sent back? That's like him going to complain to the people he's complaining *about*.' Ackerman said, 'Well, he didn't have to go back [to his commanding officers].' I said, 'Did *Barry* know that? Did they tell *him* that?'"

While Ackerman fumbled with an answer, Wally asked him if there were records of the complaint. "He said, 'No, we don't keep records.' They *were* keeping records, then they *weren't*, now suddenly they're keeping them *again*."

Pat sighs, and takes another sip of coffee. "They kept I.G. records till April. Barry was murdered in July, then they resumed record keeping in October," says Pat dryly. "They *lost* Barry's records."

Wally has a particular memory of Barry in his late teens.

"I was listening to some old records, playing an old song from 1944," Wally remembers. "Suddenly, in walks Barry." Wally recalls that his son seemed particularly moved by the song on the turntable at that moment. "Barry asked me to play it again. And again. I said, 'Look Barry, I see where this is leading. I could be playing this all day long. If you want the words, I'll write them down. I know them by heart.'" The song was called "The House I Live In," written by Paul Robeson (1898–1976), an African-American actor, writer, and singer of international renown. Robeson was an articulate and passionate advocate of black civil rights, who both loved America and saw it for what it was. His advocacy for the rights of workers made him enemies among every right-wing extremist group in the United States, from the lowest echelons up to the top. In 1950 his passport was revoked by the State Department, though he was not charged with any crime. President Truman had signed an executive order forbidding Paul Robeson to set foot outside the continental limits of the United States. "Committees to Restore Paul Robeson's Passport" were formed internationally, though the fight to restore his passport lasted eight years. "The House I Live In" became something of an anthem, recorded by numerous artists including Frank Sinatra.

Ten minutes later, Wally handed the lyrics to Barry, who left the room with them and went into his room. Wally heard him saying the words out loud, memorizing them. "Barry loved that song," Wally says. "He loved those words. He really believed in them."

When the army returned a box of Barry's belongings after his murder, Pat and Wally found them trashed. "Everything was stuffed in there like garbage," says Wally. "I thought, if I'd been hurt, is this the way my parents would get my stuff? I was really mad, and out of respect to Barry, I started neatening them out." As Wally reached to the bottom of the box, he pulled out two of Barry's medals. Jammed into the bottom of the box were the lyrics Wally had painstakingly copied for his son, who'd had them framed. The frame was broken, the glass smashed. Shards of it littered the bottom of the box. This last obscenity somehow seemed to Wally a final damning insult to Barry by the army he loved and believed in.

"Do you want to hear the words?" Wally asks me softly. "I still know them by heart." I say yes. Barry's father recites Robeson's lyrics from memory, his voice suddenly thick.

The song is a paean to a nostalgic, mythic America that seems almost beyond living memory in these cynical times. The lyrics are just this side of maudlin, but still curiously moving in their homespun simplicity. You'd probably like a man who believed these lyrics passionately. You might even admire him. But if you loved him, you'd worry about the fragility of his red, white, and blue idealism. It's the sort of idealism men die for. If the idealist who died was your son, it would break your heart.

Wally's voice cracks, then trails off. His eyes are wide and haunted. His hands unconsciously rise, palms flattening outwards, opening in a gesture very much like supplication. As with much in this terrible story, words fail at a certain point. Silence itself becomes like the sound of screaming.

∞∞∞

IN 2000, PAT FILED a $1.8 million wrongful-death claim against the army, contending that the anti-gay atmosphere and failed leadership at Fort Campbell led inexorably to the events culminating in Barry's murder. The army rejected it. Pat appealed: her last chance to seek redress was under the Military Claims Act, which allows civilian survivors to seek redress from the military for injury, death, or loss of property. The army rejected the appeal. A separate administrative procedure, provided by the Federal Tort Claims Act, was unavailable to her because of a Supreme Court ruling limiting claims against the military. For its part, the army was cruelly efficient this one last time: knowing they were untouchable, they simply waited for Pat and Wally Kutteles to exhaust themselves.

In spite of it all, perhaps defiantly, Pat and Wally give speeches, talk to reporters, and work tirelessly in the resolute hope that someday the "don't ask, don't tell" policy will be nothing more than a bad dream from a different, more savage time. They usually cover their own travel expenses. This, combined with Pat's lost wages when they're on the road, is a severe economic hardship they're not sure they can afford much longer. Still, they are grateful for the media, whom they describe as uniformly respectful and generous, and for their friends and family, who have never wavered in their love and support. Pat notes sadly that when gay seaman Allen Schindler was beaten to death in Sasebo, Japan, in 1992 by a shipmate, "half the family turned their backs on" Schindler's mother, Dorothy Hajdys-Holman, when her son's homosexuality became known.

"You get knocked backwards, then you get up and go on," Pat says. "Then you get knocked backwards again. And we have to keep on fighting. Barry used to tell me that when he first went into basic training, he found it difficult for a while. One of his sergeants used to say, *Suck it up and move on*. When I would be talking to Barry and be overwhelmed by things, he'd say, 'Suck it up and move on, Mom.' And I hear that in my head, in his voice, all the time. And that's what I do, and what I have to do."

ooooo

PAT KUTTELES AND I are driving though the frozen dusk towards the cemetery on the outskirts of Kansas City where Barry is laid to rest. A slender finger of dark amber sunlight is beckoning the coming night across the flat Missouri horizon and it has started to snow. It's tacitly understood that the name of the cemetery is not for publication, primarily to avoid a desecration of Barry's grave by

Fred Phelps and his Westboro parishioners. She smokes as we drive, her eyes steadily on the road ahead as snow dances in the headlights. Pat is a devout Catholic and her faith has become her bulwark since Barry's death. As she looks for something resembling meaning in the midst of pain and dispossession, she clings to the notion that Barry died for a reason. If her son had expired in a bar brawl over a girl, for instance, none of the fallout relating to his death would have occurred — the searing media exposure of the horrors of "don't ask, don't tell," the continuing dialogue in Congress about the army's culpability in the deaths of gay and lesbian soldiers who are victims of bashing, and the film, *Soldier's Girl*, which will bring the story into millions of living rooms. If "don't ask, don't tell" is essentially a dirty bandage on an infected social wound, it can only be cleansed and healed by exposure to sunlight and fresh air. The Barry Winchell case has, at the very least, opened another window, and it has remained open.

"I feel that Barry died for a reason, that there's a reason things happen," Pat muses. "That's also one of the reasons I keep fighting." She notes that often, when children die, it spurs society to change. "That gives me comfort, in a way. I don't know that there's anything that gives me total comfort, though," she admits. "Sometimes when we're home alone, going through our day-to-day stuff, I feel alone. I feel that there's nobody who really cares that he died, nobody who cares what kind of a person he was. No one who shares our anger and grief over what's happening to others out there. And then something will happen that reminds us that there are people who care, and who are fighting with us. Then I feel a little bit better. But often, I feel like I'm really alone, and really, really missing my child, and those long talks we had late at night."

The lights of the car play across the larger mausoleums and the gates of the cemetery as Pat pulls up in front and parks the car. Pressing close against the biting wind that has sprung up, we walk for a short distance, then come to a long row of unpretentious flat stones that seem to catch what's left of the light. Carved into one of them is *Pfc. Barry L. Winchell*, with the dates of his birth and untimely death. You wouldn't notice the gravestone unless you were looking for it. It strikes me as beautiful in its simplicity. It occurs to me that after three and a half years, and the attention of the world, it has all come down to this: a small flat stone resting stoically against the frozen Midwestern ground.

Pat crosses herself and sits down heavily on the granite bench that she and Wally purchased so that they would have a place to sit when they visited their son. She visits Barry often and talks to him. She tells him what's happening in her and Wally's life and keeps him abreast of the struggles, the disappointments, and the small incremental victories. Pat shows me where she will be buried next to him, and where Wally will someday be buried when they are all reunited. She bows her head in silent prayer and when she raises her head to speak, I can't see her face for the shadows. Her voice, though, comes tenderly in the encroaching darkness.

"I told him," she says softly, "when I signed the papers and they switched off the life-support system at the hospital and I said good-bye, I told him, 'You'd better be waiting for me when I get there, Barry. You'd better be there to show me the way home.'"

Then, because we're alone and because there is nothing else to say, Pat Kutteles and I hold each other tight against the black winter wind, and night falls.

Murder at Fort Campbell:
The Filming of *Soldier's Girl*
2003

NIGHT FALLS, AND THE mid-summer humidity lowers a heavy shawl of perpetual dampness from the bruise-coloured sky. In the glow of all-season Christmas lights stapled along the rooftops of a dozen double-wide residential trailers, a gypsy caravan of production trucks and Winnebagos have formed a pocket of Hollywood incongruity on the edge of a trailer park just outside of downtown Toronto.

All afternoon, the hatchet-faced, sunburned denizens of the park looked on in bemusement as slim, bronzed Californians barked rapid-fire, staccato orders into cellphones, and crewcut grips transformed this garish outpost of an otherwise prim Canadian city into an equally garish facsimile of a Nashville trailer park. Canadian flags were apologetically replaced with American ones, though the plastic garden gnomes standing guard in front of the trailers would seem equally at home in either locale. Many of the crew, from the screenwriter on down to the grips, sport the same crewcut. Their hair was shorn weeks earlier in solidarity with the actors, and in homage to the military theme of the story currently being filmed a country away from the locale where the tragic story, upon which the film is based, occurred.

All afternoon, they watched the same scene filmed over and over: a battered car driven by a handsome off-duty soldier pulls up in front of one of the trailers, whereupon he is greeted by a tall, tall woman, dressed not unlike many of the Wal-Mart shoppers who stand at a respectful distance, watching the scene. She embraces the soldier and draws him inside. By late afternoon, the whispered rumours in the trailer park have been confirmed. The "woman" is a male actor named Lee Pace, a relatively unknown recent graduate of a famous acting school called Juilliard, who is making a film debut in which, paradoxically, he is rendered nearly invisible. Through the magical medium of state-of-the-art makeup and prosthetics, his masculinity has vanished behind an opaque varnish of femininity. Or as the trailer park women insisted, they "can't imagine him bein' no *man*." One of the women asked me if Juilliard was the character's name.

Although they don't recognize the second actor, the one playing the soldier, he's rumoured to be "related to somebody famous." Eventually they tire of watching. As the sun goes down, they drift away, fire up their barbecues, and discuss their brush with Hollywood amongst themselves.

As for the two actors, heading back to their respective Winnebagos — one striding manfully, a trace of military-bearing artlessly asserting itself, the other unable to lose a sway of the hips, or the lacquered finger delicately brushing the long wig away from his painted face — neither seems particularly disappointed to lose the intense scrutiny of their trailer park hosts.

It's July 5, 2002, a sultry evening on the Toronto set of *Soldier's Girl,* and the film's star, Troy Garity, is almost ready to talk about playing murdered soldier Barry Winchell. The key word is *almost.*

Garity has been a distant, looming presence throughout most of the shoot, accessible to his immediate colleagues, but wary and distant to most everyone else, and completely inaccessible to anyone even remotely resembling the press. Tall and dark, at a distance, which is where one usually found him throughout the shoot, he occasionally resembles a tanned, muscular, younger version of his famous grandfather, Henry Fonda, though with his military crew-cut and white-hot intensity, he's indisputably his own man. Early in the shoot, I'd been warned by a crew member not to bring up Garity's lineage to him at any cost. The feeling among some members of the production was that the actor had fought long and hard to distance himself from qualifying titles — *son of* Jane Fonda and Tom Hayden, *grandson of* Henry, *nephew of* Peter, *cousin of* Bridget — and had earned it. His last name, Garity, is his paternal grandmother's maiden name, and it's conceivable that a great number of viewers won't make the Fonda connection at all when they see him onscreen as the doomed army private, a role that he has been fighting his way into since shooting began four weeks ago.

Inside his air-conditioned trailer, far from prying eyes, Garity and I circled around each other in the time-honoured, wary dance between journalist and interview subject. He almost apologized for his reticence about being interviewed, conceding that the role of Barry Winchell was one of the hardest he had essayed to date. He lost fifteen pounds to play the part and worked out with a trainer. Too, he was building a house prior to the shoot. "I tried to do as much manual labour as I could, putting up drywall, digging holes, and smashing tile, but the way into Barry Winchell's character was challenging. We're four weeks into shooting, and I'm still finding out things about this guy," Garity said thoughtfully. "Whenever I think I have it, I realize I don't. I probably won't have it until the movie is done and over, and I see it, and I'll say, 'Oh fuck, *that's* how I should have done it.'"

Three years earlier, to the day, in the pre-dawn hours of July 5 1999, inside the 101st Airborne "Screaming Eagles" infantry barracks at Fort Campbell, Kentucky, Private First Class Barry Winchell's head was smashed to pieces against his pillow with a Louisville Slugger baseball bat while he slept. The bat struck no other part of his body but his head, face, and neck, and the force of the blows was such that bits of brain matter and bone fragment mixed with the blood that splattered against the wall behind him like a crimson halo.

Winchell never regained consciousness after the beating, and died at Vanderbilt Medical Center the next day. His murderer, an emotionally-disturbed, eighteen-year-old, near-alcoholic army private named Calvin Glover, had been steadily provoked and manipulated into a drunken rage by Winchell's roommate, Justin Fisher, who'd taunted Glover over having lost a fight earlier that day to Winchell, "a faggot." In the previous weeks, Barry Winchell had been the object of mounting anti-gay harassment, taunts, and slurs. Though not gay-identified, Winchell had been enjoying a clandestine relationship with Calpernia Addams, a transgendered nightclub performer in nearby Nashville. Fisher had discovered the affair and, for a multiplicity of twisted reasons that remain mostly speculation, it provoked him into what appeared to be an obsessive, jealous fury. In retrospect, although Barry Winchell was murdered with a baseball bat, the real weapon appears to have been Calvin Glover, wielded by Justin Fisher.

The story captured worldwide headlines, as much for the unprecedented savagery of the attack as for the other component elements: the increasingly desperate failure of the army's profoundly homophobic "don't ask, don't tell" policy, the prurient hint of forbidden sexual and romantic scandal, and the near-Shakespearean tragedy of the circumstances surrounding Barry Winchell's murder. Here was a clean-cut, tough, all-American soldier in the classic mould, the sort the army claims to venerate, murdered for no other reason than the *suspicion* of homosexuality, in what appears to have been a masterpiece of sociopathic manipulation by a roommate with a tenebrous agenda of his own. Articles in *Rolling Stone*, *Vanity Fair*, and *The New York Times Magazine* all asked the same question: What happened?

The previous week I'd joined the filming at Canadian Forces Base Borden, 60 kilometres north-northwest of Toronto, which was standing in for Fort Campbell. It was a hot, hot day, the army camp a blaze of green grass, blue sky, and white sun. Outside the enlisted men's Spartan dormitories, the crew had set up gas barbecues and beer kegs. The scene being shot that day was the fateful Fourth of July barbecue where Justin Fisher (Shawn Hatosy) goads Calvin Glover (Philip Eddolls) into the final altercation with Winchell, the brawl that set in motion the events that culminated in Winchell's gruesome murder many hours later. As the day wears on and the sun climbs higher, the pervasive smack of gas barbecue and fresh-cut grass compounds vertiginously with the rough male voices of the actors playing the drunk soldiers. The scene of the fight is played over and over. In the shimmering summer heat, reality shifts for the observer, and the repeated anti-gay slurs begin to take on an unwhole-somely authentic tone as the actors recreate a fight that occurred nearly three years in the past with dizzying authenticity.

I notice a group of real Canadian soldiers who live on the base watching solemnly on the sidelines, and I approach them. I ask them what they think about what they're seeing.

"Man, if there was any of [that verbal gay bashing] at this base, those guys would be up on charges so fast it would make their heads spin," says one soldier in wonderment, the toe of his highly-polished black boot scuffing nervously in the dirt. "They'd be lucky if they didn't get kicked out of the army."

The Canadian military instituted a zero-tolerance policy for hate speech of any kind some years ago, around the time they lifted the ban against gays and lesbians serving in the Canadian Army. Anti-gay harassment, let alone physical gay bashing, is grounds for dishonourable discharge from the Canadian Forces. It seems ironic, yet somehow fitting, that this film, which would likely never have been granted permission to shoot on a U.S. Army base because of its subject matter and critical point of view, should be shot in Canada. When asked if he knew the story of Barry Winchell, the young soldier said yes. "Yeah, sure we know it. We've heard about it. Fucking tragic, man. There's no excuse for that kind of thing in any army, anywhere. But it's real," he says of the scene that he's watching being set up for yet another take. "It's very, very real."

Again and again, Eddolls's Glover leaps at Garity's Winchell and wrestles him to the ground, screaming with the hysterical, impotent rage of a young man with nothing, and therefore nothing to lose, punching him over and over again. Hatosy's Fisher watches the two roll in the dust with the surreptitious, cunning delight of a child trying to determine how long a fly can live without its wings.

The coarse, shouting voices swim through the sickening emerald heat.

Every time the director calls "Cut!" Garity steps off to the side, and retreats out of sight. While other actors, and the crewcut extras who aren't needed in the shot, chat with one another, or rough-house, or watch the monitor in between takes, Garity vanishes. Something appears to bleed out of the actor every time he plays the ugly scene, and whatever it takes to refill and restore the part of him that pays the cost of this role's terrible authenticity doesn't occur within the sightline of visitors.

ooooo

ALTHOUGH INSIGHTFUL, ARTICULATE, AND politically precocious, Garity's professional armour doesn't crack until I ask him, a week later, on the night of July 5, about the point at which the intensity of the role he was playing struck him full force.

"There were two moments when it became overwhelming," he says. "Through the process of reading the script so much and doing a lot of research, I began to endow certain emotions from the script, namely paranoia and fragmentation," he says. "This happened specifically during the week we spent filming Barry in the middle of the witch hunt in the barracks." Garity says that the intensity became too much for him at one point and he began to have paranoid imaginings that the crew were talking about him behind his back. "I feel *disgusting* saying that, because it has nothing to do with the hell that this kid went through," he says furiously. "The second moment was the day we filmed the murder scene." Garity's voice trails off, and he pauses. He takes a deep breath and leans forward, eyes down. When he looks up, his eyes are slick. He blinks back tears and continues, haltingly. "They had to put the prosthetics on my head to match the injuries that this kid endured. And to think of the misery that this act of complete cowardice cost and this poor kid's family —" Garity begins to weep. "I don't know how to play it honestly because I didn't know Barry and I don't know his family. He didn't tell anybody. Not once in these five months of torture he was going through did he complain. Not to *anybody*." He pauses again, then regains his composure, brushing away the tears with the back of his hand. "My goal is to take his face down off the poster and make him a real person again."

If the specific details of the last months of Barry Winchell's life remain cloaked in a mosaic of recollections by the various people who knew him, much of the question of "what happened" was answered this year at Sundance when *Soldier's Girl* swept the festival and drew critical raves. *Soldier's Girl* is the fruit of Ron Nyswaner's long fascination with the Barry Winchell story, which he encountered in 2000 in one of the magazine articles detailing the murder and its aftermath.

"I called my agent on my cellphone and said, 'I've discovered the story I was born to write,'" says Nyswaner, best known as the screenwriter of *Philadelphia*, "'and you have to make sure I get the chance to write it.'" Nyswaner did as much research as possible using public domain sources, magazines, newspapers, the Internet, and trial transcripts. The next step was to fashion a story that would interest a studio. "It always takes two things to interest me in a drama," Nyswaner muses, "and they have to be opposed to one another. There was Barry's Midwestern decency and Calpernia's articulate and somewhat ironic sense of herself. I remember her saying, 'I know my life has a somewhat Jerry Springer tone to it,' and I thought: 'This is someone who has irony and a sense of humour even though she was involved in this horrible tragedy.' Those two things coming together interested me."

Nyswaner was unaware that at the same time he was meeting with major studios about a motion picture based on Winchell's life, producers Linda Gottlieb (*Dirty Dancing, Citizen Cohn*) and Doro Bachrach (*Citizen Cohn, Truman*) were already setting up their own Addams/Winchell project at Showtime. By serendipitous coincidence, a mutual friend of Nyswaner and the producers was at a dinner party and heard Gottlieb speak about Calpernia Addams and Gottlieb's intention to make a movie based upon Addams's life and the murder of her lover, Barry Winchell. The friend reported the conversation to Nyswaner, who tracked down the two producers and offered himself as the screenwriter.

"There was no script at all, not an outline or anything," Nyswaner explains. "They had set it up at Showtime, and they were talking to Calpernia about purchasing the rights to her life story and using her as a consultant."

Nyswaner started writing in the summer of 2000 and worked on the script all through production and shooting in the summer of 2002.

"In my research, I found that Justin and Calvin had very troubled pasts and had been treated very badly by several of society's institutions. They had been dumped in the army as a last resort," Nyswaner reveals. He had spoken to several sergeants, the officers most immediately superior to the enlisted men and most directly responsible for them, who were willing to talk off the record; some of them pointed out that "there are troubled people in the military who are sent there as a last resort when schools, churches, and families fail to help kids."

Nyswaner also spent time in Nashville and New York with Addams while writing, and during shooting they often spoke by telephone. She also supplied Nyswaner with material from her memoir-in-progress (since published under the title *Mark 947*) "There was no such thing as a shooting draft," laughs Nyswaner of the script, though he concedes that somewhere in the fall of 2001, there was a draft that Showtime was willing to make, with the understanding that there would be changes once a director was attached. When the producers first approached Frank Pierson to direct, he declined, citing the complexity of the material and his own doubts that the story could be done justice. But after a week, the story continued to haunt Pierson. The director changed his mind and called the producers back to accept.

"We struggled with the role of Calpernia the most," Nyswaner says of the casting. The actor would have to be believable as a pre-op transsexual, neither a fully anatomical woman nor a drag queen. After auditioning countless actors, the production decided on Lee Pace, an Oklahoma native fresh out of Juilliard. Even so, there were challenges. "Lee's talent was so spectacular that is seemed obvious to choose him," Nyswaner notes, "but we were concerned about his physical build. He's very tall, very broad-shouldered, and he's a good-looking, lean-but-hunky guy." Nontheless, his audition stunned everyone. "In the end, someone said to the director, 'Frank, you always go with talent. The other stuff can be worked out.'"

The illusion of Lee Pace as Calpernia Addams is seamless, and during the shoot he was rarely seen on set without the three hours of prosthetics and makeup it took to turn him into a pre-operative transsexual. Male crew members fell naturally into treating him with unconscious gender-based courtesies — doors held, hands lightly touching his back as they guided him onto the set.

ooooo

"I'M CLEARLY A GUY," laughs Lee Pace today. It's the early spring of 2003, many months since the film wrapped, and the first wave of buzz and publicity that greeted Soldier's Girl following the Sundance Film Festival has called considerable attention to Pace and his performance as Calpernia Addams. The actor is just back from a weekend in upstate New York visiting Nyswaner, during which he acquired the beginning of what has rapidly become a hellish cold. Dressed in cargo pants and a sweater, he has regained the weight he lost to play Calpernia, his eyebrows have grown in,

and there is no trace of the feminine persona left. A recent photograph in *Details* magazine reveals a jockish, wide-smiling Pace with
his arm around co-star Hatosy. "You're never going to forget that
I'm six-three," Pace sighs. "That's never going away, no matter how
many prosthetics you apply. As far as playing a role this specific,"
he says of playing a transgendered person, "I had to just trust
that I was a woman and focus on Troy, falling in love with him,
and playing the scenes as honestly as I could." Pierson advised
Pace to avoid drag clubs and, instead, watch real women and let
their physical and emotional movements guide his performance,
both alone and in his scenes with Garity. "Calpernia told me that
they did behave in a very heterosexual fashion," Pace confides.
"She really valued that in him, and that's what he was comfortable
with in her."

Addams, who didn't consider Winchell gay and says he didn't
think of himself in those terms either, visited the Toronto set during
the shooting. She gives Pace high marks for the subtlety and insight
of his performance. "I walked into the theatre [where some of
the filming occurred] and it felt so eerie," Addams says, "because it
was such a close match to the theatre I used to work in. It had the
balcony and everything. There was a moment when I went into
the lobby and peeked through a crack in the open door and watched
Lee and it was like looking four years into my past."

Having recently left Chicago and moved to Los Angeles to start
a production company called Deep Stealth, Addams, whose final
gender reassignment surgery was completed just after her visit to
the set, is tall, slim, titian-haired and camellia-petal delicate, and bears
more than a passing resemblance to the actress Julianne Moore.

"It felt magical in a way," Addams confides of the time she spent
on set. "It gave me what I never thought I would have — a revisi-
tation of places and moments I thought were gone forever. It was a
surreal, cathartic experience for me." Speaking of the finished film,
she is unequivocal. "It's hard for me to see this film as I would if it
wasn't mine or Barry's story," she says softly. "It's hard to look at

this in a detached way and judge it as a film, but Troy's performance was so beautiful. Obviously he wasn't trying to clone or duplicate Barry exactly, but he got the core of it right, the powerful masculinity and the strength that was held in check by a peaceful, gentle spirit.

"The sense you get of Troy on the screen is the same sense you got of Barry in person — great strength controlled by a beautiful heart. He could have beaten up Fisher or Glover anytime he wanted to," she adds poignantly, "but he was a gentle and good man."

ooooo

ALMOST A YEAR AFTER our first interview on the *Soldier's Girl* set, Troy Garity is at home in Los Angeles. He has come in out of the sun, having spent most of the morning and early afternoon working in his yard. As he rummages around looking for some after-sun lotion, he reflects, from a less-piercing distance, on the evolution of his performance as Barry Winchell.

"In the original draft, I think Ron was a little afraid of Barry," Garity muses. "I don't know whether that was out of respect, or an inability to define his character. He was initially scripted as this 'gosh, golly' 1950s movie star, so incredibly chivalrous and shy that you wanted to vomit," he laughs. "In fact, Barry Winchell, although very decent and stoic and quiet, was very firm in his wants and desires. Barry was tougher than even I was able to portray. He was a guy who was catching people as they fell out of helicopters."

"I think I idolized Barry a little bit," Nyswaner admits in retrospect. "I felt I was making a tribute to him, an homage, and I think I initially erred in my first screenplay by making him too Gary Cooper-ish, and almost sub-articulate. I had always seen Justin Fisher as a Iago and I gave him these wonderful, florid speeches. Troy walked on the set and said, 'Why is my character not as exciting as the other characters and why isn't my dialogue interesting?'" Nyswaner laughs. "And I took that to heart. Troy really wanted to emphasize the fact that Barry was a sexual person, that he desired

Calpernia, and was turned on to her. He loved rock and roll, and the sexy heavy-metal, rock-and-roll fan persona wasn't originally present in my screenplay."

An accomplished actor in his own right, Garity is also the founder of the Peace Process Network, a worldwide anti-gang-violence network. As the son of Jane Fonda and Senator Tom Hayden, politics is something of a birthright.

"Perfect parents we weren't," Jane Fonda concedes on the phone from Atlanta, "but we lived our politics — it wasn't lip service, and he grew up with that. And it wasn't always pretty, as I'm sure he told you. It wasn't easy as a kid to grow up [in a political environment], and he saw, up close, the battle of gender issues. You can trace any issue back to hierarchy, patriarchy, and power. It's why gay people, men and women, are so vulnerable, now more than ever. They challenge the most fundamental structures of our society. For me, Troy is the perfect man: he's truly androgynous."

Early on, Garity, who is straight, approached his mother for advice on the potential impact of playing a controversial role.

"He called me up and said, 'Mom, do you think it could hurt my career to kiss a guy on the lips?' And I started listing all the actors who'd done it and I said, 'No.' As a mother, it wasn't the love scenes that were hard for me, it was the beating."

"I had heard about the Barry Winchell incident," Garity says, "but I had filed it away with all the other hate crimes I hear about day in and day out. It didn't really have much gravity in my belly, because I didn't assume it had anything to do with me. And now I see how gravely wrong I was. I see that the 'don't ask, don't tell' policy is responsible for the death of Barry Winchell and the ruination of the lives of those two young men who are in prison forever, and it moves beyond the military compound. The policy is something that exists in our homes and our schools, and the preposterous notion that silence is going to resolve conflict is absolutely crazy."

Nyswaner points out that like all great tragedies, the story being told in *Soldier's Girl* requires a complex range of interconnected characters.

"One of the reasons the movie is so disturbing is that Shawn Hatosy is so good in the role of Justin Fisher," he says. "He's Iago. He saw that aspect of the script and ran with it. You never know if Justin is being completely manipulative, or if, occasionally, some humanity leaks through. For an actor to bring that complexity to a 'villainous' role is a great contribution."

Barry Winchell's sexual orientation will never be known. He related to Calpernia as a woman, but according to Addams, engaged all of her physicality.

"Unfortunately, he died too young," Garity says. "Sexuality evolves with us. Part of our journey on this planet is the discovery of our sexuality. He was attracted to this female figure and was ultimately able to fall in love. We didn't have the luxury of asking him questions. He never complained to Calpernia or his parents. He had a slogan: 'Suck it up and move on.'"

Likewise, Nyswaner feels the film will find its audience, gay or straight, and all who watch it will bring something of their own to the table. "I write what interests me," he says, "and what interested me in this story had to do with universal themes, people who love unconditionally, and people like Justin Fisher who are tortured by repression. These themes apply to all human beings."

"What I want people to understand about this film is that the story goes beyond gay rights," says Garity thoughtfully. "This goes into the very core and makeup of our society as a whole. This story is about people not being able to express themselves, and being punished for difference. And there is no one in our elected offices who is willing to fucking sit down and deal with our issues of difference. Now," he adds, "we have a situation where we're at war and young men like Barry Winchell are out fighting [in Iraq], not for any concept of 'liberation,' but for the policies of the corrupt one per cent who run this country. We have the greatest soldiers in the world and [many of them] are constantly being abused and betrayed by their leaders. I can't expect my country to go liberate another country when we're unable to liberate ourselves."

Ron Nyswaner agrees, and furiously. "'Don't ask, don't tell' played an incalculable role in Barry Winchell's death," he says, steel in his voice. "The people who crafted it have a lot to answer for. It's a heinous policy, and one of the great political failings of the Clinton administration. The implied message is one that all gay people have had to live with our whole lives: 'We'll pretend you're okay as long as you don't tell us who you are.'"

$\mathscr{T}$he Carpenter's Hands

An Introduction to *The Highway:*
Recollections of a 21st Century Heretic
by Mark R.Braun

2003

MARK BRAUN'S BOOK *The Highway: Recollections of a 21st Century Heretic* is a personal road map of sorts, an exploration of faith by a gifted writer with his own questions. Reading it, I realized that they were my questions too, and likely the questions of incalculable numbers of men and women at the beginning of the twenty-first century. While Mark Braun in no way presumes to answer anyone else's questions, he offers up his own observations in the clearest, cleanest possible way. From a Christian author writing in the age of George Bush the Younger, it's a generous gift. Many of Braun's Christian literary contemporaries are busy churning out Christian potboilers about how the saved will all be swept up in the Rapture, leaving everyone else to perish in the coming Armageddon, while they watch and cheer from on high. These titles are then promoted locally from every fundamentalist bully pulpit in North America, then with all the dazzle of corrupt medieval bishops jockeying for political power, manipulated up *The New York Times* bestseller list, where the resulting sales figures are trumpeted as a sign of a religious quickening in America, and a sure signification that the end times are imminent. One longs to hear the bracing crack of a whip, the sound of tables being overturned, the metallic crash of coins, and the irritated, hysterical gabble of moneychangers being driven out of the temple.

The Highway, by contrast, is a true Christian literary *rara avis* — a modest, embracing, inclusive, beautifully written first-person narrative by an ordinary American Christian man offering up a personal account of the times in which he lives, and the queries of his own soul regarding what it means to be a Christian at the dawn of a new millennium. Mark Braun lives a good man's life in suburban Illinois: he works as hard, or harder than many of us ever will. In addition to physically demanding skilled labour as a construction carpenter, he provides and cares for his family — his wife, Laurie, and their three children — and carves time from his schedule to write, trying to make sense out of the chaos, as every serious writer does. His life is real, and that informs his writing. Mark Braun's personal literary quest is to understand how genuine, altruistic Christian charity and ethics were overtaken by the macabre fixations of the people who devour the aforementioned potboilers about the end times, smacking their lips and licking their fingers in anticipation of Christ's imminent return and all its attendant fire and destruction.

Like the best non-fiction writing, *The Highway* is an invitation to join him on his quest, not an instruction manual, or a fatuous Hallmark-style polemic about lambs and angels. The lodestar by which he guides his explorations is his own home life, his family's experiences, and his own soul-searching about what form actual Christianity — in the sense that its founder likely intended — might take in twenty-first century America.

In an increasingly secular age, the question of personal faith has become two diametrically opposed things simultaneously. In many ways, faith, primarily "religion," is less relevant to the culture at large than it has ever been before, while, paradoxically, it has become a keening, ravenous hunger for those who believe that the universe is governed by unseen forces that are greater than those they govern. If anything defines North American spirituality at the beginning of the twenty-first century, it is this uncertainty. The war between these two concepts has swept millions of people into its calamitous heart. Fundamentalist Christians have drawn a line of division between themselves and nearly everyone else. According to them, they are the elect of God, and anyone who falls outside of their circle is "not a real Christian," or worse. Many of them take a perverse and most un-Christlike pleasure in the thought that they will spend eternity in the company of God and their fellow conservatives, while the rest (Catholics, Jews, Muslims, Buddhists, pagans, liberals, gays, lesbians, feminists, and other so-called "Satan-friendly" people including, presumably, Democrats) serve out their sentences burning in hell.

In the late nineteenth century, proper Bostonian Unitarians, perpetually at odds with their Episcopal neighbours, joked that the American Episcopal bishop Phillips Brooks, was "an Episcopalian — with leanings towards Christianity." This *bon mot* was typical of the dry Yankee wit of the day, but it has some applicability to the current disconnect between American fundamentalists and other people. In many ways, the phrase "fundamentalist — with leanings towards Christianity," is an apt description of this most modern incarnation of Christianity.

Fundamentalist Christians, as a species, are rarely celebrated for their subtlety of thought, much less their sense of irony or humour. When they look to the Bible for reflections of — and justification for — their brand of Christianity, they find a bitter, jealous, vengeful Yahweh, who "loves" His children by creating them only so that they can spend a lifetime walking along a narrow, treacherous moral ledge where one false step will consign them to agony beyond description for all eternity. Forgiveness is like applying for a bank loan: the outcome is uncertain, and the penalty for irregular payments is terrifying. The God they find is white, male, Anglo-Saxon, heterosexual. He's pickled in righteous hatred for "moral deviates," especially for those who "choose the homosexual lifestyle," though He allegedly "loves the sinner and hates the sin." He votes

Republican. America is His chosen New Jerusalem, and George W. Bush is His instrument of cleansing fire.

In short, they find themselves. Their own attributes become, in their minds, divine.

They miss the fact that Christ was, himself, a radical liberal. The conservatives of His day — the direct spiritual antecedents of today's conservative Christians — were not the early Christians, but the conservative Romans and Pharisees, both of whom lived by strict, harsh, unforgiving codes that left no room for dissent. Christ's message of love and forgiveness was a radical and frightening concept in its day. Today's fundamentalist Christians would dearly love to see themselves shoulder to shoulder with the persecuted early martyrs of their faith, but in fact they have more in common with their persecutors. As a gay Christian, I have been told that my claim to that title is an obscene affront to the teachings of Jesus, and that the title itself is an oxymoron. When I weigh that opprobrium against the silent blue hours of my own personal, private communion, and the manifold blessings of love, health, wisdom, and friendship that have flowed into my life, it leaves me questioning the authority of those who condemn me, and leaves me straining to see where Christ even exists in the word Christian as it is currently understood by fundamentalist Christians, let alone in their harsh, exclusionary dogma.

Reading *The Highway*, I realized that I was not alone, and that Christianity is the personal choice of anyone who is interested, willing, inclined, or prepared to open up to Christ's ultimate directive, as expressed in Matthew 22:36-40: "Love the Lord your God with all your heart and with all your soul and with all your mind. This is the first and greatest commandment. And the second is like it: 'Love your neighbour as yourself.' All the Law and the Prophets hang on these two commandments."

So simple, and yet oceans away from so much of what passes for contemporary Christianity. One of the most powerful questions posed by *The Highway* is this one: Who are these self-styled gatekeepers of Christ's teachings, and what monstrous blasphemy is it to set yourself against your brother by claiming that you have a direct line to heaven, and to claim you speak on behalf of God?

As I write this on a rainy morning at the beginning of May 2003, the world outside the windows of my study at the top of the house is in turmoil. Bush the Younger has just announced that the war in Iraq is won, and while the United States and its tiny band of allies removed a brutal dictator from power in a country a world away, they have also opened a Pandora's box of options for how to deal with future conflicts. Those options include many things we in the self-styled civilized world told ourselves were long finished with: war for profit, illegal detainment, neighbours spying on neighbours, political witch hunts, and torture in the name of security and freedom. At no time in recent historical memory is the question of where Christ would stand on political and moral issues more relevant, and at no time is *The Highway* a more relevant document. Like the consumers we are, North Americans peruse all-inclusive Christian theologies in the same way we gobble fast food meal deals — thoughtlessly, hungrily, and hysterically, almost as though we had to supersize faith itself, something that by definition ought to be the centre of a believer's life. The result is a bloated, growth hormone-enhanced mutation of a religion that already has a dark past in serious need of reparations, and which threatens to take on a political aspect that it has no right to in a society where church and state are constitutionally separate.

What *The Highway* proposes is that we turn *inward*, and attempt that most difficult (and most overlooked) Christian challenge: humbleness and genuine kindness of the sort Christ preached. All true human goodness flows from that precept. The word love is bandied about by many contemporary North American Christians like a dirty copper penny, and has been used over the years to grease and shove the worst social atrocities through the narrow portals of a nominally moral society, from homophobia, to sexism, to racism, and beyond. Genuinely loving your fellow man is hard work, something to be struggled for. It's an eventual goal, not something one automatically does just because one has a religious conversion, or claims the title of Christian. Until true *love* can be attained — and one suspects that even Christ knew it would be a lifetime journey — there is a long highway of faith, every step moving towards the ultimate perfection, oneness with God and the universe.

Mark Braun is many things: among them a writer, a husband, a father, and an American man. All of these things are brought to bear in his book, and in his life. All of these things inform the outcome of both. He is one more thing, however. He is a carpenter, a crafter of beautiful and practical things, and he shapes them with his rough hands and artist's heart. In this profession, he is in the most illustrious, and indeed, if you choose to believe the subject matter at hand, celestial company. Although his book is a beautifully written narrative that I, or indeed any serious writer, would be proud to claim as my own, I see a carpenter's loving, calloused hands at work here as well.

There are such sights, and there is such beauty.

The Preacher's Life: God, Gay Rights, and the Reverend Dr. Brent Hawkes
2004

Consider the work of God: for who can make straight that which He hath made crooked?

— ECCLESIASTES 7:13

FROM THE OUTSIDE, THE Metropolitan Community Church of Toronto on Simpson Ave. — usually called by its acronym, MCCT — is not significantly different from any of the dozens of others nestled in the red-brick heart of the new gay yuptopia of South Riverdale. The faithful, men and women alike, greet each other on the sidewalk with a mid-century neighbourliness that seems out of place in a city like Toronto. Other than that, you could drive past the church and never notice anything remarkable. Inside, however, it's a different story. As the choir warms up with a rocking hymn, informally joined by some of the more musically inclined congregants, gay men, lesbians, leathermen, and transfolk begin to take their seats, nodding to and/or embracing their neighbours.

In the silver drizzle of November rain outside the sanctuary, a rogue explosion of late autumn sunlight suddenly streams through the stained glass windows, scattering a prism of rainbow-tinted luminosity across the patient, long-suffering faces of the etched saints.

The first impression of the church and its congregation is a stunning lack of irony. In a culture as narcissistic as urban twenty-first-century gay culture, it's absurdly touching to see "ordinary" GLBT people of all shapes and sizes socializing happily at a *church*, some with children in tow, none fuelled up on anything stronger than non-alcoholic communion wine. Denying themselves the frumpy, preening sartorial one-upmanship that might mark an equivalent mainstream church, the MCCT assemblage lays bare the stripped bones of creed and community in the classic sense. The congregants are there for prayer, for joyful celebration, and for "fellowship," a time-honoured Christian term meaning sharing psychic space, bonded by common faith. The knowledge that many of the congregants have crawled, wrecked and bleeding, from a holocaust of homophobic persecution and expulsion from their home religious traditions — often clinging to their faith by a frayed, bloody tendon — is the church's emotional cornerstone.

The Universal Fellowship of Metropolitan Community Churches, of which MCC Toronto is a member, was founded in Los Angeles on October 6, 1968 in the living room of the Rev. Troy Perry, an openly gay clergyman with a then-radical vision for a church that welcomed gays and lesbians in the spirit of Isaiah 56:7: "My house shall be a house of prayer for all people." Then, like now, mainstream heterosexual Christians were loath to concede that the "all" in Isaiah 56:7 included gays and lesbians. In the almost forty years since that date, the church has grown, in the face of opposition, adversity and persecution, to over forty-four thousand members in over three hundred congregations in seventeen countries around the world, and has become a powerful worldwide political force for gay liberation and social change.

Never was that change more in evidence than in 2001, when MCCT's senior pastor, Brent Hawkes, launched a lawsuit in conjunction with two same-sex couples whom he had married using a Christian tradition called reading banns. The process, a little-known legal alternative to city-issued marriage licences under Canadian law, requires asking the congregation on three consecutive Sundays if anyone objects to a couple's marriage. When the city refused to grant marriage licences, Hawkes and the two couples joined another lawsuit brought earlier by eight gay and lesbian couples who had been refused marriage licences by the City of Toronto. On July 12, 2002, the Ontario Supreme Court ruled that the Ontario government must recognize same-sex marriage under the law, making Canada the third country in the world to recognize same-sex marriage, and fulfilling, at a stroke, one of Troy Perry's original dreams for his church. Though it might be overkill to attribute the entire success to Brent Hawkes, it was his stance as a man of the cloth that brought worldwide attention to the issue.

Since the roots of Western homophobia are inextricably bound up in a monotheistic Judeo-Christian model that has rarely had to answer for its hatred of, and violence towards, gays and lesbians, this renegade Christian preacher's involvement in the resulting court decision struck the religious right with the force of a wooden stake through the heart, dragging them screeching and writhing into the searing sunlight of a new century.

This first weekend of Advent, the official start of the Christian year, the MCCT sanctuary has donned its finest gay apparel in preparation for Christmas. "I heard that they needed people to help with the decorating," said the man in front of me. "I found out too late," he sighs, regret evident as he surveys the shimmering red and green. "It's beautiful, though, isn't it?"

Once settled, the congregation turns expectantly as the organ swells to the magisterial opening strains of the processional hymn, "Jesus Came, The Heavens Adoring." Rising, they join the choir. Leading the procession is the purple-robed, bearded man whose face and name have become recognizable across the country. Indeed, in gay and civil rights circles, they are recognized around the world. Firebrand pastor, social activist, gay liberationist, gay marriage advocate, bane of conservative Christian leaders, media darling,

imperial pain in the ass, hellraiser, and knocker on heaven's door —
The Reverend Doctor Brent Hawkes is all those things, and likely
many more. But here, in his home church, he's just a preacher on
the first Sunday of Advent addressing his flock.

"Welcome to the Metropolitan Community Church of Toronto,"
he says. He smiles widely, arms opened in a gesture of benediction,
and the congregation know they are indeed welcome.

∞∞∞

IN THE YEARS SINCE his ordination as an MCC pastor in 1977, Brent
Hawkes has dovetailed his calling to the ministry with his longtime
fascination with the civil rights movement, especially as it applies
to the gay rights movement that caught fire at the Stonewall Inn
riots in Greenwich Village in 1969. Certain specific media images
of Hawkes are indelibly etched onto the history of the Canadian
gay liberation movement in the bleached silver-and-black of photo-
copied newsprint: Hawkes in 1981, slowly starving himself on the
steps of the Legislature to protest the 1981 raids on several Toronto
bathhouses, an event that precipitated street riots on a scale never
before seen; addressing the crowd's rage, thundering, "No longer
will we stand idly by while the police abuse us and the right wing
lie about us!"; Hawkes in 1995, shouting, "Shame! Shame!" after
the defeat of the same-sex benefits legislation Bill 167; Hawkes
triumphantly performing marriages of gay and lesbian couples in
the summer of 2002, the images flashed across the world via CNN.

"I think one of the criticisms that the church has had over the
years that has been unfair, in my opinion, is the assumption that we
are a church like every other one, and therefore sex-negative,"
Hawkes says in response to the question about MCCT's openness
to the full spectrum of the gay community and its experience.
"The assumption, for instance, that the church would condemn the
baths, or open relationships, or would condemn a variety of sexual
choices. Most of the criticism, I think, has come from people who

have never been to our church. I don't believe open relationships are immoral at all. I think they are not practical for many people, but people are free to choose that. It's not a moral issue, it's what's right for this couple." Nor is he impressed with the notion that these attitudes are in conflict with traditional Christian doctrine. "We can argue that homosexuality itself is in conflict with it," he says. "But we can also argue that women clergy are in conflict. Jesus came with unconditional love. He came because much of traditional faith, religion in his day, needed to be corrected. And it's amazing, because fundamentalist Christianity is *not* Christianity. We have to be careful not to be judgemental," he adds cautiously, "but it *isn't*. Fundamentalism does not follow the Christian tenets. It has shifted Christianity to a road that requires you to believe certain statements over and over again. I don't think that's what Christianity is. It's not a set of beliefs, it's a way of living. It's a path. So whether you believe Jesus died for your sins or not, or whether you believe in the resurrection or not, you can believe or not believe. You don't have to buy the party line in any of that stuff. The issue is: Are you on a path? Are you going deeper on that path? Most people want to sit on the fence. And they don't want to pick a path. The illustration someone gave is, if you want to dig for water it's better to dig one well sixty feet deep than ten wells six feet deep. Jesus came to save the church from the fundamentalists in his day, and now we have to do it again."

Today, dressed conservatively in a white button-down shirt and khaki slacks, he is sitting at the dining-room table in the Toronto townhouse he shares with his spouse of twenty-three-plus years, John Sproule. From upstairs comes the frustrated whining of the couple's two dogs, which have been penned up in order to afford their master a measure of peace during this interview.

"When I was eight or nine years old, I knew I was gay," says Brent Hawkes without a dollop of hesitation. "When they say, 'I used to dream about cowboys and Indians,' I really was dreaming of cowboys and Indians," he says wistfully. "And of swinging on the vines in the jungle with Tarzan, sitting in the treehouse and watching the sun go down together."

Born and raised in Bath, New Brunswick, Hawkes distinctly remembers watching some local youths playing basketball at an outdoor court near his house. He heard them joking about "homosexuals," and waited until one of the boys was practising alone to ask him what the word meant. The youth told him to look it up. "I vividly remember going home and getting a dictionary, trying to spell 'homosexual,' and finding out that it meant something about a man attracted to a man." The next day, the basketball player asked him if he had looked it up. "I said yes," Hawkes remembers. "He said, 'What did you find?' and I told him it was something about being a man attracted to men. I said, 'That's me!' He picked me up and sat me on the fencepost and looked me in the eye and said, 'That's *dirty*! That's *evil*! Don't ever tell anyone about that!'"

Demonstrating a uniquely Maritime pragmatism, his Roman Catholic mother and Pentecostal father raised their children in the Baptist tradition as a sort of ecclesiastical compromise. His father owned a grocery store, and his parents were pillars of the community.

Paradoxically, Hawkes's fierce identification with the church was his bulwark against any guilt he might have felt about his burgeoning awareness of his homosexuality. "I had this really personal connection with God," he says. "God was my best friend. We would go on walks, and we would talk. To me, it seemed like the church must be wrong." He smiles, and adds dryly, "Because it was a Baptist church, so many things were 'wrong.' It was 'wrong' to dance, 'wrong' to smoke, 'wrong' to hang around with Roman Catholics. I had Catholic friends who were wonderful people. It was easy to lump homosexuality in with everything else that was 'wrong.' I knew that my feelings were my feelings, and I didn't feel dirty and evil. I felt that God loved me, but the church was wrong. I kept disconnecting God with the church."

Still, he wanted to change. The only image of homosexuality available to young Brent was an elderly man who lived in the town, "very effeminate, whom everyone used to ridicule. He would dress up as a woman in the privacy of his house with the curtains drawn." The townspeople would peek through his windows, and pelt his house with eggs. Though moved by the man's plight, Hawkes couldn't identify with anything about him. "I knew that wasn't me," he says. "I didn't want to dress up as a woman, so I thought, 'Maybe I'm not a homosexual.'"

Like millions of gay men before him, Hawkes channelled his adolescent stirrings into church activities, and into schoolwork, at which he excelled. Neither activity precluded occasional sexual experimentation with other boys. "Afterwards, there was no discussion," he admits. "Never any discussion. There was a huge disconnect."

He developed an early fascination with the American civil rights movement of the 1960s. "There was no gay tone to it at all, but it was about people wanting freedom, of people finding solidarity with each other. I felt a connection with it, and wished there was that kind of a movement for me."

One day, in junior high, Hawkes intervened when an extremely feminine male classmate was being bullied. "I stood up for him, and someone said to me, 'Why are you standing up for him? Are you gay?' Everyone was shocked, because I was so popular. I stayed silent. I wasn't going to lie, but I wasn't going to say I was gay. I often thought afterwards that I stood up for him, but I let him down by not being fully honest." At the same time, he was feeling a powerful call to the ministry, a decision he announced on career day. "As soon as I said 'ministry,' everyone said, 'Oh God, a minister! He's a religious freak!' And so I learned to keep even more quiet."

As his awareness of his homosexuality became impossible to ignore, he realized that he could never be a Baptist minister and be gay. "It had less to do with inner turmoil for me, and more to do with an awareness that it wasn't going to work," Hawkes says. "I knew I wasn't going to be able to abide the party line on this issue, that I would be too outspoken."

The decision broke his heart. Eschewing a Baptist university for Mount Allison, he felt as though he had deserted God. "I felt like I had abandoned my best friend," he says quietly. "It was an awful decision." He attended a Baptist church during the first of the five years of his B.Sc., but at the end of it, the pain of listening to vitriolic sermons was too great, and he stopped attending church completely.

"I was in university for five years," he recalls, "because I got a full Bachelor of Science degree. The last four years of university and my first three years of teaching high school were a real learning curve. But I had no church. Church, at its best, offers comfort and challenge. The comfort is a sense of God's presence, God's promises, the hope, the strength, and the courage. But I also valued the challenge the church offered, because every Sunday there is a sermon that challenges you to think. Someone once said that the church is the only place people voluntarily go to be told they need to be different. It's a place which, at its best, challenges people to grow and expand their horizons, to be more committed to changing the world. So, for seven years," he says of his wandering in the spiritual desert, "I didn't have that."

ooooo

BRENT HAWKES HEARD GOD's second call in a 1972 Pinto in the parking lot of a Halifax bookstore in the freewheeling spring of 1975.

Like thousands of gay men in the United States and Canada, Hawkes, a high school teacher in Nova Scotia, was surfing the wave of post-Stonewall, pre-AIDS gay liberation. Ever the student, in addition to visiting the gay bars of Halifax, with trepidation at first, then with increasing authority and joy, Hawkes read everything he could about the burgeoning gay world into which he was coming out. On the afternoon in question, he entered the bookstore, which had a gay section.

"I bought one copy of everything," he remembers. "One of the things I had was *The Advocate*," then, as now, the gay and lesbian newsmagazine of record. "I was flipping through the magazine, and there was a display ad with a cross. It was for the Metropolitan Community Churches. And I just cried, and cried, and cried. I knew I was home. I knew that was where I belonged. I could try a Christian community again, answer God's call to ministry again. I just couldn't believe it."

Hawkes wrote to Troy Perry in Los Angeles. Perry wrote back and told him about the church in Toronto, and the one in Boston which was closer to Halifax. "I'd heard about Provincetown," he says about his impromptu holiday that summer. He stopped in at the MCC in Boston and attended a Wednesday night service there. He bought a copy of *The Front Runner* and took it to Province-town with him. "Here I was in Provincetown," Hawkes says softly, the years falling away. "Here I was in Provincetown, at a gay resort, playing in the dunes in the gay beach area, reading *The Front Runner*, and crying my eyes out. It was blowing my mind. I was seeing gay people everywhere, some holding hands."

Upon his return to teaching in the fall of 1975, Hawkes faced a dilemma. There was no doubt in his mind as to where his future lay. This second calling to the ministry was, to Hawkes, inarguable. And yet he loved teaching. Perhaps, most practically, becoming an MCC pastor would mean definitively coming out to his parents. Hawkes knew where he needed to be. On a field trip with his students to Ottawa, Hawkes sidetracked to Toronto and met with the pastor of MCCT who urged him to leave Nova Scotia and move to Ontario.

"I gave notice that I would be leaving at the end of the school year, and I also decided that I had to tell my parents. So I wrote a letter, and re-wrote it. I drove to the post office and parked my car. I remember getting out and walking in the front door, past the tellers to the drop-off, dropping off the letter, and having this instant panic: *I've done it!* I had two feelings, panic and joy."

That was Friday. The following Tuesday, his father called in the morning before Hawkes left for school. "He said, 'Your mother got the letter, and if I hadn't been there when she opened it, she would have killed herself.' And he said, 'What's wrong with you? What happened to you in university? What went wrong?'" Hawkes tried to explain to his father about his searing call to the ministry as a gay pastor in the Metropolitan Community Church. "He said, 'Don't mention the word *church*! It's foul coming out of your mouth!' But during the whole time, I felt someone holding my hand," he adds, with a trace of wonderment. "I felt a physical presence sitting there while I was talking on the phone, to keep me calm enough to have the conversation. As soon as the conversation finished, I just collapsed."

That night, with two gay friends who had also just come out to their parents, Hawkes watched a television program about Leonard Matlovich, the decorated airman who was discharged for being gay, and whose grave would later record: *When I was in the military, they gave me a medal for killing two men, and a discharge for loving one.*

There was a temporary ban on bringing any "gay friends" to his parents' home. "They just assumed that every single friend I brought home was gay," Hawkes confirms with a chuckle. "I never had a gay friend home." There was also an aborted meeting with a psychiatrist at his father's behest. After several long talks, the tension eased.

One conversation, though, struck Hawkes powerfully.

He was driving his father back to the airport one evening. "He was saying to me that he didn't want me to hurt Mom anymore and stuff. And I said that I just had to be me. He said to me, 'Well, no, you have to sacrifice for other people.' He said, 'For instance, what if I told you that *I* was "that way?"'"

He answered his father, telling him, "If you were 'that way,' I would say, 'That's the way you are, but you are married to my mother, so make a decision.'"

His father answered gruffly that he had just been using it as an example, and quickly ended the conversation. The phrasing of his father's question gives Hawkes pause today.

"I always thought my father was gay," he says neutrally. "We would be working in the grocery store. It would be a busy, busy day, and he would be at the counter cashing in some groceries. Then a cute young man would come in, and Dad would say, 'Oh Brent, can you take over the cash?' And he would go up to the young man and say, 'Oh, can I help you? Is there anything you need?' And he had his drinking buddies that he would always go off hunting with. My family would have been horrified," he says wryly, "but I often wondered."

ooooo

HAWKES HAS ACQUIRED HIS share of detractors over the years, both within the gay community and without. He often has to wear a bulletproof vest when he goes out in public. He has received death threats, and he has been stalked. Those who utter threats are usually hate groups and their adherents, often driven by hatred for what he represents: a clear-cut challenge to opponents of gay rights, but one who, instead of coming at them from the comforting bestiary of cherished gay stereotypes, comes at them from the very heart of the Christian faith, and with all the authority that, to many, accompanies it. The presumed temerity of that position is sometimes too much for his enemies to bear. Hawkes shrugs it off as the cost of being a controversial public figure, and insists that the day he allows death threats to keep him from his ministry is the day he resigns that ministry.

Gentler disaffection is closer to home. Many gay people have suffered bitterly at the hands of the church, any church, and there is something about an authoritarian male figure behind an altar and the image it conjures that proves to be a barrier they can't quite clear, no matter how hard they try. Though it saddens him, this is something that Hawkes understands intuitively. He realizes that the church will always be seen as something other than benign by a significant segment of the population, and for excellent reasons. He observes that the longstanding antipathy many gay people feel towards the church and other ecclesiastical organizations is deep-rooted, in many cases almost a collective cultural sense-memory.

"No question about it," he says, noting the sixteenth-century etymology of the word *faggot*, which has its origins in the witch and heretic burnings that devastated Europe between 1450 and 1782. Accused homosexuals were often forced to help condemned heretics gather the wood that would be used to burn them, at which time the homosexuals themselves would be thrown on the fire, tied fast to each other like bundles of twigs, in order to make the heat of the fire more intensely hot. In its own right, burning was a sentence carried out against homosexuals in Christian Europe, inspired by, and mimicking, the Biblical fate of Sodom and Gomorrah.

"John Boswell [author of *Same Sex Unions in Premodern Europe*] wrote that in the early centuries of the Christian church, gay people were welcome and appointed to leadership positions, were married, et cetera, until the twelfth and thirteenth century," Hawkes points out. At that point, a cultural and religious shift towards a shame-based view of sexuality replaced the old model, leaving little room for the non-procreative and the emotional. "When sex becomes 'bad,'" Hawkes says wryly, "and it's only for procreation, gay folk get left out, because we are seen as not procreative. So from that point on, gay became bad in society, and in the church."

Hawkes points out that in 1513, when the Spanish explorer Vasco Nunez de Balboa threw fifty homosexual Panamanian Indians to his dogs, which disembowelled and tore them apart, he laughed and shouted that "the only thing [the Indians] need to be women are teats and then they can give birth." That one mass murder was praised by the King of Spain as the Christian act of "an honorable and Catholic Spaniard."

"I think that there is so much historical damage done," Hawkes says with a sigh. "And the church's comparatively more recent history has been awful towards minority groups. Again," he adds rhetorically, "it's hard for people to understand [the reason gay people remain members of a church.]" Still, the Metropolitan Community Church creed is an inclusive one, which its clergy and congregants insist is much closer to Christ's intended message than is Christianity as it is manifested by fundamentalists.

"I think fundamentalist Christianity is more focused on an angry God, and secondly on Jesus being sacrificed," Hawkes says with a sigh. "It's like that old saying, 'Fundamentalist Christianity is so busy crucifying Jesus that they never will let him say a word. They're afraid what he'll say.' So," he adds, "with an angry God, you need to sacrifice. They saw Jesus as being perfect and so therefore Jesus would make the perfect sacrifice. I think that by approaching it this way, by making Jesus this super-human, they lost the strength of the message, which is that Jesus was this human being who did phenomenal things, started an amazing movement, and was willing, for the sake of being a peaceful movement, not to start a violent overthrow of the community. I don't believe Jesus's life was about being crucified. He came to try and transform people and transform the world, to get people back on a path. Again, it was a healthy path. It wasn't about a God of reward and punishment, but about freedom and justice. And Jesus tried to re-focus that again and they killed him. The religious and political league killed him for what he did. Our church chose as one of their faith statements that we believe there are many paths to God, and Christianity is one of them," he adds, stating that after a recent sermon series, he declared that he didn't believe Christianity was "the only way" to heaven, something that would bring down the wrath of the more dogmatic traditionalists, not that he gives a whit.

"It is one of *many* paths," Hawkes adds unequivocally. "It's a great path, but it's one of many paths to God."

ooooo

DURING THE SUMMER OF 2004, many Canadians, both gay and straight, watched the United States with growing disbelief, then bewilderment, at the realization that they had been living so close to neighbours they clearly didn't know. For many Canadians, it was like discovering that they lived in an apartment in a house directly above a ground-floor apartment where the tenants smoked in bed, and occasionally passed out drunk before extinguishing their cigarettes. It wasn't their choice of candidate — the world had already had four years to get used to George W. Bush and his swaggering, Texas-inflected "cowboy for Christ" brand of Americanism, whether it liked him or not. No, what was striking to Canadians was the orgasmic religious zeal of his adoring followers, many of whom came just short of calling him the new Messiah who had been called to rule by Divine Right.

As happens whenever modern Christianity is imposed on politics, it wasn't long before the moral danger of gays, this time the specific threat of gay marriage terminating society as they knew it, became the major rallying cry. Who could forget the circus of hypocrisy and political expediency that was the sight of vice-presidential wife Lynne Cheney sitting silently by while the Christian Coalition vilified her lesbian daughter, Mary, in order to not offend her husband's conservative Christian fan base? And who then turned on John Kerry like a pitbull when he had the temerity to *mention* her daughter as an example of parents loving their gay children? Nearly lost in this Grand Guignol spectacle of political buttock-parting was the inherently humorous and perversely ironic notion of Lynne Cheney trying to paint John Kerry as homophobic for invoking Mary Cheney's name during a debate over the merits of a just society for gay people.

"Communism had declined," Hawkes observes wryly. "They had civil rights, they had abortion rights, though right now it seems a little tenuous. Homosexuality is the last thing American fundamentalists can rally against for money and for a cause: *'Homosexuals are taking over the world!'*"

Playing to the fundamentalist Christian vote, George W. Bush initiated a Constitutional amendment to ban gay marriage. Although the measure was defeated, if it had passed it would have been one of the few times that the U.S. Constitution had been amended to curtail civil rights rather than expand them. Under the shopworn guise of defending "patriotism" and "family values," the powerful evangelical Christian movement in the United States mobilized with an unprecedented ferocity to elect Bush to a second term. Using the spectre of gay marriage as a sign of moral decay, the lobby stirred the slumbering homophobia that lay at the root of a significant portion of the self-identified "Christian" segment of American society, convincing voters that Senator John Kerry who, in spite of being on the record as believing that marriage was "between a man and a woman" (though in favour of same-sex civil unions) was a sort of gay marriage Antichrist tool of the "homosexual lobby."

"It wasn't even the gay community who put gay marriage on the political agenda," Hawkes says pointedly. "Some gay people wanted to get married, and took it to court. And now, it has become the major issue of the political agenda."

In the end, several anti-gay initiatives would pass on election night, leaving the rest of the world to wonder, perhaps naively, what on earth the Americans thought they were doing, and what homosexuality, or gay marriage, or God had to do with choosing a president, especially when, a world away, a war was raging that was killing at least one American soldier per day, and which was costing hundreds of thousands of Iraqi lives.

"Fundamentalist churches in the United States are not budging on the issue of gay rights," says Hawkes, referring specifically to the gay marriage issue. "In Canada, 57 per cent of the population support gay rights. In the States, the best percentage was 40 per cent in one state. But most were between 25 per cent and 30 per cent. So they have half the support for gay marriage. They have never managed to secure universal job protection, and only recently did the U.S. Supreme Court decriminalize gay sex."

During the run-up to the election, several networks treated viewers to up-close views of a world of home-schooled fundamentalist children whose Christian Republican parents were prepared to sacrifice the quality of their offspring's education in order to keep them from interacting with people of other races, sexual orientations, or political affiliations. It was a world of home Bible studies several times a week, church at least twice a week, and a casual, chatty relationship with God and Jesus, as though the Almighty and His Son were just another "dad and lad" who happened to live up the street, and who might drop by at any moment to borrow the lawn-mower; or, for that matter, to scorch the world with cleansing fire and Armageddon. One CNN special featured a pretty little girl who looked confidently into the camera and declared that she "couldn't wait" for the end of the world so that she could "see Jesus." Though not without fundamentalist Christianity within its borders, the Canadian national identity wasn't shaped by seventeenth-century Puritanism, with its witch trials and its superstitions, nor have Canadians been regularly swept by periods of religious revival and "spiritual awakening." Nothing, as it happened, could have made many Canadians feel more like Canadians, and less like Americans, than this up-close view of obsessive, sweaty religious hysteria, or this new and egregious breach of the barrier between church and state that is the cornerstone of American democracy.

"Gays in the United States are in deep trouble," Hawkes says. "A full 37 per cent of the U.S. population identifies as evangelical fundamentalists. Thank God we don't have that kind of influence in Canada," he says fervently. "And it's not just because Canada is multicultural," he qualifies, noting that many new Canadians come from violently homophobic home cultures, and bring those prejudices with them as part of their heritage. "Many tend to be not as helpful in terms of support for gay rights," he cautions. "Right now, we are importing hate. Canada has to have a better immigration policy. I'm not remotely racist, but I *am* saying that no matter what countries people come from, they need to be told that *tolerance* is one of the primary Canadian values. If you support these values, please come to our country. You don't have to *like* homosexuality, but you have to *respect* your homosexual neighbours. You have to *tolerate*, at minimum, your homosexual neighbours. If you are not willing to tolerate them, then don't come to this country. I think, in Canada, because we've done it incrementally, we've built a movement, and more and more people have been able to come out, and have influenced their friends in the process. And," he says, not without passion, "as a country and as a community, we've been able to undercut the 'God versus gays' thing."

ooooo

BRENT HAWKES WAS THE cheapest date John Sproule ever had. Although the two had met in early 1981 at the now defunct gay bar, Les Cavaliers, Sproule fell irrevocably in love with Hawkes during the latter's hunger strike on the steps of the Legislature as he protested the 1981 police raid on Toronto bathhouses.

"The whole situation was really big at the time," Sproule says softly. He is an intensely private person who has necessarily become a public figure as the spouse of a Canadian religious and political leader. "[The bathhouse riots were] Canada's Stonewall, or at least that's how people refer to it. Brent really kept the situation under attention through what he was doing."

Hawkes, who would eventually lose thirty-five pounds, had vowed to starve himself to death unless then-Attorney General Roy McMurtry acceded to his demands for an inquiry into allegations that police used excessive force during the raids.

"I would come out to communion on the Legislature steps every day, and we grew closer," Sproule says. "We started hanging out after the services." Sproule was attracted to Hawkes's "resoluteness. It's hard to put into words. He was very, very committed to the community — incredibly so. He was an admirable person, a solid person."

They didn't fall in love right away, Sproule clarifies. "It was a slower thing," he says thoughtfully, "a growing thing. It continues to be that. The longer I'm with him, the more I respect the guy. Which is a really good thing if you're going to have a long-term relationship. The number one thing for me about being with Brent is that I got a good guy. After all these years, I see a commitment to the community, to his church, the hours he puts in to do his work. And also the fact that, in many instances, he's really put himself on the line."

Part of "putting himself on the line" is the matter of personal safety, something that is never far from Sproule's mind when Hawkes is out in public. He worries about his partner's safety.

"One of the things that has been a worry has been the stuff around political action, when he's been attacked by the right wing," Sproule says in his soft voice. "It kind of goes with the territory. But sometimes things are going on that are bigger than yourself, and you have to buck up. That means, if you're feeling uncomfortable and nervous for a good reason, that's part of the deal. You can't allow people to dictate the agenda by phoning in a random bomb threat. That's the flip side of Brent's role in the community," he adds. "You can see Brent on Sunday, and it all looks really nice. You don't see the evening meetings all the time in the office, the weekend work. You also don't see the fact that there is a security threat. And the security threat has become more intense at various times, particularly when there is political action. The precautions that were necessary at various times made you feel worried. It makes the threat that is there real. You just keep going. I remember one time when we were both kind of worried, and I said, 'We're in God's hands, and we always have been.'"

The two are an easily identifiable couple on Church St. Although "the pastor's wife" is an established role with a built-in respect factor, especially in small towns, there is no precedent whatsoever for the gay male variant, which is a decidedly new animal.

"I looked around for role models of my own," Sproule reveals. "I made some connections with other clergy spouses." Male spouses, or female? "Both," he says. "I can't say that I was really that successful. Perhaps I didn't make as concerted an effort as I could have. I did subscribe to a clergy spouse magazine, but it didn't register with me. It was very 'Midwestern-straight.'" He pauses delicately. "I think you understand what I'm trying to say ...?"

"You mean tacky?" I ask him. "It was a tacky magazine for ministers' wives?"

"I'd never say that," Sproule says diplomatically. "In culture and language it didn't resonate with where I was at. I had to figure it out for myself a lot. The basic response I've had is: be supportive of Brent and have my own role in the church. And do something positive with the time I have."

The couple had a Holy Union (a declaration of intent, and blessing, which was MCC's only offering to couples prior to legal marriage) on their fifteenth anniversary. [Author's note: The couple married on March 7, 2006, nearly a year and a half after this interview was conducted.]

"Many ministers' spouses talk about it like living in a fishbowl," Sproule says pragmatically. He adds, not without humour, "I was raised Roman Catholic, and the only thing a pastor's wife does in the Roman Catholic tradition is not exist. So when I first settled down with Brent, I needed to figure out what the expectations were that people had around a pastor's spouse, and where I fit into that. What I aim for is to utilize that role to make my contribution to the community by supporting Brent's work, and, when possible, helping others. Basically, though, in the church, I've maintained my own identity and role," he says, referring to his work directing instrumental music ensembles, teaching Sunday School, playing recorder along with the hymns. He works hard to avoid the perception of abuse of his position. "It's a bit of a delicate position," he admits.

There is something wonderfully old-fashioned about Sproule. It is clear, watching them interact, that to Hawkes, Sproule is literally his "other half."

George Ripley (1802–1880), the Harvard graduate and Unitarian minister who founded the idealist communal experiment, Brook Farm (1841–1847) near Boston, once stated proudly that his marriage was not "founded upon any romantic or sudden passion," but instead "upon great respect for [his wife's] intellectual power, moral worth, deep and true Christian piety, and peculiar refinement and dignity of character." Writing about his wife, Ripley might have been Hawkes talking about Sproule, or vice versa. The nineteenth-century Boston Unitarians were great social reformers. It seems almost inconceivable today, in the era of Jerry Falwell, Pat Buchanan, and Fred Phelps, that over one hundred years ago, denominations could be such powerful forces for social good — for social betterment, for intellectual change, liberation, children's rights, women's rights, and the rights of minorities. There are strong parallels between the social and civil rights movements these firebrands spearheaded in New England, and the striving for social reform that is the consuming passion of the Metropolitan Community Churches in Canada and the United States today. In both instances, the denominations were facing fierce opposition from the conservative Christian establishments of their respective days. In the case of both Ripley and Hawkes, the spouses of these clergymen were solid helpmeets in a way that is, perhaps sadly, less the norm today.

"Our relationship has gone through a lot of changes over the years," Hawkes says, love clearly evident in his voice. "We're good for each other, and looking forward to growing old and retiring together some day. We have two dogs we love, and we are both very close to our families."

Both families were initially a challenge to the couple, but Hawkes says they have come around and are "very, very supportive of us. We know we are very lucky. John is involved in the church, and is not in my shadow. Part of that is more than affection," he says.

"It's about creating 'safe space.' There are limits, there are certain boundaries beyond which John doesn't want to hold hands, and he'll push away. But lots of folks come up to us, and talk to us, and thank us for the church and for what has been done. People who have never been to the church are just really thankful for what the church has meant, as an important institution in our society."

"Younger gay people probably don't have a vision of what it was like to live in a closed society," Sproule murmurs. "Of not being able to hold hands walking down the street, of not being able to mention anything at the office." When Brent and I were first together, you could get fired on the spot for being gay," says Sproule. "You could be thrown out of your house if you were renting. There were no protections. Early on, we had to make all sorts of wills in case anything should happen. To see things like George Hislop," Canada's first senior citizen to be retroactively awarded his life-partner's pension, "getting survivor benefits is a wonderful thing. To have been a part of the 2001 marriages which were covered worldwide ... to be a witness to that is an incredible thing. One of the things I realize is, if you think about the struggle of women, blacks, Jews, and gays, there have been dozens and dozens of generations that went by with absolutely no improvement. Here we are, you and I, seeing a time when there has been actual social change. Where our lot in life has become better. The amount of change that you and I have seen, it's like having a front-row seat on a miracle."

ooooo

BRENT HAWKES CAN LOOK back and see the little boy who was propped up on a fencepost and told that homosexuality was a dirty thing. It was a long, long time ago, he knows, but he still sees that little Baptist boy. Or rather, he qualifies, a *version* of the little Baptist boy.

"I can more see the rebel who was arguing with the Baptist minister about why I couldn't hang around with Roman Catholics," he says, smiling. "And why smoking was wrong. I'd never smoked a day in my whole life. But I would just argue: why, why, why? And that kind of rebel spirit — I can't say enough about the degree to which watching the U.S. civil rights movement on television affected and shaped me. I would still like to go back," Hawkes says thoughtfully. "I haven't been back to a Baptist church for meetings since I came out. I would *love* to go back," he says, his eyes twinkling with genuine merriment. "But I don't know if I'd be welcomed or not."

$\mathscr{T}$he Reinvention of Scott Merritt
2003

ON THE FIRST TRULY warm day of summer's outer edge, Scott Merritt, *Playgirl*'s thirtieth anniversary centrefold, is sitting in a leather club chair in the bar of the Sutton Place Hotel in downtown Toronto, remembering life on the other side of the closet door.

Like many extraordinarily handsome men, especially those whose primary medium of exposure is the super-terrestrial Olympus where celluloid Adonises walk the earth in the pages of magazines, he appears slighter and somehow more accessible in person. In his photo spread in the June 2003 issue of the magazine, which famously, and with no discernable irony, bills itself as "Entertainment for Women," he appears as remote as a Donatello carved from alabaster, posed poolside in the searing Miami sunlight. Today, the ex-model turned events promoter is tanned, tousle-haired and unshaven, dressed in faded jeans and an elegantly shabby sweatshirt. His eyes are the same vivid cerulean as in the photographs, but there is a warmth and immediacy that seems somehow new. Scott Merritt looks exactly like the sort of thirty-year-old guy who would rate at least a second glance on the street of any metropolitan city. He looks the way you'd want a *Playgirl* centrefold to look off-duty: hot enough to inspire fantasy, but real enough to imagine taking in your arms and kissing, first gently, then with all the passion his celluloid image was crafted to evoke.

Merritt was chosen as *Playgirl*'s thirtieth anniversary man from hundreds of photographs that poured into the magazine from across America in response to an announcement by the editors that the magazine was looking for a one-time birthday beefcake to represent their thirtieth year. After three decades of successfully exploiting and marketing the male form, initially to straight women, then increasingly (though unofficially) to gay men, the magazine was looking for the jewel in its crown. Merritt had emailed his photograph in to *Playgirl*, and when he was selected, he was flown to Miami and photographed. Even by *Playgirl*'s standards, the resulting images were stunning: clean, elegant, classically masculine but not aggressively sexual. The spread begins with Merritt dressed in white jockey shorts, then unfolds from there until he is nude. His expression is mischievous rather than predatory, almost elfin. Compared to Merritt, the pneumatically macho Shannon Fuller (*Playgirl*'s brawny Man of the Year, whose own nude pictorial ran alongside Merritt's in the June issue as well as claiming that issue's cover) looked positively simian. There is no subtlety to Shannon Fuller's appeal, but Scott Merritt looked like he could have a mystery side.

"It's taken me a while to get to this point," Merritt sighs, "but I'm gay. It's time to live truthfully. I've always been gay, and I'm done playing the part of a straight man in any context at all, in photographs or in life. The road to this point has been personally rocky at times, but I'm tired of keeping my head down. I don't want to hide anymore, period."

Contacted in New York, *Playgirl*'s editor-in-chief, Michele Zipp, acknowledges that Merritt's coming-out is a surprise.

"I didn't know he was gay," she says. "But I don't have a problem with a model being gay or coming out, and I don't know why anyone would. It's about a gorgeous guy, and if he's gorgeous, I really don't care about his preferences. I just write, generally, to women, because most of our readers are women. It really bothers me when

I get mail that says, 'That model was gay, and you *lied* to us.' That's not the case. We don't *ask*," she adds, laughing.

"Any time anyone comes out in a public way, it's a good thing, even a great thing," says Dirk Shafer, *Playgirl*'s 1992 Man of the Year, who famously came out on the cover of *The Advocate* in 1995. "It's a positive step forward. *Playgirl*, for the longest time, never admitted that they were a gay magazine, or that they had a gay readership. When I came out, they took a lot of different stances. When it first happened, they said they didn't know [I was gay] and [that I] had misrepresented myself. When they saw how much attention my film [*Man Of The Year*, Shafer's 1995 mockumentary about a gay *Playgirl* centrefold] and my story was getting in the gay press, they turned around and said they knew the whole time and didn't have a problem with it. They did a big turn-round. Look," he sighs, "the magazine is very clearly geared towards gay men. Look at the ads in the back and the kind of men they choose for their centrefolds."

In 2003, it's a popular truism among urban gay men that coming out is something that happens early and fast. A thirty-year-old man, especially an uncommonly handsome one like Scott Merritt, who has appeared nude in a magazine read all over the world, seems an unlikely candidate for the closet, especially given the social wealth his beauty might afford him in urban gay male culture. At the same time, Merritt's reluctance to discuss his sexual orientation up till now is a noteworthy reminder that, even today, gay men and lesbians come out of the closet at widely divergent points in their lives, for widely divergent reasons. Furthermore, the decision of when to do so is as personal and unique as the individual in question. In Merritt's case, the reasons stretch back across years.

Born in a rural Ontario farm town, his parents separated when he was two. "My earliest memory is that night," he says softly. "I remember phones being ripped off the walls, slamming doors, grown-ups storming around. It was very intense. I asked my dad where he was going and I remember I wanted to go with him." In short order, his father remarried and Scott went to live with his father and new stepmother. Two half-brothers followed in quick succession.

As a young man, his father, a police officer, had been scouted by the Chicago White Sox, and he passed that athletic ability along to Scott, who threw himself into athletics as a way of processing the tensions at home. He showed a particular precocity for track and field, settling into the decathlon as his primary event. "In the world of athletics," he says, "if you're the decathlon champion, you are considered the greatest athlete in the world. I ate, drank, and breathed track." Athletics also served as a receptacle for another powerful tributary of personal stress and tension: an evolving — and to him, confusing and frightening — attraction to men.

"I loved the way guys were, they way they looked. I loved it," he remembers. "But I also had to protect myself. I wouldn't shower when we had gym class, or go anywhere where I could physically see a guy's penis, because I was afraid of getting turned on, of having an erection and being picked on for that." Nor, he says, did he explore sexually with other boys. "I didn't experiment physically with other guys," he says. "I explored [these urges] by viewing magazines. I remember looking at the pictures in one of them and I realized that I liked the poses the models were doing. They were sexy, they turned me on. I have a vivid memory of one particular image — a guy, lying on his back, stretched out, muscles flexed. It was in *Playgirl*. You could see his penis. Looking at that picture, I felt something I had never felt before." One day, at age seventeen, his evolving sexuality came to a crashing halt when his stepmother found the collection of erotic magazines he had hidden behind the washstand in the family's Victorian farmhouse. "My stepmother didn't really want to deal with it," he says, his face darkening at the memory, "so she told my father." His father's fury at the discovery was towering and, ultimately, emotionally scarring. "I said to myself, 'Oh God, I can't be gay! How could I ever tell my father I'm gay?'" He buried his secret urges as far into his subconscious as he could, redoubling his athletic ambitions and shutting down his sexuality completely. If anyone wondered why the handsome and popular jock seemed sexually frozen at a time when his peers were stirring to sexual life, no one paid much attention. In the bovine arena of high-school society, his track and field achievements bought him a sort of public peace and no one looked too closely at anything else.

At nineteen, tensions at home were near a breaking point and he moved out of the house. He met a young woman (Merritt requests that her name not be used, to protect her privacy), and they began to date. "At the time, I wasn't looking for a relationship, or a girlfriend, and I saw this girl in my class," he says. "She was very intelligent, a very quiet girl. We just kind of hit it off, and the next thing you know, I ended up having sex with her." The two began a relationship, and moved in together. "She took control of things," Merritt says, adding that it was welcome control at a time when his life seemed chaotic. They both applied to college and the day before the acceptance letter arrived, the woman discovered that she was pregnant. They briefly discussed the option of terminating the pregnancy, but decided against it, a decision Merritt says he hasn't regretted from the moment he first laid eyes on his tiny blonde daughter.

When student loans came through, the woman returned to school, and Merritt took a job as a home-care worker and looked after their child. Although he says he was faithful to his partner, his attraction to men began to resurface. Due to many "contributing factors, one of them being the natural breakdown of the relationship," and the woman's desire to leave southern Ontario, the relationship ended. She moved, first to Vancouver, then Los Angeles, taking their daughter with her. "The relationship ended and right afterwards, I had my first experience as a gay man. I was twenty-five years old. I did it once and I figured, 'You know? This is right.' It was a huge weight lifted off my shoulders." Still feeling a need to protect his ex-partner and their child from the stigma, real or imagined, of being a gay father, Merritt did not identify himself as gay. His ex had been livid at his announcement of his sexual orientation and she turned on him in a fury. "[She] said, 'Scott, do you ever stop to think what it's going to do to your daughter? When she goes to school, she may not want to have friends! Her friends may not want to be friends with *her* because her father is gay!'" Reeling with guilt, Merritt shut down again, more severely even than when he was eighteen. Furtive sexual encounters left him wracked with guilt. Perhaps as a result of the pressure of the closet, he spiralled into a period of hard living and drugs. He began a modelling career that took him to Asia and Europe, and began his first serious relationship with a man. Scott Merritt was, by then, almost thirty years old.

∞∞∞∞

WHILE SCOTT MERRITT WAS overhauling his attitudes towards gay life, so was *Playgirl*. Although the magazine still presents itself as completely heterosexual, its tacit gay-friendliness today has evolved significantly from its stance just a few years back. According to a gay former senior-level editor whose tenure at *Playgirl* spanned the early nineties, the magazine was aimed at women, end of story.

"There were gay men who read it, but the editorial wasn't tailored to them," explains the editor, who asked that his name not be used. "The concern was *Playgirl* models showing up in the [gay erotic magazines] at the same time. I used to peruse the gay magazines — a real chore," he says, laughing.

Back then, the editor says, "a model coming out as gay would have been a problem, because the fantasies the magazine was creating were styled to be women's fantasies. 'Did women want to look at erections?' The consensus of the women on the staff, and I was the only male, was that they didn't."

In the last decade and a half, *Playgirl*'s policies have evolved with the times on models, sets, and, yes, erections.

"The gay readership is about 30 per cent," Michelle Zipp says definitively. "It's 'Entertainment for Women' because there's no other magazine out there that caters to women in the way we do, but we love our gay readers as well. These days, both gays and straights occasionally accuse *Playgirl* of being a 'gay magazine,'" says Zipp. "I find it interesting when people make that observation. I've read a lot of the gay [erotic] magazines and looked at the photos. I don't see *Playgirl* as being similar to them. The pictorial 'eye' is just a little bit different."

Judging by the feedback she receives, sexuality is in the eye of the beholder. "I get letters from our gay readers that say things like, 'I love *Playgirl* because it's *not* a gay magazine.' For them, we provide an 'insider' view, enabling them to share in a fantasy that although guys are straight, they might be able to turn them around. Then I have women readers who say things like 'These guys look a little *gay* because their chests are shaved,' to which I reply, 'So? Do you think he's sexy or not?'"

Amid the ceaseless debate about *Playgirl*'s market, one thing is clear: As far as Zipp is concerned, gay boys no longer need to worry that *Playgirl* is not for them.

"The overall mission and the overall attitude of myself and the staff we have now is very positive and very accepting," Zipp says firmly. "We have something in common, straight women and gay men. We both like men and they have to be good looking."

As encouraging as all this is, most gay teens still have no idea of the acceptance *Playgirl*'s creators might feel for them. The story they expect, the story that Scott Merritt grew up with, is that everybody in the world is straight and if you're honest about being gay, you'll be hurt.

Playgirl and its men are the incubi of adolescent gay dreams. However inevitably we may outgrow the all-American boys of *Playgirl*, trading them in for rougher, more overtly gay imagery, more men than not have memories of their discovery of the magazine, and what it meant to them growing up. In his luminous debut novel, *The Year of Ice*, author Brian Malloy renders the coming-of-age story of a gay teenager, Kevin Doyle, growing up in the late seventies, whose discovery of his own sexuality is abetted by stealing copies of *Playgirl*. Kevin befriends a straight college student who begins to buy him copies of the magazine, as well as copies of *The Advocate*. When Kevin is forced to move to his aunt's house following a fight with his father, he only has room to hide one set of magazines.

"He throws out copies of *The Advocate* because, he says, they're 'too boring,'" the author says sheepishly on the phone from Minneapolis, "and he keeps the *Playgirls*. In my own experience, in the mid-seventies, I stole *Playgirl*. I never bought them. I always stole them, because I didn't have the nerve to pay for them at the cash register. I also wasn't old enough to buy them. I got to look at non-threatening, clean-cut guys, which was all I could handle at that point. I think graphic depictions of gay sex would have been too startling for me when I was in my mid-teens. As an adolescent, your hormones are raging, but it's also a very romantic time. When I was a teen, I could imagine that the *Playgirl* model was my boyfriend and that he was there just for me, because he posed alone. I also liked the fact that they started out with clothes on, so I could imagine a process of flirtation and dating. So it was romantic and erotic at the same time. It would have meant an awful lot to me," he muses, contemplating how an out *Playgirl* centrefold would have opened up his world as a teenager. "I was convinced that it was me alone on the planet. You hear the insults on the playground, but you don't think 'people like that' really exist. It would have made a huge difference, because I would have been able to go through that stage that other teens got to go through. I think teen girls go through it earlier, when they put pictures of rock stars on their walls. With teen boys, their rite of passage is getting their first girlie magazine and talking about it with their buddies. With gay teens, you don't put the picture of the guy you have a crush on up on the wall and you don't swap the magazine with your friends. You feel so alone. Knowing that the guy I was looking at was also gay would have done two things: it would have ended the isolation, and brought him into the realm of possibility. You'd know you'd never meet him, but it would have been a possibility."

According to Dirk Shafer, *Playgirl*'s evolution has surpassed the mid-seventies imagery that Malloy and many gay men in their thirties and forties remember with fond nostalgia.

"The idea is that *Playgirl* centrefolds are fantasy images for *women*," Shafer says wryly. "But I think that in the last ten years, the way things have changed, it's a fantasy image for *people*. Men or women, at this point. The line has become blurred. I'm sure there are still women who read it, but there are just as many men, if not more." In the last thirty years, societal sexual mores have shifted again and again, making space for a kaleidoscope of sexual possibilities that would have been inconceivable in years past. "A lot of straight women are turned on by gay men," says Shafer. "I didn't have a lot of negative reaction from women when I came out. Even to this day, I run into straight women who are attracted to the notion of two men together." He recalls a recent visit to what he calls his "first titty bar," where he had a lap dance. The dancer wriggled her bottom between Shafer's famous thighs, at which point he gallantly pointed out that he was gay and introduced his boyfriend. The stripper smiled knowingly and said, "I knew you guys were gay. Your teeth are too good."

ooooo

ON FEBRUARY 1, 2003, Scott Merritt found himself poolside in Florida, with two female *Playgirl* editors, a photographer on a mission, and no wood.

The humour of the situation wasn't lost on him. He was trying not to be nervous. He'd done runway shows where, in the pandemonium of backstage, models of both sexes changed at the speed of lightning, flinging clothes everywhere, and modesty was too expensive.

"You tell yourself, 'You're a professional!'" Merritt laughs, remembering how he tried vainly to summon his composure as the editors waited patiently for him to strip. He gingerly stepped out of his trousers, and put on the "official" *Playgirl* underpants. The photographer shot some film.

"We decided to have lunch," he says. "But before lunch, I was thrown into the pool. They did some shots there, and I froze my nuts off. So I stood in the shower for forty-five minutes trying to warm up."

In preparation for the shoot, Merritt had dieted himself down to low single-digit body fat, and in sixty-five degree water, he was chilled. As he lay in the sun trying to warm up, he called his boyfriend in Toronto. Just then, they announced that it was time to take the "hard" shot. Oblivious to Merritt's sexual orientation, but wanting to be helpful, the editors offered him a huge stack of *Swank* magazines to stimulate his imagination, and sent him behind a privacy screen. *Swank* is a magazine aimed at heterosexual men with very flexible and eminently negotiable standards of what constitutes feminine beauty. Merritt frantically flipped through the ocean of rippling female flesh, cheaply photographed and printed on luridly glossy paper, desperate for one of the few shots of men engaged in sex with the female models. He was relieved to find a few and he focused on the naked men in the pictures before facing the camera on the other side of the curtain.

"The photographer was very professional, which helped," he says. "Plus, I had time with him before the shoot. We'd had dinner and he'd explained all of the shots to me. I couldn't be one hundred per cent aroused, but we'd do a shot, then I'd go behind the screen and look at some images, then come back out. He'd say, 'Look sexy, look like you're enjoying this.' And he made it easier, so we were able to pull the photographs off."

He answered all of the questions on the questionnaire honestly, Merritt says. When asked about his most memorable moments with women, he talked about the mother of his child. It didn't feel like lying, and in fact, technically, it was the truth. *Playgirl* faxed him the layout and he was impressed by the quality of the photos. The poses were far from vulgar, the photography was beautiful, and the entire layout was one any model would be proud of.

But somewhere along the way, he began to wonder what he was doing. He knew there would be a perception on the part of *Playgirl*'s readers that he was straight. "On the one hand," he says, "I didn't really care, because I saw it as a modelling job, and I did it well. They didn't ask me if I was straight, and I didn't lie." On the other hand, in moments of increasing private honesty and introspection, he began to feel as though it was one more in a long series of masks he had worn since he was a teenager, framed in half-truths and technicalities. "I think that, in my mind, the possibility of being thought of as straight wasn't at all disturbing to me," he says. "I could rationalize all sorts of reasons to stay in the closet — protecting the feelings of family members, colleagues, the people around me. But suddenly, it didn't seem nearly worth the personal cost."

While freely admitting that no one had forced his hand by posing, he realized that somehow in the midst of it all, he himself had bought into the image of the "*Playgirl* man" as a heterosexual icon, the ultimate totem of fantasy masculinity as "entertainment for women."

And, with the photographs about to hit the stands, Scott Merritt looked inwards and decided it was time to be honest with himself, and with everyone else.

"The biggest handicap is not being true to yourself," says Scott Merritt. "Not being who you are meant to be and who you should be. There are a lot of people who go through life pretending to be who they aren't, and in whatever way and for whatever reasons I've done that in my life — I'm tired of faking it. I'd like to think that I'm evolving. I'm thirty years old. That's young. Some people don't ever come out of the closet. I'd always put 'coming out' on the back burner. I thought I was 'partially out,' and that was okay. But it wasn't. I've got to be true, one hundred per cent. It's never too late to address that sort of honesty, and to live that way" adds *Playgirl*'s Thirtieth Anniversary Man, "but it's really time to start."

$\mathcal{D}$reaming in the Land Beyond the Forest
2004

I'VE WAITED MY WHOLE life to carve these words into a non-fiction essay. This season of Halloween's frost and cold blue moonlight seems the ideal time to do it, so here it goes:

> *I'm writing this in the courtyard of Castle Dracula. The low westering sunlight slants down through the distant, forbidding vista of the blue-green, mist-shrouded Carpathian mountains, edging the rough cobblestones and the stone-cut mullioned windows of the ancient castle with blood-tinted late afternoon shadows that seem oddly patient, though somehow hungry.*
>
> *Soon it will be night, and the moon will rise behind the turrets of the castle, and whatever lives when the sun dies will walk the earth again. I have come to this ancient, forgotten land whose soil is enriched by centuries of spilled blood in search of answers. I fear I will have them shortly. I pray that I will have the strength to bear the knowledge that will soon reveal itself to me*

Not bad, if I may say so myself. I like it. A little over the top, a little purple, but then again, horror fiction is one literary genre where a touch of the grape isn't just forgivable, it's actually encouraged.

The thing is, it happened. I was *there*. It's non-fiction.

I wrote those paragraphs on May 9, 2004, in Bran village, in Transylvania. They are paraphrased from some notes in my journal, written specifically for this October essay, which would be crafted many months later. My literary intention in writing them was to see if I could take the elements around me — the village of Bran deep in the heart of Romania, the courtyard of Castle Bran, the mountains, the sunset — and merge the journalist's eye for detail with the horror writer's inner-eye for colour and atmosphere through the power of imagination. The facts are technically accurate: the sun *was* setting, the Carpathians *were* blue-green, the land *is* largely forgotten, and the soil of Transylvania *has* seen more bloodshed than most in Europe. I *was* in search of answers, all of them journalistic and pertaining to the film I was there to cover for the magazine that had flown me halfway across the world. None of the questions were about vampires. Whether the shadows seemed "hungry" or not is a matter of artistic vision, and since I wrote it, I am the ultimate authority. That's the magic of the writing craft, and one of the gifts of imagination, to bring a waking dream to life on the page.

If I say they were hungry, then they were hungry.

In the popular imagination, Castle Bran has become the de facto "Castle Dracula," one of the seats of power of the fifteenth-century Wallachian prince, Vlad the Impaler — the Saddam Hussein of medieval Transylvania if you will — whose historical identity was the genesis of Bram Stoker's novel *Dracula*, published in 1897. I first read it in 1971 when I was nine years old.

My mother started me on this twilit road with the grisly "bedtime stories" of the Brothers Grimm, replete with ogres and demons and ancient wind-blasted castles where witches dwelt. I graduated to British fantasy writers like Alan Garner, then to English ghost stories of the M.R. James school, and American horror comics. Laced throughout were the Christopher Lee Dracula films I adored, among the best of the Hammer Films oeuvre. I read Mary Shelley's

Frankenstein at our house outside of Geneva when my father was posted to the United Nations there in the mid-seventies, learning early what I would later rediscover upon re-reading *Dracula* in Transylvania in 2004 — that there is power in experiencing a writer's work by reading it in the milieu in which it was set.

As an adult, my professional writer's life to date has been largely comprised of non-fiction and essays, but I have managed to make horror fiction my avocation, not only with my own horror fiction, but with the *Queer Fear* anthology series, the first collections of horror stories to have gay protagonists and themes as a matter of course. I'm a proud member of both PEN Canada and The Horror Writers Association.

Being a gay horror writer is a lot like coming out a second time. Readers, editors, and friends see you one of two ways. They either regard you as a spooky fellow whose predilection for things that undulate by moonlight is an amusing, endearing twist in your character, or they see a massive incongruity between what they think of as your "serious" literary work — articles, essays, reviews — and this weird shit you seem to love. I occasionally feel the pressure to disavow my horror work as literarily "unserious," as though I couldn't possibly be thought of as a "serious" writer if I didn't.

I always decline the invitation.

For every patronizing mainstream book editor who chuckles indulgently across an elegant dinner party table when the subject of "that ... *horror* stuff you like" comes up, for every insecure, highbrow gay literary fag who feels his own queer-themed work is hanging by its manicured fingernails above the abyss of being considered "genre" by virtue of its gay theme (and who therefore refuses to confer on you the title of colleague for fear of being tainted himself), there are a dozen smart, articulate, well-spoken readers and fellow writers who celebrate your speculative work. Writing is either good writing, or it is bad writing. I don't acknowledge the barriers of genre, and neither do the writers I most admire.

Having separately interviewed both Stephen King and Peter

Straub on this topic, I am comforted to know that this prejudice extends to the highest levels: King is the Dickens of our age, the most widely read author in history, and Straub's Jamesian prose has elevated the horror field again and again to the highest echelons of American letters. You'd think they'd be immune, but they're not. Horror, like desire, is a visceral emotion. Anything that makes a reader feel those emotions that society would rather leave behind closed doors is bound to make these prim worthies uncomfortable.

Back in May, I was on assignment in Bucharest for *Fangoria*, the American horror film magazine of record, for whom I have been writing for nearly twenty years. My editor, Tony Timpone, has become a great friend and confidant over the years, and he has sent more fun my way since 1987 than any journalist has the right to expect. I was covering the filming of *Seed of Chucky*, written and directed by out-director Don Mancini, and starring two gay icons, Jennifer Tilly and John Waters. A group of us from the production had chartered a minivan and departed from the Bucharest Marriott, an oasis of eastern European luxury that borders on the ultimate in vulgarity, to make the occasionally bumpy day trip "deep into the heart of Transylvania," as Roman Polanski wrote in the screenplay of 1967's *The Fearless Vampire Killers*.

My fellow travellers were superb company. As difficult as it was to get into the "vampire mindset" with the van's radio playing Blondie's "Heart of Glass" and other hits of the 1980s while we swapped film, travel, and boyfriend anecdotes, we *did* see genuine Transylvanian peasants with goiters driving ox-carts, as well as gypsies and wild dogs everywhere — just like the movies — through the windows of the van.

As we left metropolitan Bucharest, the land became flatter and sparse, until we began to climb into the mountains. Great fields of dark earth gave way to soaring rock and black-green pine forests. The air grew cold and clear. Here and there we drove through villages where humble-looking wooden houses were interspersed with stern, rigorous municipal architecture. In the distance, every now and then, we would catch a glimpse of a monastery, or a sinister-looking *castel* jutting out from a mountain ledge, sometimes, delightfully shrouded in mist. Given the loathing many Romanians feel for the co-opting and casting of their national hero, Vlad the Impaler, as a vampire horror staple, we kept the delight largely to ourselves.

The ubiquitous Romanian street dogs, mute victims of Ceausescu's savage uprooting and the forced dispersal of their owners, wandered the city and countryside. When the late dictator appropriated the homes of ordinary Romanian citizens in order to use the land to construct what would later be acknowledged as grotesque monuments to his megalomania, families were forced to settle in government-owned city apartments that forbade pets. Abandoned, the dogs are Romania's other orphans. They interbreed and wander freely along the treacherous roads by the tens of thousands. The ones who survive form a parallel Romanian population to the human one. During my stay in Bucharest, a good day was seeing only one dead dog along the side of the road as I was chauffeured to the studio. A bad day would be nearly unthinkable to the average modern North American city dweller, especially a dog owner.

Midway thorough the journey, our driver stopped the van and sauntered over to a group of gypsies standing in front of a store to ask them directions to Castle Bran. The gypsies suddenly became agitated, and an exchange of rapid-fire Romanian exploded between them and our driver. As we watched, our driver raised his hands and waved them away. The gypsies lurched after him, keening and wailing and crossing themselves. He jumped into the driver's seat of the van and slammed the door, locking it. Inserting the key into the ignition, he put the van into reverse, gunned the engine, and swerved away from the gypsies who were by now spitting on the ground and glaring at our departure.

"What were they saying?" queried one of my travelling companions, turning her head and looking back. The whole spectacle had been quite dramatic, and we were all by now aroused from our travel-induced torpor and quite taken with the entire passionate exchange.

"They are wanting money," said our driver, manifesting the urban Romanian's universal contempt for gypsies. "I have not given money. Gypsies angry."

Nonsense, I thought with a private smile. *They were saying, "For the love of God, stay away from the castle!"*

After an hour or so we parked, turned off the radio, and stepped out into the cold wind to stretch our legs. We stood on the edge of a desolate stretch of highway. The fields were dead and yellow, life not yet returned to them after the savage Romanian winter, and the Carpathian Mountains in the distance seemed cruel and implacable, though no less majestic for their cruelty.

I listened to the wind, closed my eyes, and tried to dream of Dracula.

For a moment, the world as I knew it vanished. I heard Jonathan Harker's calèche clattering along the Borgo Pass through spectral blue fire on *Walpurgisnacht* and the distant baying of wolves. Then the dream vanished as quickly as it had come, reality closing over the dark obsidian stone of fantasy as surely as the surface of a bright green lake.

And yet, later, the moment occurred again, this time after our arrival at the castle. With a sense of reverent pilgrimage, I split off from the group and went to explore, on my own, the rugged, gloomy castle, which was momentarily blissfully free of tourists. I sat on a rough-hewn wooden bench in the courtyard and looked up. I closed my eyes and again summoned my waking dream of "the land beyond the forest," the Transylvania of myth and legend that I've carried in my head and heart since I was a very young boy.

5 May. — I must have been asleep, for certainly if I had been fully awake I must have noticed the approach to such a remarkable place, wrote Jonathan Harker in his journal, describing his arrival at Castle Dracula. *In the gloom, the courtyard looked of considerable size, and as several dark ways led from it under the great round arches it perhaps seemed bigger than it really is.*

The sudden arrival of a clutch of hearty, beaming, white-legged German tourists in black socks and sandals, wielding cameras, snapped me out of my reverie. I opened my journal, made a few notes, then gathered up my things and went to join my friends.

∞∞∞

AS I WRITE THIS, October has come to my Toronto neighbourhood. The leaves are turning and there is a bite in the air that hints at winter's inevitable, carnivorous arrival. Halloween has been my favourite season ever since I was a child. I first became aware of it when we were living in Cuba in the 1960s during my father's diplomatic posting there. The embassy threw a Halloween party for the children, complete with a costume masque — also my first.

Shades of things to come, I went as Maleficent, the evil queen from *Sleeping Beauty*.

Perhaps it was the Halloween colours, black and gold, which struck me so incongruously in the pastel-hued Havana twilight. I had never seen an autumn leaf in 1968, nor had I seen Canadian snow. But the idea that on this one magical night the world could be transformed into a candle-lit diorama of glaring pumpkins with fiery eyes, flying witches with green faces, and drifting ghosts suggested an appealing world of metamorphic possibilities. Gay people are, if nothing else, masters of plural identities. It's either bred in the bone, or it's the first lesson we learn as children. It often starts as a way to protect ourselves from a hostile world, but harnessing it is a power we grow into and one that makes us special. That, and the ability to take a world that is often mundane and brutish and turn it into something that glitters with autumnal light through the sheer power of our own imagination.

Ultimately it didn't matter to me last spring that Bran village had become something of a *mittel Europa* "Dracula Disneyland," with peasants and gypsies hawking bread and cheese and everything Dracula-related to tourists who were there to celebrate Stoker's vampire count — a count who never was.

Or that after visiting the tomb of Vlad the Impaler on the monastery island of Snagov a few days later, the "silver crucifix" I bought to commemorate the occasion began to glow in the dark — and not because of the presence of anything unholy.

No, what mattered was that, as I gazed across the fields at whose edge the brackish marsh water lapped the muddy shores of Snagov Island, I was able to remember the island's gruesome history, and its legends. Over the centuries it has been put to a series of grisly purposes — prisons, torture chambers, the site of monstrous impalements, many supervised by the inhabitant of that elaborate Byzantine crypt beyond the line of trees at my back.

I was able to close my eyes and see a storm coming in over the water, lightning flickering at the centre of boiling, tenebrous clouds in a sky gone black and violent. Behind me, in my waking dream, loomed the rain-lashed medieval monastery that allegedly contained the last earthly remains of a fiend whom many believed was immortal.

I found that even after I opened my eyes and blinked in the sunlight, Snagov Island was nowhere I would want the dark to catch me.

Plural identities, plural realities.

Imagination.

For a writer, they're powerful tools. For a horror writer, they're the air we breathe.

Before leaving Castle Bran that late-afternoon in May, I ran my fingers lightly along the stone walls in tribute to the boy I was in 1971. I committed them to memory, again not without a pilgrim's veneration. I won't forget the feeling of that rough surface of Dracula's castle beneath my fingers as the sun went down, or my rediscovery of the secret doorway in my mind that had swung inward with the soft click of memory.

I knew well the ancient thing that waited for me inside.

After all, I was nourished on blood.

In Praise of Queer Fear

An introduction to the anthology
Queer Fear: Gay Horror Fiction

2001

THERE'S A STORM COMING.

The air is paralyzed, sweating ozone. The late-afternoon sky is blue-black and swollen with the sure promise of violence. I like storms. A perfect one can take you to the very edge of creation. In 1816, Mary Shelley, a houseguest with her husband, Percy Shelley, at Lord Byron's rented Villa Diodati on the shores of Lake Geneva, first dreamed of her monster during a furious lightning storm that her husband noted was like the end of the world. "What terrified me will terrify others," Mary Shelley wrote in her "Author's Introduction to the Standard Novels Edition" of *Frankenstein* in 1831, "and I need only describe the spectre which had haunted my midnight pillow."

My partner Brian and I live in a 135-year-old farmhouse on a tree-lined street in a leafy Toronto neighbourhood. In the summer, when I draw the blinds against the sun, the house smells like time sleeping. The ceilings are high and, sometimes at night, by candle-light, the shadows seem to move at their own discretion. As a writer, I spend hours alone with the blinds drawn, inhabiting other people's lives. Readers who have lost themselves in a well-written tale of terror on a stormy night will understand what I mean when

I say that I sometimes wonder if we don't bring the stories back into the world with us by reading them alone, whether or not they stay contained. A board creaks in an upstairs room, and it makes you start, even though you know you're alone in the house. A tapping on the glass has to be a branch tortured by the wind. A sigh in the shadows of the far recesses of the next room has to be a draft. The slumped figure drifting just out of your line of sight is a shadow cast by the candles.

You're alone, reading.

Keep telling yourself that as you read the stories in *Queer Fear*. The creatures that live in these pages, monsters, both human and otherwise, are better confined between the covers of the book you are holding in your hands. The authors of these stories, among whom are the darkest jewels of the horror fiction field, have written in the spirit of Mary Shelley's maxim: what terrifies them will terrify you as well.

ooooo

WHEN I WAS A little boy growing up in Ottawa, Ontario, in the early 1970s, my allowance was twenty-five cents. In those days, that was enough for a twenty-cent comic book and five cents' worth of candy. As I remember my childhood summers, some of the clearest, purest memories are of gold and green Saturday mornings. I would ride my banana-seated Schwinn up Kilborn Avenue to the Kilborn Confectionary, a neighbourhood grocery store run by a Lebanese family whom, it seemed, had always been there. The store was air-conditioned in the summer and faintly scented with pine floor cleaner and some indefinable powdery perfume that I have always associated with that innocent, vanished time. The radio behind the counter would always be playing music — Janis Ian, Bread, The Monkees. It was there, in that store, on the creaking metal turnstile racks near the entrance, that I first discovered the field of horror fiction, both in comic book form and also in the form of cheap paperbacks with titles like *The Frankenstein Wheel, Dracula's Brothers*, and *Power Through Witchcraft*. The novels cost as much as seventy-five cents, so if my mother wouldn't buy them for me (which was a rarity, since my parents believed that reading, something, anything, was better than not reading), I would save up and buy them myself. I could always afford the comic books — *Tomb of Dracula, The Witching Hour, Werewolf by Night*, and *Dark Shadows*. I was fascinated by the beautiful, lurid covers, and something in me soared at the power and the magic — and yes, darkness — inherent in the stories. Heart pounding, I would place the comic books and the candy in the basket of my bike and pedal home, wind in my face, pretending that I was flying like one of the night-creatures in my comic books. I would land in our driveway, curl up in the porch swing in my mother's cutting garden in the backyard, and proceed to lose myself in the wash of acid-toned storytelling in the comic book I was reading. My friend, Gordie Brown, lived nearby and we would often swap comics. He was a die-hard *Dark Shadows* fan and he had the best collection of horror comics of anyone I knew. His father had made him a silver wolf's-head cane, like the one Barnabas Collins carried. Gordie also had a large cardboard "coffin" in his basement, which I thought was very cool, for when we played vampire.

What I know now, but didn't know then, was that I was living in what would become a clearly-delineated pop-culture moment. The early seventies coincided with the beginning of the end of a period of grand and garish gothic storytelling that had begun in the fifties, both in fiction and in film. Indeed, the second-last of Hammer Films' Dracula pictures starring Christopher Lee was *Dracula A.D. 1972*. In 1972, I was ten years old and my imagination was the key I was using to unlock the world around me.

Around the same time, I was beginning to detect something about myself, my nature, that was at odds with what I was seeing around me in my friends. Although they were still too young to be much interested in girls, neither were they in love, as I was, with Bobby Sherman and David Cassidy. They were interested in war games, fort building, and hockey. My interest in horror comics was a neutral area, a socially-acceptable DMZ where I could rest, observe, and try to figure out what was going on. If I identified with Rachel Van Helsing, the glamorous blonde vampire hunter in *Tomb of Dracula* who, pre-*Buffy*, was fast on her feet and handy with the crossbow (and in love with handsome Frank Drake, Dracula's tormented descendant), no one was any the wiser.

Gene Colan, the artist who drew all of my favourite Marvel Comics characters, had an unerring eye for the male physique. The male characters in Marvel Comics were usually well-muscled, so a pre-adolescent appreciation for big shoulders, strong pecs, and corded forearms was queerly inculcated into my nascent sexual psyche by those comic books in a way that I'm sure Colan never intended when he put his pen to paper. In 1998, when Wesley Snipes fired up the screens in New Line Cinema's action vampire epic *Blade*, all muscle and leather and attitude, it was *déjà vu*, like meeting an old boyfriend. Blade is a character created by Marv Wolfman in *Tomb of Dracula*, Issue Ten. Seen from the vantage point of almost thirty years later, infatuation makes me smile. There's nothing quite as queer as having a crush on a comic book character, unless it's wishing you could be one.

As childhood segued into adolescence, horror novels and stories were my still my preferred reading material. The perpetual October country of horror fiction was a haven in which to escape what I perceived as my body's betrayals of the norms I saw all around me. My nose was always buried in a book and there was a certain sanctuary accorded to boys like me. Teachers liked us, and even if our peers didn't, they thought we were "brainy" and left us alone for a little while.

At some point, though, my male and female friends began pairing up. I dated girls for two reasons: the first, a defiant attempt to fit in; the second, a desperate hope that somehow the real magic of the world (as opposed to the magic in the supernatural novels I was reading, which I always knew didn't exist) would touch me and transform me into an insider with normal desires instead of the perpetual sissy outsider I and everyone knew I was. As I got older, in the later 1970s, when the market was flooded with horror novels, and filmmakers had decided that the market was hot enough to begin to flood it themselves, my friends and I would load ourselves into our parents' cars, and watch movies like *Halloween* and *Friday the 13th* at the mall or the local drive-in. It's hard to think about those movies without remembering what it felt like to be pressed up next to a guy with feathered hair and tight Levis I had a mind-blowing crush on: smelling his soap, Clearasil, and cheap after-shave as we watched slash after slash, especially if his girlfriend had decided to stay home because horror movies were "too gross." Talk about developing a gay horror sensibility. As a dear friend of mine, who grew up to be a great horror writer, recently reminded me, "It was good to be a big old sissyboy terrified of a butch monster." He was only half-joking.

At thirty-seven, I can afford to look back at the horror influences of my youth in the seventies with warm nostalgia, with a sense of a more innocent era caught in amber and, perhaps, with some aware-ness that some of the messages contained in those influences were ultimately not all that desirable, especially for a young gay boy fumbling in the sticky darkness in search of a sexual identity. While my peers saw their own sexuality played out on the silver screen (albeit with lethal results), adolescents of my persuasion were left somewhat out in the cold.

The horror films of the seventies and eighties were morality fables of the first order. There were five basic "types" with occasional variations: boys, "good" girls, scantily-clad "bad" girls, virginal and/or homely girls, and "neuter" boys. Boys wanted sex with girls. "Bad" girls wanted to give it to them. When they had sex, they would be killed, and there would be a lot of screaming by the girls as they checked out. The boys, however, never screamed. They shouted *uuuuuhhh!* or went to their deaths silent, and surprised.

Although virginal and/or homely girls more often than not survived, "neuter" boys, possessed of bland, sexless tag-along tendencies, were dispatched without a look back. I doubt that many gay boys watching those movies had any doubt at all where we fit into that paradigm. We rolled with it. Everyone shrieked, but nobody was surprised when the neuter boy was skewered. It all seemed very normal — the way of the world.

The girls in those movies were the eye-candy, spilling juicily out of lacy bras, silky panties, and wet towels. Never the boys, whose pre-Nautilus 1970s bodies remained coyly draped under the sheets as they performed the death-fuck that would earn both them and the girls a pointy reckoning. Girls, or closeted gay boys, who wanted some beefcake, were out of luck.

Except occasionally.

In 1982, on a pre-university catalogue modelling job, I happened to meet Richard Rebiere, the handsome blond French-Canadian actor who played Greg, the hapless, star-crossed jock in *Happy Birthday to Me*, released by Columbia Pictures the previous year. As one of a series of inventive murders suspected to be the handiwork of the character played by Melissa Sue Anderson of *Little House on the Prairie* fame (the camp possibilities in this film are virtually limitless), Greg is killed, pumped-up and sweaty, while lifting weights.

In a pre-Freddie Prinze Jr./Ryan Phillippe moment in the history of horror films, when handsome guys were not a requirement for casting directors, Richard Rebiere was a knockout.

I had seen that movie several times in 1981, but didn't think it appropriate, on that snowy afternoon at the photo studio in 1982, to explain to him why. Today, I would. So, if you're reading this, Rick, thanks for the memories.

By the time the horror genre was resurrected by director Wes Craven in 1996 with his neo-slasher, *Scream*, the pansexual vampire novels of Anne Rice had long been in the best bookstores in the world. Poppy Z. Brite, a brilliant writer whose elegant novels embraced queer themes with gusto, had become a superstar. Clive Barker, a writer whose extraordinary literary sensibilities have often led him to explore the monster as a beautiful, redeemable outsider, had unleashed the S/M-inflected *Hellraiser* in 1987, and, in 1990, *Nightbreed*, a visually stunning and genuinely affecting film about an underground city of monsters who are portrayed as heroes who must battle the forces of "good" for their very survival. Whether it was Barker's intention or not, the film serves, in some ways, as a powerful gay allegory, dexterously illustrating how those who society sees as "evil" can, in fact, be intrinsically gallant paladins, whereas the titular guardians of "decency" are often the truest monsters. All of these writers demonstrate how, under the deft pen of a gifted author, a queer sensibility or theme can be focused through the prism of contemporary horror fiction, yielding a result at once terrifying and illuminating.

In 1998, Michael Marano published *Dawn Song*, an award-winning first novel that, for me, stands as one of the most ethereally lovely, poignant, yet terrifying novels of the decade. The protagonist, Lawrence, is a fully developed and evolved gay man, whose homosexuality is merely an aspect of his character, and he interacts with the other characters in the novel without explanation or apology for it.

The application of this aesthetic by authors such as Marano — and indeed, many of the best horror writers working today, some of whom appear in *Queer Fear* — may be the foundation upon which a new genre (let's call it "gay horror fiction") rises. Unlike novel readers of previous generations, gay men and lesbians today can find themselves represented as part of the general literary mosaic with increasing regularity. This new inclusiveness will hopefully, someday, yield newly-inclusive mainstream horror fiction that would make the notion of "gay horror fiction," if not unnecessary, then, at least, not the only place in horror to find fully developed gay characters.

Goth culture, now more part of the mainstream than ever, continues to further blur the boundaries. In many horror circles, being gay, or bisexual, is cool. Even desirable.

Even horror films, formerly the near-exclusive province of red-blooded heterosexual boys, now feature buff, shirtless himbos with washboard abs and tight butts, being rescued by empowered girl-power girls — all of whom still scream, but now sound like they mean it, and, more often than not, scream loudest just before they deliver the sort of roundhouse kick to the masked killer's groin that would do Jamie Lee Curtis proud.

In horror literature, vampire fiction continues to be a good barometer by which to measure the acceptability of gay imagery in popular horror fiction. Intrinsically sexual, invasive, and necessarily wet, vampire fiction has expanded the classic Victorian paradigm of evil, corrupt male versus virginal, delicate female to encompass a much wider net of possibilities. In 1996 and 1997, Thomas S. Roche and I edited two well-received gay-themed vampire anthologies, *Sons of Darkness* and *Brothers of the Night*. The stories we collected in these two books demonstrated how easily gay iconography could be incorporated into horror fiction. It requires a certain amount of imagination to visualize a world of ghosts, vampires, werewolves, and other night-creatures. Imagination is a stock item for gay people, who have traditionally needed to literally imagine themselves into existence by visualizing a world in which they could exist.

The difference today, of course, is that we have a social climate that has evolved beyond the female beauty/male beast strictures that kept horror fiction so mired in a type of sedentary, torpid homophobia perfectly portrayed in 1974, when a popular but dreadfully-written novel called *The Sentinel*, featured a now-hilarious encounter between the protagonist, Allison, a fashion model, and "a bull dyke and her lover," in which Allison delivers a scorching diatribe about "... sickness! Masturbation and lesbianism!" then portrays a "lisp[ing]" gay fashion show announcer with a "high-pitched voice," a few pages later.

In those days, we took our monsters where we could find them.

Even today, though, the question that I find myself answering even more than anything related to being a gay man, or a gay writer, is this: *Why horror? What is it that attracts you to horror? Isn't there enough horror in the world already? Do you like being afraid? Does violence turn you on?*

The stories in *Queer Fear* aren't an attempt to answer that question, which has more to do with taste, and perhaps a peculiarly suspicious, puritanical reluctance to acknowledge the legitimacy of a literature that isn't a serious moral duty to read.

Never mind that Charles Brockden Brown, the first professional author in the United States, admired by Sir Walter Scott, Keats, and Shelley, was arguably the father of American literature when he wrote *Wieland, or The Transformation*, a gothic horror novel, in 1798.

Never mind the notion that no marginally aware gay man or lesbian at the beginning of the new millennium is going to have a moment's difficulty differentiating between vampires, werewolves, and ghouls, and the true horror of hate crimes, AIDS, or the abandonment by parents of their gay children. Yes, there's more than enough *horror* in the world. A passing glance at CNN confirms that.

As Robert McCammon, today sadly (for us) retired from horror fiction, but whose oeuvre has included some of the best horror fiction of the twentieth century, wrote, "Horror writers are simply trying to make sense out of the chaos."

And yes, there are real reasons to feel terror today. I don't care to be in fear for my life, or for the lives of people I love, but that has nothing to do with reading Stephen King, or Clive Barker, or Robert McCammon, or Douglas Clegg, or watching *Urban Legend* or *Deep Blue Sea*.

Horror fiction incites the same response in the mainstream reading public as erotica does. Both of these "outlaw" genres deal with strong emotion, violence, and a lack of control that is uniquely human. The imagery is often violent. Fear, like lust, is only truly acceptable to the mainstream reading public when it is confined within strict boundaries. In the case of lust, marriage and adultery are okay; rape fantasies and S/M are suspect. For its part, horror places the reader squarely in the middle of conflict, invites visceral responses, and doesn't provide the "easy out" of an antiseptic, dispassionate, cerebral literary experience. Like those snobbish Victorian physicians who used to look down on surgeons as little better than butchers, an element of the literary establishment dismisses horror as vulgar entertainment for the unwashed.

Among gay men, although we have provisions in our canon for a variety of sexual and emotional variations on "the norm," I have found, over and over, that open horror fans are a clandestine group, best known to each other. When we meet, there is often a joyous sharing and celebration of our joint histories. Sometimes, for gay "horror people," the path from adolescence to adulthood has that extra dimension of shared cultural flashpoints that our less-imaginative brethren may have missed completely. What we have read, seen, and loved, has made us what we are. This is true for everyone, but it is especially true for the lover of horror fiction.

Ultimately, though, it's about the stories.

We can place gay-themed horror in a myriad of different socio-political contexts, but if the stories don't frighten, disturb, or cause us to question reality as we know it, they're not horror stories. This is one genre, thank God, where it's impossible to hide behind political rhetoric or polemic.

ooooo

THE SKY OUTSIDE IS now black, and the wind is blowing hard against the windowpanes, making them rattle like old bones. The lamps are flickering, and I think we may lose power. I'd better wrap this up and find some candles to light the coming darkness.

Hold tight. I think all hell is about to break loose.

*R*ed Nights: Erotica and the Language of Men's Desire
2002

THERE ARE CERTAIN NIGHTS in late August, in Toronto, when the swollen summer sky presses itself down upon the city, making shirts cling damply to backs, and blood rise to the surface of sweaty skin, stroking to life every sensation that we might overlook, or even suppress, on a cooler evening when the heat is less physical. The humidity wraps the street lights in a gauzy aureole, and every sensation seems stronger somehow because of it — sight, sound, taste, touch, smell.

My friend Ron and I called them "red nights" when I was in my early twenties and life was less complicated than it naturally became later. I dream of them today, and even when I am awake and walking though the city at dusk, I will occasionally catch the ghost-edge of some scent or other in the indolent lagoon of summer night air and it takes me back along the paths of memory to the place where I first discovered the pleasure of loving men openly and celebrating what makes them beautiful.

The August heat might have exhausted the suburbanites far beyond the city's core as they sat fanning themselves on their patios, but for Ron and I, walking downtown along Yonge St. in the subtropical dampness of those August nights, there was an erotic call-to-arms implicit in the sinuous warmth, an alertness to the sexual possibilities all around us. Neither Ron nor I had the inclination to describe or discuss what we were feeling. Neither of us were connoisseurs of written erotica, nor were we inclined to verbalize, much less rhapsodize, the particulars, beyond the verbal shorthand of young gay men. *Arousal* was too specific a word, certainly at the start of the night. Even when we weren't looking to score, the visual buffet was there if we wanted to sample it, or even just admire its presentation. *Awareness* came closer, but awareness of *what*? The men in the streets were not all handsome, nor were they all to our respective tastes, which have always been diametrically divergent. Ron and I are able to spot each other's type as only longtime best friends are able to and we often marvel at how two gay men with such different views of what constitutes sexual attractiveness could belong to the same gender, let alone the same sexual orientation. They all were, however, indisputably male.

On those nights, the most eclectic sexual tastes could be visually indulged.

There were the ethereally handsome gay men, alone or in groups, dressed in Lycra dancing-queen mufti, or leather, or denim. There were the young suburban bulls with K-car muscles and crewcuts, arms draped around their teased and frosted girlfriends who seemed to wear them like bulky bronze jewellery. The boys themselves, firing macho scowls and sweating testosterone, looked everywhere except down at the girls who flaunted them with such passive possessiveness. There were the depleted straight businessmen coming home from late meetings, jackets slung over their shoulders, sweat plastering their white shirts to their backs, hinting at broad shoulders and racquetball triceps. The humidity caused the summer-weight poplin of their suit trousers to cling suggestively in a way that was too well-bred to be overtly lewd, yet was inviting enough to have disturbed (or intrigued) them if it had been pointed out. There were the men returning from the gym, the ones who wanted to dry off in the summer night air, the ones you could easily imagine naked, who carried with them the faint, clean scent of soap and sweat as they strode home in damp sports gear. Their striated thighs shimmered under a dew of sweat in the refracted neon light, their biceps twitched with exhaustion, and their beautiful, sweaty faces were always, somehow, perfect, no matter what they looked like.

And suddenly, at some point in the night, awareness became arousal. The visual became a language, the flesh made itself word. The men's beauty derived not from any particular aesthetic attribute, but from a gender-based, sexual one. It was enough that they were *men*. Like us in many ways, unlike us in many other marvellous ones. Their maleness, their oppositeness from women, became a keening red night-song that hummed through our young bodies without a sound. It left us bursting with a soaring euphoria that we were alive, that we were gay, and that we were able to appreciate the men who stalked through these red summer nights with such assurance, and appreciate them in a way that only a gay man could. My communication with Ron remained non-verbal, but in that parade of heat and sweat on those red nights, most words would have been superfluous anyway when measured against the unspoken, inarticulate language of our desire.

ooooo

I DISCOVERED WRITTEN EROTICA in college. The visual variety had never interested me. I'd never been one of those boys who hid stacks of porn magazines under his mattress as a teenager. I attended a rough, tough prep school in the wilds of western Canada and the male form was all around me, twenty-four hours, seven days a week. My friend David, himself a man of extraordinary physical presence, recently told me that he was gay because of straight men. He wasn't making a statement of fetish; he was referring to his own youth in an all-male boarding school, where the seasons were marked by a shifting array of shucked sports uniforms and locker rooms, and the years were marked by a litany of developing musculature and the salty scent of boys ripening. Winter's paleness (wide, lean chests and body hair flowering wild, like dark wheat) gave way to summer's gold (strong young legs flexing in the gilded green sunlight, supple arms reaching, catching a ball in mid-flight, sweat cascading like a sun shower.)

The hierarchy of age and strength is as inviolate in a private boy's boarding school as any caste system anywhere else, and as cruel. There was little quarter available to those of us who were effeminate, or uncoordinated, or in any way conspicuously different, as I was. The younger boys looked up to the older ones. We marvelled at the shadow of incumbent beards, of lengthening muscle, of more private development, and the braggadocio of sexual adventure and conquest. We dreamed of being these boys, or of having them, but when we dreamed the latter it was never talked about.

By some miracle, I took my first lover from this number, at the age of seventeen. I can still remember the moment rough, chapped lips first kissed mine, the moment a calloused, male hand first touched my cock, stroked my thin chest. I can still hear the blood thundering in my ears, see the red darkness behind my closed eyes, and feel my heart stop, then take flight. My first lover, Barney, is still my friend today. We're both much older and his beauty, especially as he ages, is the only hint I ever had that God might have a sexual preference.

But the affair was a secret one in those days. Revealing it would have meant the end of both of us. There was no language available to us for what we were feeling; the bittersweet adolescent *chiaroscuro* of lust, confusion, and longing for love.

For any of us who grew up in an environment like this, mere photographic images would have to achieve something superterrestrial to compete with those heady, early memories. I *have* seen photographs that suggest those times, however, photographs where the beauty of men is so pure and clean and golden that it needs no reference to art, or history, or politics. It is unchallengeable and it, therefore, exists beyond the boundaries of envy or acquisitiveness. These men exist in a place where light and muscle meet, the place where glamour wears the armour of strength and athletic grace. There is a place where sun and shadow sculpt powerful limbs, strong backs and broad shoulders, where the planes of a face are wide and virile and uncompromising. It's the place where art and beauty fuse on celluloid, in the fraction of a second, in the photographer's clinched eye, in the click of a shutter, in the ephemeral flash of strobe light. It's the place where the photographer and his model become, briefly, the lover and the beloved, and their dazzling offspring is the photograph itself, more beautiful than either of its parents, etched in black, grey, and silver. The photographer and the model will grow into age and wisdom and, eventually, die. The photograph itself, born of their passionate communion, will live forever. Beauty and art are eternal in a way that mere youth and vision are not and will never be.

But the visual never really engaged me once I'd known the real thing, and had seen what it cost.

The written erotica I discovered in college was by a man named John Preston and it was as different from the carnal imagery I had known as a youth as night is from day.

Having come out and having discovered the bounty available to me as a gay man, my erotic imaginings shifted to underground sexuality. In the leather bars of Toronto, Boston, and New York, I discovered a world where male sexuality could be rough and endurance-building without being exclusionary and hurtful. As beautiful as the demigods of my childhood were, they were also cruel to those who fell outside their golden sphere. In a leather bar, roles could be assumed at will and there was respect either way. That the brain is "the biggest sex organ" extant is such a cliché, but frankly the world of S/M, as it revealed itself to me on the printed page, engaged my fantasies in a way that video, pornographic photography, or even the memory of the platinum young gods of my school life didn't.

Preston's erotica, books like *Mr. Benson* and *I Once Had A Master*, and stories in magazines like *Drummer*, were my first window to the sexual power of the written word. The very nature of S/M erotica presupposes fantasy, and, through most of my twenties, I explored its imagery for my own enjoyment. I noticed that in Preston's work (and the work of such writers as Aaron Travis, and the then-disguised Anne Rice, writing as A.N. Roquelaure) there was a level of literary quality that expressed desire and lust in ways that played the mind like a sexual Stradivarius. Clumsy writing, bad "porn" dialogue of the pulp variety, did the opposite. I went to Harvard to take a writing program there during the summer I was twenty-nine. I met Preston in Portland, Maine, that summer and we became friends. Later that year, he took me under his wing as a mentor, and began to coax new work from me.

"You write about everyone else," he told me once, referring to my mainstream journalism. "When are you going to write about your own life? When are you going to use your own language?"

By that time, he was as well-known for editing mainstream hard-cover anthologies as he was for his erotica, though it was significant that America's most famous gay pornographer was responsible for starting erotica's inexorable social rise as a valid mainstream literary genre when the first book in his *Flesh and the Word* series appeared in hardcover from Dutton in 1992.

Under Preston's tutelage, I began to write the essays that appeared in his anthologies *Friends and Lovers* and *Sister and Brother*. I wrote erotica for *Flesh and the Word 3* with my friend Ron, whom you met at the beginning of this essay. My focus turned towards the lives of gay men, our commonalities, and our private language. My first book, *Writing Below the Belt*, was an exploration of the lives and writing of fourteen erotica writers, and a portrait of where they, and we, saw erotica in the broader cultural context. John Preston never saw the book, which was dedicated to him. He died from complications relating to AIDS just before its publication in 1994. The most significant literary friendship of my life died with him, and I miss him with every word I write. Through our friendship, and his mentoring, I learned that there was indeed a language for what I felt as an adolescent, watching my fellows in prep school grow into men around me. There were words for the aches I felt, the terrible keening desire to own them, without understanding what it was I wanted from them. There was a nomenclature for those red nights of walking Yonge St. with Ron, when the humid neon-lit twilight was the stage for a ballet of desire and the unaware, nameless dancers were men who moved and shook us without ever knowing it.

There was a vernacular for the beauty of men in their most private moments: Barney's rough hands on the wheel of car as he drives; Geof's great golden head, blue eyes, wide smile, his broad shoulders tapering into a narrow waist, the way he looks when he bends down to pick something off the floor with an athlete's unthinking ease; the anonymous sunburnt, tired, sweaty young leatherman in the dying sunlight after the Pride parade dressed in chaps and a harness — too drunk to affect a tough pose, too happy to care; James, painting shirtless, passionately intent on bringing his vision to the canvas; Chuck, cradling his newborn daughter protectively in his arms while his wife watches.

It is the sound of men's voices, the way they move, the way they smell, the way they taste, what they look like, asleep and dreaming. Erotica is more than a form of gay men's vernacular literature. It is more than the language of desire. It is the distillation of our lusts, private and public, into written form.

PORTRAITS

Hollywood Darkness: Clive Barker on *Coldheart Canyon*
2001

CLIVE BARKER, RUGGEDLY HANDSOME at forty-nine and looking vaguely piratical in a black shirt and gold earring, sits at a wooden refectory table in one of the three houses that comprise his residential compound high in the canyon country above Beverly Hills. He has a cigar in one hand and a cup of tea in the other. Behind him, like a stained glass window to his imagination, stands a selection of three hundred of Barker's paintings, the heart of an eight-million-dollar deal he signed with the Walt Disney company in April of 2000 for film and ancillary rights to *Arabat*, a quartet of fantasy novels for older children that HarperCollins will bring out in the fall of 2002.

In front of him on the table sits his most recent novel, *Coldheart Canyon*, the story of a narcissistic, washed-up action hero named Todd Pickett in flight from the media while he attempts to recover from a botched facelift. The novel is at once a full-on ghost story and a blistering satire of modern Hollywood. Pickett selects as his hiding place the remote estate of a once-famous silent film actress with a taste for sexual sadism, which, he discovers, is haunted by its original owner, as well as by a cabal of ghosts of old movie stars.

In spite of its innately camp premise, the novel is as dark, violent, and hyper-sexual as Barker's best-known work.

Although the George Hurrell-style photograph gracing the cover looks like the portrait of a handsome 1920s movie star, it is, in fact, Barker himself, shot by Barker's husband of six years, the photographer David Armstrong. This particular move is pure Clive Barker, a sly nod by the acknowledged lord of illusions, an invitation to the reader to try to delineate where the novel becomes more than a novel, or, indeed, Barker's own commentary on Hollywood as seen from his current vantage point on the cusp of turning fifty.

"I was lucky enough, seven years ago, to be drawn into Roddy McDowall's circle," Barker says, his voice cigar-roughened, like broken glass wrapped in black velvet. "Roddy had Friday night dinner parties regularly throughout the year." Barker describes nights in the company of such luminaries as Elizabeth Taylor, Gore Vidal, and Maureen O'Sullivan.

"What do you say when you have that degree of history and intelligence and storytelling?" Barker asks rhetorically. "You shut the fuck up, and you listen. The only time I raised my voice at one of those dinner parties was when Gore Vidal was in the room and he opined that there was no such thing as homosexual literature, which I think is nonsense."

As the stream of dinner-party anecdotes took root in his imagination, Barker realized that there was a story growing, though he was unsure of the direction it would take.

"Talk about six degrees of separation," he says wryly. "In Hollywood it's three degrees. Everyone has known — or slept with — everyone else."

At the time, he had a friend who worked at a facelift clinic that catered to a privileged Hollywood clientele for whom immaculate discretion was essential. The author wanted details. "I said, 'Fill me in!' and he said, 'I can't! I can't!'" But eventually the friend caved in and revealed some of the names and circumstances. At Barker's request, he also passed along some literature dealing with the surgical process. "He smuggled out these big books which had these horrendous photographs of what happens when really simple things go wrong," Barker says delightedly. He realized that he had the beginning of his story, which he imagined as a 70,000 word novella about a world-famous movie star recovering from a botched facelift.

"It would be almost a Burroughs-esque kind of novel, like *The Western Lands*, one of the later Burroughs novels where the narrative hangs together very strongly, not the stuff that flies off in all directions, which I love, but isn't my style as a writer. But it would be a book in which a guy would have things go wrong with his face-job and, because of the amount of medication he was on, he wouldn't know if these were real ghosts or not. And at the end of the 70,000 words, he'd decide that Hollywood wasn't for him and he'd go back to Ohio."

As he pondered the specifics, Barker realized that even his Beverly Hills home provided grist for his creative mill.

"Here I am," he remembers thinking, "living in a nameless canyon in a house that was built by Ronald Coleman back in the 1920s, who, according to those who know the history of this town, had quite an orgiastic time of it."

A nice moral novella, in other words, but not what readers have come to think of as a Clive Barker tale. As the author pondered his story, dimensions began to reveal themselves to him. The more he researched the peripheral characters, many of whom were composites of people he had known over the course of his years in Hollywood, "the more I realized that I had a deep-seated hatred for these people that I wasn't going to be able to throw off in a few sentences. I had a lot of resentments and rages inside of me. The rage I felt surprised me."

According to Barker, the genesis of his rage was the process of getting the 1998 film *Gods and Monsters* made. The film, adapted from Christopher Bram's novel *Father of Frankenstein* was executive produced by Barker and won the Oscar for its writer and director, Bill Condon.

"I don't know if I would have felt the same way previous to the experience of going around Hollywood with Bill Condon and Ian McKellen trying to get *God and Monsters* set up," Barker muses. "That really changed my idea of what this town was. Bill is an extraordinary talent and we had Ian and this wonderful book. The hypocrisy of the people who you knew were gay but wouldn't say it, or who would say it but wouldn't support [us]." The spoor of hypocrisy gelled, in Barker's mind, with Hollywood's parallel obsession with appearances and surfaces. "All of these things were factored in when I started writing, uncharacteristically for me, without a detailed chapter breakdown," he reveals. "And the story began to tell itself."

Barker was writing from things he knew. The novel is a mine of devastatingly accurate cameos of people Barker has known and loved, or otherwise. When presented with a reader's speculation as to the identities of certain characters, Barker laughs like a madman and claps his hands delightedly, then refuses to confirm or deny.

"There wasn't much of a leap of faith here," he says in response to a question about the novel's believability factor. "People know that Hollywood is a corrupt place. It seems that we are more in love with celebrity and its nonsense than ever. The *National Enquirer* and other tabloids tend to get short shrift, but we're all closet readers," Barker sighs. "We're picking them up in the supermarket and slipping them back into place before we pay for our low-fat yogurt." Barker, for his part, admits to actually buying them. "There's definitely a way in which we're more attracted to the fall from grace than we are by the elevation. The elevation seems steeper than it ever was, and the fall from grace more vertiginous than it ever was."

Although he has no intention of downplaying, either in the novel or in interviews, *Coldheart Canyon*'s supernatural themes, he will concede that they act as a framework in which other motifs are also explored in depth, as befits a writer of Barker's maturity, namely the cost of fame, the relationship of a superstar to his fans, and the corroding effects of narcissism. There are traces of Barker's personal experiences in every one of these sub-themes. Even the character of Katya Lupi, the (literally) immortal film goddess under whose sadomasochistic spell Todd Pickett falls, bears his sexual imprimatur.

"It was certainly written with a woody," Barker says slyly, in reference to a particular blood-drawing sex scene. "I can write with a very open-minded erection. I found the stuff with Katya and the whipping very fun to write and rewrite." As to whether or not he is invested in writing from a woman's perspective, Barker shrugs. "There is certainly peer pressure within gay society not to find women [sexually attractive]," he says. "But the gay man gets to play all kinds of sexual head games. You can be active, you can be passive. You can swoon, you can dominate. There is a wonderful menu of sexual possibilities which is put in front of the gay man, in terms of role play. If you watch gay men at Carnival in New Orleans, or on Santa Monica Blvd. at Halloween, you will see how really happily confused and delirious people are. The muscle-boy who suddenly decides he wants to go in drag. The little guy who never said boo to a goose is transformed by some leather and a whip into a sex-master from hell. We play those games and we play them pretty openly. Straights don't."

Although Todd Pickett's narcissism is impossible to ignore, and is very much an actor's trait, it is also a *leitmotif* of gay male culture. Although Barker doesn't identify with Todd Pickett, he isn't entirely unsympathetic to his plight either.

"This culture — and I mean the southern California culture — is a body culture. It's a culture which is in love with surface and I'm not about to condemn that. I take great pleasure in seeing beautiful men and it would be deeply hypocritical of me to say, 'Oh, who cares about that?' I care a lot about it. The question is, what is beauty? Is it determined by going to the gym or [plastic surgery?] This book hopefully deals with some of my confusion about this, which, I think, on one hand, is ludicrous. Still," he admits, "I want my heroes on the screen to be beautiful."

Although Barker lives and works in the selfsame Hollywood that has helped Todd Pickett destroy himself with its image obsessions, Barker seems reasonably indifferent to those obsessions.

"I don't go to the parties," he says. "I don't go anywhere I think I would feel that pressure. When I do go to The Faultline [an L.A. leather bar], I feel nothing of that pressure. I mean, absolutely *nothing*. I go to the gym, I look after my body to a not-obsessive degree, and the only person I care about making a judgement on me sexually is my husband."

He and Armstrong have been a couple for six years. Each wears a wedding band. They have had two private marriage ceremonies, one in their home in Los Angeles, the other in Hawaii. If readers of his work are discovering Clive Barker as *paterfamilias* here for the first time, so be it. Here's where the loveless Todd Pickett and his creator diverge most sharply. Barker freely admits that his relationship with Armstrong is the place from which he launches himself into his frenetic life, and their life together with their daughter, Nicole, is where he returns at night to draw strength.

"Relationships provide armour against anxiety, against depression, against the world's woes," Barker says. "It's great to roll over in bed and find somebody's head on the pillow beside you. If that person is somebody you've known for a long time, as I've known David, and not a casual trick, I think it's hugely more comforting to me, personally.

"I adore the simple pleasures," he says, sounding like a very contented man. "We have dogs, we have our daughter to look after. Doing *homework* with the *daughter*?" he laughs, perhaps imagining how it must sound coming from a hell-raiser. "Whoever knew? But my life has always been filled with paradoxes like that."

When *The Books of Blood* were first published in 1984, the public didn't know who he was. When he began to appear on television and in the media, his new fans had a dewy, wholesome face to attach to the crimson prose that prompted Stephen King to declare Barker the future of horror.

"They said, 'You're the guy who wrote this stuff? We thought you were really old and twisted!' I'd say, 'I really *am* twisted; it just doesn't show.'"

In those days it might have been just a smile of recognition, or a request for an autograph. Today, Barker admits, the Hollywood element often overrides the sweetness of past encounters.

"I get into limos," Barker says ruefully, "and the driver will give me a smile that I instantly know means trouble. He'll say, 'Mr. Barker, I really loved —' fill in the blank, 'and my entire family are actors. Here are our resumés and pictures.' Or worse, 'Here's my idea for a script. If you write it, I'll share the profits with you fifty-fifty.' Some variation on that theme happens every third time you get into a car, and it gets very old. But I can't bring myself to be mean to them, because what they have is your attention for a few minutes and getting *anyone's* attention in this town is bloody difficult. I've had times where *I've* needed somebody's attention! But what it gets to is the desperation that this town engenders."

If today Clive Barker is an openly gay literary superstar whose fans have multiplied many times over, he's still moved when someone shows up at a book signing with a stained and tattered copy of one of his books. This stands in stark relief against the many writers at his level who instruct booksellers to refuse to allow fans to line up unless they are holding newly bought copies of whatever current bestseller they are flogging.

"When I met Ray Bradbury," he says, thinking about his encounter years previously with the legendary fantasist, "I was a bumbling heap of a man who needed to say, 'I wouldn't be a writer if it wasn't for you.' Everybody has somebody like that in their lives, and if they don't, they're the poorer for it. There should always be room for genuine adulation, room to say, 'I love what you do. What you do changed me. It gave me room to dream.'"

If some of the themes in his work today are more contemplative and reflective than when he was younger, readers shouldn't start sending him Dockers and golf shirts anytime soon.

"Occasionally, David and I will go to a premiere with our daughter," he says wickedly. "You've got a black man and a white man, and a girl who is mixed-race standing between us ..." Barker trails off and begins to laugh. "And then it's like, '*What have they finally learned to do, those bastard fags?*'" Barker laughs delightedly at the thought of inciting, even inadvertently, such confusion about the apparently supernatural reproductive powers of gay horror writers and their photographer husbands.

And then, thinking of the place where his art diverges from his private life, the Coldheart Canyon of his imagination where his readers can visit him anytime they like, he admits, "I'm very keen to push the boundaries whenever I can, but I tend to do so with a smile on my face, which takes the edge off it a little bit. I don't have much patience for game-playing anymore. I never had that much anyway. And that might just be the fact that I'm coming up on fifty and I still have a lot to do. I'm not satisfied with what I've made, not remotely. I'm very ambitious to make more and better work."

Eloise on Church St.:
A Portrait of Angie Moneva
2005

ONE SNOWY JANUARY AFTERNOON when she was a very little girl at Catholic school in East York, Angie Moneva came home to the comfortable Bathurst and Lawrence-area house she shared with her parents, Vince and Leticia, the owners of Café California on Church St. in Toronto.

She had something to ask her mother.

"She was *very* serious," says Leticia Moneva in delicate, Spanish-accented English that suggests her patrician Chilean upbringing. She smiles at the memory. "Angie said to me, 'What do you want me to be when I grow up, a prostitute or a lesbian?' I said, 'Why do you ask me that, my darling?'"

Angie told her mother that one of her teachers had told her that the two things were equally bad, and that she was a very naughty little girl.

"I told her, 'My dear, if you are a lesbian, you will make another girl very happy.' At that point, I said '*Angicita*, if you love a man and he makes you happy, Mummy is happy. If you love a woman and she makes you happy, Mummy is just as happy. I just want your happiness. But it's not a matter of choice. You're born with certain preferences.'" As for being a prostitute, Leticia said, "'We'll talk about that in a few years.'"

What Leticia would later discover is that the teacher had presented her daughter with an even uglier paradigm. Angie had told some of the older kids that she knew gays and lesbians through her parents' restaurant, and word had gotten back to the teacher, an older woman. The teacher had said to Angie, "I hear you're around lesbians and gay men. You do know, don't you, that they're unclean and promiscuous, and that they go around prostituting themselves?"

The teacher told her that all lesbians were prostitutes, and the kids, upon hearing about Café California, told Angie she must be a lesbian too, and therefore a prostitute in the making.

"Needless to say," Leticia adds wryly, "that was Angie's last day in Catholic school."

After what Leticia coolly refers to as "a very nice talk with the teacher," she and Vince withdrew Angie from Catholic school and placed her in a public school. In light of the fact that the teacher had presented their daughter with a narrow, and typically homophobic, range of career options, Vince and Leticia weren't about to allow their daughter to be educated in an environment where the life and people — the chosen family — in fact, that the little girl knew at the restaurant would be denigrated

More than a decade later, a Café California customer would ask who the comely young girl with the flawless hair and makeup and sense of style helping bus tables was. One of the waiters told him, "That's Leticia's daughter, Angie." When the customer complimented her on her hair and makeup, the waiter said, "Of course she's glam, we raised her!"

ooooo

IN ORDER TO BETTER understand the circumstance leading to Angie Moneva's withdrawal from Catholic school that day so many years ago, one might be tempted to paraphrase the opening line of Kay Thompson's *Eloise*, the legendary 1955 storybook about the little girl who lived at the Plaza Hotel in New York City this way: "I am Angie. I am a city child. I live on Church St." If her childhood was *encantada* — enchanted — it couldn't have been any other way. Like Eloise, Angie had grown up surrounded by a cast of worldly adults — in her case, gay men — who never treated her like a baby, and through whom she was exposed to a dazzling array of life possibilities. Any effect on her life, or in turn, her effect on the life of anyone else, can be distilled through this social prism. If nothing else, how many graduating seniors can claim a prom dress designed by drag queens, who also did her makeup? Birthday cards from the Mayor of Toronto? Or a big-brother waiter figure who, with his partner, a flight attendant, would whisk her off to New York when she turned eighteen for an impromptu weekend of shopping and theatre?

"I can't say, [my husband and I] raised her," Leticia admits with disarming honesty. "We *all* raised her, the staff, the regular customers, the gay community have had a great impact on the way Angie was raised. She's the most giving and generous person. She's the kind of person who will do anything to protect someone vulnerable, because of the way she was raised in the restaurant."

The superficial effects of that sophisticated upbringing are clearly visible today. On this early autumn afternoon, twenty-year-old Angie Moneva is sitting with her parents on the deck of their townhouse on the edge of Church St. She is wearing a simple tank top and jeans. A discreet gold crucifix gleams against her lightly tanned skin. She wears the barest touch of expertly-applied makeup, and a pair of smoky Versace sunglasses are perched on top of her sun-streaked light brown hair. The pale pink polish on her nails is chipped slightly, keeping the illusion from being too *Vogue*, an oddly touching reminder that she's a university student, not a fashion model or a Barbie. The Bayview Village house in which she lived as a child was sold when Angie was accepted to the University of Toronto in 2004.

"I consider the gay community more my family than my actual extended family," she says. "I adore my aunts and uncles and cousins.

They're my blood. But I see them every two years. The people in the community have raised me, and taught me to be who I am today, and to have a wonderful sense of humour. People like Richard and Peter," she says, naming two legendary dowager staffers, "have been around since I was a little girl. They have that big brother instinct to protect me, and that big sister instinct to advise me on my appearance, and go shopping with me."

ooooo

AN ILLUSTRATIVE MONTAGE OF family photographs can add a dimension to a story in a way that words often can't. Here are a scattering of snapshots of a pretty little girl holding a variety of adorable dogs — not holding them like possessions, or accessories, in the way many little girls do, but with an awareness of her privilege as a human being, albeit a young one, and her responsibility to their fragility and difference. In all the photographs, she is smiling, and her eyes are luminescent with joy and curiosity. Here is another: a school portrait, probably, of a little girl with enormous brown eyes, staring frankly at the camera with no hint of fear, but no hint of defiance either. Here are some others — she is older. She is water-skiing in one, her adolescent body firm and supple, in control. And others — Angie with her friends (she's the one with the magenta streaks framing her face), with still another dog in her lap; Angie wearing a yellow one-piece swimsuit, sitting on a large inflatable yellow plastic banana, the water of the pool brilliant blue; Angie dressed as a witch for Halloween, surely no more than fourteen, her costume perfect, her Halloween makeup perfect; Angie older still, her face and body now those of a young woman, long and lean, her bones fragile and delicate like her mother's. She is standing in front of her house in an inky-midnight evening dress on prom night. The dress has a plunging v-shaped bodice, and her décolletage is pale as milk. Angie is leaning slightly into her boyfriend's gallant embrace, but again, there is no hint of the clingy, simpering, jejune, veal-calf quality of so many young girls on the occasion of this particular threshold of womanhood. Instead, she is looking serenely at the camera as if to say *Isn't this fun? On to the next adventure!*

The last photograph in the montage is Angie at her high-school graduation. She is lovely, sun-struck. Her streaked blonde hair blows in the early summer wind. She's wearing a dark blue top that sets off, rather than clashes with, the generic cerulean of her graduation robes. A gold crucifix gleams against the indigo.

As in all of the images, Angie doesn't seem to seek out the light, *it* finds *her*.

An amateur anthropologist looking for a thematic visual link in these photographs would likely look past the superficial, evolving beauty of the subject and be struck by her confidence. In Angie's case, there's a reason for the confidence. Like many strong young women, she is the product of a strong mother. Angie's life might have been very different if her mother, Leticia, had not dared to venture beyond the cloistered upper-class Chilean milieu which asked nothing of her except that she accept and accede to the role of society matron for which Leticia Martinez, as she was then known, had been groomed her whole life.

Thirty years later, petite, her russet hair worn in an elegant crop, Leticia Moneva is still a very beautiful woman. Her skin is pale and smooth, and her eyes are the colour of warm sherry. When she moves her hands to talk, her gestures convey that inbred femininity that Latin women seem to wear as a natural birthright, be they women of Angie's age, mothers, or grandmothers.

"I grew up in a very homophobic society, where men and women have very defined roles," Leticia says, her face darkening slightly. "There was no room for gay people. If there were any gay people in my life, it was the biggest secret they kept."

In the fiercely conservative Chile of her youth, criminals, homosexuals, and prostitutes shared the same distinctions and fate in the eyes of the law. Similarly stratified, and perhaps even more inflexible, and intolerable to the young woman, were the inviolable gender barriers.

"Oh yes, men are superior to women, the rich are superior to the poor, and everyone is superior to gays," she says wryly. "That's one of the main reasons I'm in Canada: I rebelled against that type of society. I couldn't just accept it. In my family, there were five girls and two boys. Girls could only be teachers and nurses. Boys could be anything they wanted to be. I couldn't deal with that. I knew I had to find — somewhere, somehow — some place I could be what I wanted to be."

Her work in hospital administration taught her unforgettably cruel lessons. She came to realize that, in Chile, money was often the determining factor in whether or not one lived or died.

"For the poor," she says ruefully, "when [the hospitals] ran out of blankets, they used newspapers, even to receive babies." Corruption, as well as class prejudice, was rampant. "When you went to a clinic, you wrote a blank cheque. No cheque, no treatment."

"I also came to Canada for political reasons," she says, noting that, in addition to the personal and moral convictions that led her to experience Chile's radically stratified class hierarchy as unbearable in spite of her own upper class, professional background, her left-liberal political work had caught the attention of Chile's new rulers, the fascist state established in 1973 by General Augusto Pinochet Ugarte. After overthrowing the democratically-elected socialist president Salvador Allende in a coup backed by the United States and various South American military governments, Pinochet declared that Chile was under siege by what he called communist subversives. "I was involved in political activity, and when Pinochet came to power, it wasn't safe for me to remain." History would later record that the dictator's early reign of terror included the executions of some three thousand suspected "leftists" and "subversives," both male and female, and the torture of thirty thousand more.

Leticia came to Canada in January of 1976 on a visitor's visa for three months. She spoke no English, but she had five hundred dollars in her purse, a wardrobe of summer-weight clothes, and what she calls a great sense of adventure and joy.

She met Vince Moneva in Toronto in 1978. A native of the inland city of Zaragoza in Spain, Vince was something of a playboy about town, a man who had enjoyed a peripatetic career managing restaurants all over the world. He was managing an Argentinian restaurant near the Lakeshore called Casa Mendosa. At the urging of a friend, he interviewed "this girl from Chile who had come to Toronto" for a position in the restaurant's gift shop. He hired her on the spot.

"When I first saw her," Vince says, suddenly looking very boyish, "I said 'I'm going to keep this one!'"

One day, Vince was in the midst of a tirade about the "lazy Latins" working in the Argentinian restaurant, and how none of them could be counted on to show up on time for work, much less do what they had been assigned due to their slovenly work habits. From behind the counter at the gift shop came an amused, crystalline voice.

"Remember, my dear," Leticia Martinez scolded, "I am also Latin." Dismissing Vince's grumbled reply, she added, teasingly. "I tell you *this*, my dear. I make you a promise — like a witch, making a curse: you will *marry* a Latin girl!"

After a romantic whirlwind courtship, Leticia's "curse" came to pass. The newlyweds first restaurant was near Bathurst and Lawrence. In 1988, they sold it and bought a garishly decorated Church St. eatery called Papa Peachies that was in steady popular decline among the notoriously fickle diners along the strip, largely due to spotty customer service and uninspired cuisine. Initially, the Monevas had no real sense that they were buying a restaurant in a gay neighbourhood, much less what it meant to be restaurateurs in that milieu. Suspecting that there might be more to doing business on Church St. than merely serving smart food, they took on a gay partner to help them navigate the terrain. Vince ran the kitchen, while Leticia served as hostess.

"I was in the background, with the kitchen and the organization and the menus," Vince says. "Anything to do with the face of Café California was, and is, Leticia. I always say, Café California is Leticia. Our gay clientele identifies with Leticia. She has something I don't. She's charming, she's well-spoken, well-dressed. She's beautiful."

Nor did they encounter any judgement on the part of either customers or business associates for being straight business owners on Church St. Not that it would have mattered to either Leticia or Vince, they decided early on.

"It was up to us to learn to live with the area," Leticia says modestly, with quiet grace. "It wasn't up to the area to learn to live with us."

The deceptively simple concept worked. Café California was an instant hit. The partner stayed a little over a year to help build the new restaurant's gay cachet, then left on excellent terms for greener pastures when the Monevas bought him out. Over time, Café California evolved into a Church St. landmark of sorts, with the tiny, chic Leticia as its *doyenne*.

Leticia explains, "I always told [the waiters], 'Here, there are no queens, my darling. The only queens are the customers.'" And, she adds, smiling sweetly, "'The Queen Mother is me.'"

Many of the waiters the Monevas hired became almost surrogate sons to the family, and Angie — an only child with no brothers — suddenly had several gay ones. This was her first introduction to one of the most unique gifts of gay life: the ability to create chosen family nearly at will. Although Angie would occasionally get jealous when the staff called Leticia "Mama," to a little girl, this was magical. And to a woman as highly maternal as Leticia, it filled a void that might otherwise have remained empty.

"I've always loved my role as mother," Leticia says wistfully. "That is my biggest enjoyment in life." When Angie was three, Leticia carried the little girl in her arms when she went to visit the hospital room of a Café California customer who was dying of

AIDS. "When I started interacting with the gay community and started to get to know them a little bit, I noticed that in many cases there wasn't a mother in their life as a presence. So to me, it was almost selfish. I always dreamed of having many children, and I realized that this was my chance to have many."

Nor was the para-parental model restricted to Leticia. Vince, too, felt a paternal version of the heart-tug of chosen family. Along with it came a dawning awareness of the stories that lay behind gay life, not only in Canada, but closer to his macho Latin roots.

"The first employee was a guy from Argentina," Vince recalls. "It was from him that we learned what it was like to be gay in South America. He told us that when he was young he didn't want to be gay, so he went to a doctor friend of his to see about getting a lobotomy. He would rather be a vegetable than be gay." It was through this young man, says Vince, that gay men finally became completely real and fleshed out to him. "That's when I completely understood — it wasn't what they told us in the Catholic Church that these were a bunch of perverts. These were human beings who grow up with this orientation. They have the same desire for men that I have for my wife." The Monevas eventually sponsored the waiter from Argentina when the Canadian refugee board denied his claim that there was enough homophobia in Argentina that it was a danger to stay there.

To Leticia, in many ways, her work with the restaurant on Church St. became almost an extension of the political work she had done in Chile, though obviously less formally.

"To me it's all about acceptance," she says, the sound of steel ringing faintly beneath the ladylike, motherly tone. "As I said, Chile is very class-oriented. It was a great joy to me to accept people who, in many cases, had been rejected by the larger society.

ooo00

ANGIE REMEMBERS FIRST BEING consciously aware of gay men when she was very young. Even as a child, she was struck by the male couples, and noted their tactile comfort with each other, and not infrequently, their mutual expressions of attraction and/or romantic interest.

"My mom would send me to the tables and say, 'Bring them their bill,'" she recalls. "The customers thought I was adorable, and they gave me a toonie, or whatever. That would always make my day."

"When she was three," Leticia remembers, "Angie asked me, 'Mummy, why do boys hold hands in your restaurant? Why do they kiss on the mouth in your restaurant?' A customer said to me, 'Leticia, answer your daughter!' I said, 'My darling, because they love each other.' Angie said, 'Two boys can't love each other!'" Leticia went on to explain the various combinations and permutations of love that were possible.

Angie was spellbound. "I actually went up to one of the waiters," she says, "and I asked him, 'Why are two men kissing and holding hands?' One of the things I always admired about them is that they were brutally honest with me. They never made anything up. The way they explained it to me so that I could understand it at three was that there were male and female 'roles' that gay people can take on. As I grew up," she laughs, "it became *top* and *bottom*."

Another waiter eventually explained to Angie that the roles were fluid. "I never really questioned it after that," she muses. "It became the norm. In Catholic school they told me that a man and a woman were together for procreation, and no other reason, certainly not for pleasure. So I didn't understand why men would be intimate with each other. I would see gay men at the restaurant with kids — how did they do that? I asked my mom, and she said that two men couldn't make a baby with each other, but that they could adopt. I didn't understand why they would be intimate if they couldn't have babies. She didn't know how to explain to me that it was pleasurable, so she said, 'Well, when two people love each other...'

"I thought it was just that they were *trying*," she says, laughing. "And it wasn't *working*."

At five, Angie had twenty Barbies and one Ken. Her friends all had more than one Ken, to match up with the Barbies. "Ken had seventeen girlfriends," she explains. "My girlfriends all told me that I had to have more Ken dolls, because each Barbie needs a boyfriend. Going to the restaurant and seeing that men could be with men, and women could be with women, I eventually threw out my one Ken doll and dressed Barbie in his clothes. I figured that if the girls in the restaurant didn't need boys, Barbie didn't need one either."

If it was the norm in her Church St. world, it wasn't the norm at her Catholic elementary school, where questions about who was the top and who was the bottom weren't discussed, at least not by her friends.

"I was very proud of my gay friends at the restaurant," she says. "If there's one thing the gay community taught me even then, it was pride. There was no need to hide, and in fact there was a reason to celebrate. I would talk to everyone about it. That's when [the staff] realized I was teaching kids things they didn't want them to know. 'Seriously! Two guys kiss!' And the kids would be, like, 'No!' And the teachers didn't want the kids to know that. As if kids could live in a bubble." In Grade 5, she had a fight with a young boy who was "badmouthing" gay people. "My parents always taught me not to take anything," she admits. "I'm a non-violent person, but my father had taught me never to take shit from anyone. So I started to get into a fight with this person." The fight landed Angie in the principal's office, and the school called Leticia and asked her to come down for a meeting. "They said, 'Your daughter brought this disgusting thing to our school, so she's in trouble for it!'" Angie remembers. "Me. Not the boy who started it, me." Upon her arrival at the school, Leticia furiously lit into the principal on the subject of homophobia. "I've never seen my mother that angry," Angie says. "She almost physically threatened every teacher there. It was a very, very serious argument."

When they returned home, Leticia sat Angie down and tried to explain to her about how she couldn't fight every battle, every time.

"Growing up alone in a country where we didn't have any extended family, and where I was an only child, it was very important to have my big brothers — or sisters — in the gay community," Angie says. "They were my family. I would defend them to the death. But eventually I realized I couldn't fight every war. As much as I'd like to show the whole world what a wonderful community it is, I can't win every war."

When Angie was eight, she met a waiter at Café California whom she credits with beginning the process by which the world around her became her world too.

"He was really into drag," she says, "and he did an amazing Marilyn Monroe. He was the first person to take me around the neighbourhood. We went grocery shopping together. He took me to his apartment on Isabella Street. He had all these crazy things there." For instance? "He'd written on the walls, 'Do Not Feed the Bears' and 'Do Not Fuck the Bears.' He'd built clocks made out of Coca-Cola cans, and there were a lot of posters of men, and gay art. I was really overwhelmed, because I'd never seen anything that sexual. I didn't realize that adults painted the 'F-word' on their walls! He was an adult, but he was such a kid at the same time. I was always with him, and I remember thinking he was the most amazing person in the world. He was one of the first people who took me out of the restaurant — he'd take me out shopping, he'd introduce me to his 'weird' friends — things like that. He just scooped me up and took me around. He was proud to be with me."

When the waiter contracted HIV, Angie was nine, and heartbroken.

"My idea was, you get AIDS, you die. I didn't know that there were treatments, or that you could live a very happy life for many years. I just expected him to die. I approached him, and I was crying. He asked me why I was crying, and I told him, 'Because you're going to die.' This must have been very hard for him, because he had just found out himself. I was crying because I thought he was going to leave me. He said, 'No, I'm not going to die. I could live for many years.' He said there were many ways you could get it. I don't think that, at nine, he thought I was ready to hear that he got it sexually."

The waiter left the restaurant to be near his family. She met him again, years later, and was struck by the passage of time.

"I realized the impact of age. Looking back at some of these guys I grew up with, who were the coolest people in the world, they seem much more human. I told him about my school, and my life. He's so proud of me. He said he always regretted leaving me, that I was like a little sister to him."

The first dead body Angie ever saw was at an AIDS funeral when she was eleven, the partner of one of the regular customers. She was the only child at the memorial service.

"It was the only dead body I'd ever seen," she says, suppressing a faint shudder. "Being Catholic, my mom said, 'You have to go up to the casket and pay your respects, bless it, and walk away.'" Angie found the idea horrifying. "She dragged me. I was trying not to cause a scene at the funeral, but at the same time, I was like, 'Oh God!' I can't even remember what he was like when he was alive, all I have is a picture in my head of this dead guy I barely knew, and the knowledge of this disease I barely understood. I was in pure shock. I've never gone to another viewing."

Not all of Angie's friendships with her "big brothers" on staff were leavened with such life-altering gravity. She recalls another waiter, a handsome, dark-haired young man named Billy, for whom she retains undiminished affection and respect even though he has long since left Café California, and her memories of their interactions are shot through with humour.

"I remember when Billy got his tongue ring. I was ten or eleven," she recalls. "I asked him why the hell he would get a tongue ring — this was way before I got mine — and he didn't know what to say at first."

Perhaps weighing the consequences of explaining lingual piercing to his employers' adorable ten-year-old daughter, Angie recalls, Billy mumbled something about it "looking cool."

"Finally, he told me that it had a 'sexual component' and I was like, 'Why? What function?' I kept bombarding him with questions, because at ten I couldn't imagine how this could enhance anything sexually. I didn't get it. I was still trying to wrap my head around two guys having sex, let alone the specifics of oral sex!" she says, laughing at the memory. "Four years down the road, I came to Billy and told him I wanted to get a tongue ring. I was going through a piercing phase. My parents told me I couldn't pierce anything on my face because it would look trashy." She asked Billy if getting his tongue pierced hurt. "He said, 'I'm not going to lie to you, it hurts a little,' but he said 'Yes, go out and get it. You'll love it.' My mom nearly killed him. Anything Billy did I would have done."

In retrospect, she admits that although Billy did eventually explain the "sexual component" of tongue rings as an oral sex enhancement, "I hadn't really put it together that [gay] guys did that as well." Besides, she said, "Billy would never have spoken to me as though I was a child and said, 'No, tongue rings and piercings at your age are *bad!*' He respected me as a person, even though I was a child."

When Angie entered Earl Haig high school in Grade 9, she decided she wanted to become a psychologist. There was a peer counselling program at the school, and she joined it as an apprentice. The "peer helpers," as they were called, gave presentations on bullying, among other things. None of her friends wanted to do it with her.

"You had to give up your spare, which would have been the only time you get to eat, or go out," she says.

By Grade 11, she was a full-fledged peer counsellor herself. The peer counsellors had their photographs on the board. She became known as the girl with the blue hair with pink streaks.

"That's when a few of the kids started to come up to me and talk to me about being harassed, about homophobia. They were like, 'I think I'm gay, but I don't know what to do about it.'"

Angie's reputation as the daughter of restaurant owners on Church St. had preceded her. "Even in an arts school [which Earl Haig was], where all my guy friends were dancers, it was sad to see even my friends involved with verbal harassment of gay kids. I got called out of class to talk to kids. I sat down with a couple of them, one of whom had been rejected by his parents." Another was being gay bashed by his older brother. Angie met two lesbians in high school, including a thug of a tomboy who was never harassed in the way effeminate boys usually were.

"Everybody just assumed that was the facade she had to put on to protect herself in her neighbourhood," she says.

Oddly, the same people at school who could accept the fact that her family had a gay restaurant couldn't recognize the incongruity of that acceptance with their own anti-gay harassing at school. "I think it was just a show when they were pushing around the gay kids, to prove that they were cool and macho, superior. Even my boyfriend's friends. When I met him, he was really homophobic." She sighs, but tenderly. "We've been together for five years. He's my childhood sweetheart, and literally the only person I've ever been with. He started off homophobic, but one day I sat him down and said, 'This is my world. These are my people. If you want to love me and accept me, you have to love and accept them too.'"

ooooo

I'M SITTING AT A patio table at lunchtime, midweek, with Angie and her boyfriend, James Debenham, an extremely handsome, very macho, twenty-three-year-old security specialist with plans to go into law enforcement as a police officer in a year or two. The sun is very bright for this early fall day, and James has chivalrously given me the seat in the shade. He squints slightly as he talks. He wears casual clothes that hint at the bank of muscle beneath. His hair is cropped military-short. James draws more than one appreciative glance from the gay men who pass our table, but if he notices, he gives no hint of it except to smile warmly and wave at a very young, very pretty drag queen who he and Angie know, and who Angie knows has a crush on him.

"James treats her like a lady, which she loves," Angie tells me proudly, reaching over to touch James's hand lightly, her slender fingers covering his large ones. "There aren't a lot of men who give her that courtesy, much less straight men."

This is James Debenham's first interview, and although there is precious little he wouldn't do for his Angie, the process of talking about his life — *emoting* to a stranger about his introduction to gay life via the intermediary of his beloved girlfriend — is still uncharted waters. Still, he's game.

"At first, I was very uneasy," he says honestly of his entry into the Church St. gay milieu. "Prior to meeting Angie, I didn't know about this neighbourhood. I was pretty homophobic."

What was his worst case scenario?

"Being hit on," he says, with a hearty laugh at his own expense. "My friend would tell me to keep my ass to the wall when I went to visit her at the restaurant."

James was seventeen when he transferred to Earl Haig, Angie's high school, to play football. As luck would have it, that was the year that York Region decided to eliminate competitive football from the curriculum.

Ever the pragmatist, James switched his focus to photography and sculpture.

When he met Angie Moneva in 2002, he says, he was immediately smitten. Entranced with the pretty, punkish fourteen year old, they began to date. Although he knew Angie was beginning to apprentice in the school's peer counselling program, with a specific focus on gay and lesbian teen issues, it never occurred to him that he would have a girlfriend whose double life was lived partly on Church St. By his own admission a classic high-school homophobe, he was initially appalled at the notion of gay men in any configuration.

Angie was quite adamant, however. She quickly made him aware of Café California and her Church St. pedigree, making it clear that she and her gay friends came as a package.

"It was very difficult," he says honestly. "She gave me the ultimatum. She said, 'You deal with my life, or I'm leaving you right now.' So I thought, I'll suck it up and see what's going on."

Most teenage boys, if they have to deal with brothers at all, usually only have to contend with one or two. James Debenham had to pass muster with a dozen.

Eventually, the restaurant staff, always protective of their Angie, relaxed around James.

"When James first came on the scene," Angie says, laughing softly, "Richard would tease him. Mercilessly. He would make suggestive comments to him, pretend to grab him, describe sexual things that he'd want to take him into the bathroom and do with him. James was still getting used to the area, and he wasn't sure how to identify what was joking." Richard would suggest swapping boyfriends. "James wouldn't know if I was kidding or not, because I played along with Richard. Ryan, Richard's boyfriend, is a flight attendant and he's gorgeous. I'd say, 'Well James, he could fly me all over the world, and he's so beautiful,' and James would be, like, 'No!'"

"The waiters started teasing me as they became comfortable with me and I became comfortable with them," James recalls, noting the strangeness of having "gay men who were that protective of your girlfriend." Still, he says again, "I respected that." They interrogated him about his intentions. "I learned to love it, and to appreciate the fact that there was always someone looking out for her here."

His peers were appalled at this new dimension of his life. However wolfishly they might appreciate his hot girlfriend, the notion of their good buddy having his ass checked out by fags on a regular basis filled them with horror.

"My friends were all homophobic," James says. "This is a world they didn't feel they — or I — should have anything to do with. It's kind of the way I felt. They didn't shun me, but they'd tease me here and there and call me 'a homo.' I would say, 'Hey, I'm the one dating the pretty girl, not you, so shut your mouth!' My friends still felt that they should punch [the gays] out. I said, 'Yeah, *you* try to punch out some guy in the "gaybourhood" and see what happens to you.'" Over the years, his own self-esteem has been radically boosted by his exposure to Church St., something he has tried to share with his buddies. "These guys are always down on themselves," says James. "I tell them, 'Come downtown! These guys will make you feel like a million bucks!' You won't get that from girls," he adds mischievously. "Girls aren't going to say to straight men, 'Oh my God, you're so handsome!' Nope, it isn't going to happen, unless they actually know you. Gay guys are very blunt. I like that. They'll tell you straight up if they like you."

From where he's sitting, his old world looks a lot smaller. There was a situation, recently, where James was at a straight bar with some colleagues from work, including Angie and a gay friend. At the next table a group of men were casting surreptitious, disdainful glances in their direction and laughing among themselves at "the queers."

"All they could do all night long was talk shit about our group, and about gayness," James says. Later in the washroom, he over-heard two members of the group talking about "those faggots" at the next table. He walked up to them and said, "Do you guys have something to say about my friends?"

When the two men challenged him, he told them, "'If you have a problem with gay people, you're in the wrong fucking area. Church St. is one block over, and you guys are talking smack about gay people?' They said, 'What are you gonna do, tough guy?' I was gonna crank this guy right in the mouth, knock him flat on his ass. I realized if I did, I'd get fired from my job." Instead, he offered them the chance to leave the bar, or else.

Or else what? came the predictable sneered reply.

James turned around and punched the mirror clear through to the drywall.

"They looked at each other and bounced out of the washroom. I never saw them again." James hesitates, then speaks with poignancy that is powerfully moving for its naked need to communicate his own evolution, and his new understanding. "I have *so much respect* for you guys," he says furiously. "I wish *everyone* knew what I know now."

Although Angie abhors violence, in this one instance, she says, she understood James's protective fury. "He wouldn't hesitate to protect me, or himself, or one of our gay friends. He's a very physical man. And for those guys at the next table to focus that much attention on something they wanted so badly to hate ..." she marvels, trailing off. "We're still growing up in a society where being macho and violent and driven to acceptance makes that acceptance unlikely. We're *slowly evolving*. But I do think that as a society we need these 'roles' to reassure us. If everyone was open to gender fluidity it would be amazing, everyone would be afraid of losing their identity. People seem to have a need to define themselves in opposition to something else."

"I do owe it all to Angie," James says of his evolution, "because if I hadn't met her, I wouldn't have ever thought to change my ways. When you don't understand something, you insult it and you're afraid of it. This area has brought a lot of me out. I'm more confident, more outspoken. I've met a lot of really great people. I don't see 'homosexual' anymore, I see people. It's a lot different than it was before."

ooooo

AT OUR THIRD AND last interview, I am sitting at Café California in the middle of the afternoon, an hour after the lunch rush, and more than two hours before dinner. Over coffee, Angie, Leticia, and I are chatting.

Angie is telling me that last year a lesbian girl she'd counselled back at Earl Haig had come into Café California unannounced. After the two had hugged, the girl said that she'd always assumed that Angie knew she was gay. She asked Angie to show her the village.

"I took her to Tango and Crews," Angie says, with the satisfaction of someone who has seen her life come full circle, from Church St. child, to teenage mentor, to university student on the verge of adult independence. "We had the most amazing time."

Leticia has been sending Angie to Temuco, Chile, every couple of years to keep her in touch with her roots. Her conservative, upper-class Chilean family has never accepted the fact that Angie was being raised in such close proximity to gay people, and it has been the source of severe friction over the years, particularly with Leticia's very traditionally minded brother.

"They can't even begin to understand my world," Angie says, sighing. "Even if I tried to explain it, they wouldn't understand. A few years back, I got into a terrible fight with my uncle. At the time, my whole world was a protest. My uncle knows he can push my buttons, so he called homosexuality 'the plague,' *la plaga*. He said that gays should all be lined up and shot, and condemned to hell. I got very upset, and I would fight. And that was something which, in the Spanish culture, I wasn't supposed to be. I was taught respect of elders at all costs. For me, at fifteen, to start screaming at the table was awful."

When Leticia heard about the altercation, she was livid. Although her brother naturally expected her to discipline Angie for her insolence, it was her brother upon whom Leticia turned her wrath.

"I told him, 'That was not very mature. You're a man, you need to act like one. To pick on a little girl when you know how much these people mean to her is unacceptable. You raise your children your way, but this isn't the way I'm raising mine!'"

Although nothing changed in her brother's attitudes, Leticia continues to send her daughter home every second summer. One suspects that there's more to it than keeping her daughter in touch with her Chilean roots after all. For a woman who escaped a repressive, sexist, homophobic culture to make a new life in a new country, with a new tribe of gay men as part of the new life, there must be enormous satisfaction in being able to send her daughter — the proof of Leticia's own survival, the fruit of her own independence and freedom — back home like a message in a bottle from a brighter, kinder time and place.

"This summer, I insisted that Angie return to Chile as an adult," Leticia says with serene maternal pride. This time, when her uncle tried to push her buttons, as Angie calls it, she laughed at him. "I'm so proud to be her mother, because I think she's a wonderful human being. The last time she was there, she was still a teenager, fighting with everyone and defending the gays against my brother. But I wanted to show them what kind of human being Angie has turned out to be, having been raised in the gay community. To me, it was very personal. I wanted to show off my daughter, and to say, 'Look my darlings, this is my daughter! This is the product of a child being raised in a gay community.'"

The Dealer Behind Fashion Cares:
A Portrait of Phillip Ing
2003

WEDNESDAY, APRIL 16, 2003

Twelve hours spent with your feet on a concrete floor, in an anonymous office-loft high above Adelaide St., watching buff young models
parade up and down like so much *Vogue*-grade sirloin, is apparently murder on your heels, sitting or standing.

Yesterday, the first round of Fashion Cares 2003 auditions lasted
well into the night. This afternoon, Phillip Ing, producer, occasional
director, and thematic conceptualist of the legendary annual Fashion
Cares fashion show, is hoping for an earlier wrap. His young
colleagues couldn't be more in accord.

"Our feet were killing us yesterday," says Michelle Holmes, Ing's
crisply efficient co-producer. She's sitting in front of a long table
littered with empty water bottles and a stack of model composites
and Polaroids. "We got out of here rather late," she adds ruefully.

The assembled *fashionistas* are not taking any chances one way
or another. Like battle-hardened glamour warriors on some surreal
parallel-earth battlefield, where fat and old age (twenty-five-plus)
is the enemy, they've good-naturedly armed themselves with their
own weapons of mass distraction. Designer tote bags bulge with

emergency supplies — Advil, lip balm, bottled water, and Diet Coke — in preparation for the beauty siege to come.

It doesn't take long. As we watch in shock and awe, the attack begins.

A beautiful young Russian woman sweeps across the floor in front of us. One of Ing's colleagues asks her if she'd mind taking off her hooded sweatshirt.

"Is too cold in here," the girl pouts prettily in a silvery-accented voice that makes you think of caviar and samovars of smoky tea. In modelling, thirty-five-year-old women are also "girls." She shivers delicately, but she's a pro after all. Launching a klieg-lit smile as wide and dazzling as a sun-struck snowy Ural steppe, she gamely shrugs off the hoodie and casts it aside. She sashays into the audition, her body in perfect strut with the dance music on the ghetto blaster.

As the model glides across the floor, a smile of recognition flickers across Ing's face.

"Did you do the MAC show at GUM [the former Soviet Union's answer to The Bay], in Moscow?" he asks softly. Many of Ing's pronouncements seem equally gently uttered. Unlike the bored, metallic staccato of countless fashion mavens with a fraction of his power and prestige, Ing's voice is the sort you'd hope to hear if you were being talked out of jumping off a window ledge — warm, calming, eminently reasonable.

The model looks up, surprised, and smiles at him, answering in the affirmative.

"You wore the Mohawk," he continues smoothly. "I remember you very well."

"You were there?" she says, rolling her r's excitedly. Model auditions are usually short and often curt, and the young woman is inexorably drawn to Ing's candour. In a field where beauty is the entry-level norm, and, consequently, most often anonymous, there is a powerful allure to a personal touch, especially from a potential client.

"You were *fabulous*," Ing says sincerely. "We were all very impressed with you in that show."

"*I miss Moscow!*" the girl wails, smiling brightly all the while. Her hair glitters, and light refracts off her impossibly perfect Slavic cheekbones.

"You don't miss Moscow, you miss your friends there," Ing says soothingly. The girl immediately and joyfully concurs. The two chat briefly about the GUM show and enjoy a laugh about how Ing was stopped and interrogated by burly Russian soldiers in the streets of Moscow, who thought he might be some sort of smartly-tailored, Prada-clad international spy. Ing compliments her on her audition and promises to book her, assuring her that Fashion Cares will be lucky to have her. Volunteer-driven though the show is, with everyone donating time, talent, and beauty, the show is a prestigious gig for a model. Given this, it's no less of an audition, and Ing's kindness strikes a golden note. The girl floats off on a cloud of happiness.

"She's *fabulous*," is the murmured edict of the assemblage. "*Fabulous*."

The next model is very male, very long haired and muscular, and tattooed. He looks like Bon Jovi might look if the Jersey-bred rock star been raised on tuna and Creatine in an enchanted forest somewhere, nursed by three magic model agents dressed in pink, blue, and green. Marching ruggedly across the floor, he appears to shimmer under a slick of palpable testosterone. You could count his abs from a plane.

"Do you dance?" asks Ing, smiling.

"I haven't danced in, like, oh my God, so long," the model replies, clearly pleased to have been asked.

"Are you okay with wearing a G-string?"

The Fashion Cares show is as well-known for its edgy, fantastical erotic theatre as it is for the fashion, Ing points out. Is the young man all right with that?

"Sure," he shrugs. He pauses, then confesses, "I hurt my shoulder, though. I haven't worked out in a while. When's the show?" he asks worriedly.

Ing gives him the date. The model does some quick mental calculations, then grins, relieved.

"Good," he drawls happily. "That'll give me time to get in shape."

"This is *bad* shape?" Ing queries artlessly, the flattery as light and natural as air.

The model laughs warmly, any audition tension vanishing in the face of Ing's unaffected goodwill. He leaves, smiling as happily as the Russian girl before him, both clearly psyched at the prospect of working with Ing on Fashion Cares.

Welcome to fashion, where even perfect men need to do party crunches before a big show. You get the feeling, though, that they'd joyfully do them for Phillip Ing anyway, if he asked in that gentle voice. There's something about the self-described "ultimate back-stage guy" that keeps everyone willingly on their toes, doing their best work, and has for seventeen years. What is it?

Don't ask Ing. He's his own best-kept secret.

ᴏᴏᴏᴏᴏ

TUESDAY, APRIL 22, 2003
"I'm very conscious of that," says Phillip Ing almost a week later, when I ask him about the way he treated the models at the audition. We've just finished an off-the-record dinner at a downtown restaurant. Dressed in the uniformly flattering MAC dress code of black-on-black, his fingers are long and slender and his posture is imperial. It's rare to apply the word *elegant* to a man (outside the confines of fashion) but it's an apt word to describe Ing.

Over dessert, Ing is reluctantly — but again, graciously — submitting to an interview. He prefers to stick to the topic of Fashion Cares, however, and dodges personal with the dexterity of a downhill ski racer. "It's such a huge volunteer effort," he says of the event. "You want to treat everyone with respect for what they bring on board, be it looks, talent, or brains. If you can't walk away from a charity event experience with that, what *can* you walk away with? Especially with the models. We see probably six or seven hundred models every year, from which I know I'm going to pick seventy or eighty. The least we can do is make it a civil experience for the other 620. It's important never to forget that this is a fundraiser for the AIDS Committee of Toronto."

Phillip Ing is one of the most elusive and reclusive figures in Canadian fashion, no mean feat in an industry where everyone's best-toned muscle is a hyper-aerobic tongue. More people seem to *know of* him than *know* him. He is rarely interviewed and has never been the subject of a full-length magazine profile in the eighteen years since he first became involved with Fashion Cares. Under his aegis, the annual glamourama has become the most successful AIDS fundraiser in Canadian history.

"The nature of Phillip's work is not so much as an innovator of fashion, but as a purveyor of glamour, which is such a rare bird in this country and in the fashion industry here as well," says Jeanne Beker, the one-woman media supernova who is best known worldwide as the face and voice of *Fashion Television*. "He's such a visionary and such a creative artist. That's why we treasure him so much as part of the industry."

Uniquely, Fashion Cares brings together the disparate worlds of high society, the media, and millennial gay culture and its community. The event has raised millions for AIDS since it began in 1987 and, at the same time, with the corporate sponsorship of MAC cosmetics, made it an acceptable and viable association for more buttoned-down companies who might otherwise shy away. But perhaps the most telling testament to the enduring appeal of Fashion Cares is that it's still volunteer-based, from the front-line, hands-on volunteers right on up to Ing himself.

"In the Chinese culture, it's important to give back to the community," he says. "I know it sounds clichéd, but I honestly feel I've been trying to do that for a long time. I've never paid lip service to that line the way you can. The line is so maligned. If it's a cliché, I really think that for twenty-odd years I've been trying to live that cliché."

Born in Windsor, Ontario, ("a car town, not a fashion town") some forty-plus years ago, he delicately declines to reveal his exact age, one of his few obvious vanities. Ing was raised in what he calls a "classic first-generation Chinese family." His father was brought to Canada as one of the last "paper sons" of immigrant Chinese railroad workers, a system rooted in the Canadian government's then-willingness to allow liberal immigration for Chinese workers in the name of cheap labour. The government often looked the other way if the paperwork wasn't quite spot-on, as it was in Ing's father's case.

"A 'paper son' was somebody who was a son on paper only," Ing explains. "The person who brought him over might have been a relative who said my father was his son, when in actuality, he wasn't. I don't know who that would have been, though my father knew."

By the time he was in Grade five and six, he was working in his family's restaurant, bussing and waiting on tables, sometimes up to forty hours a week, all the while keeping up with schoolwork. He read magazines assiduously, dreaming of the gilded world that beckoned him from beyond the pages. "I've sublimated a lot of that stuff," he says, conceding that they were difficult years. "I've always been a private person, even as a kid, and when you're a private kid, you withdraw into what you're reading. When you're in high school, and you're waiting for the end of the month because that's when your favourite magazine is hitting the stands because that's the high point of your life, it says something about your life."

Because he worked, Ing always had more money than his classmates, and he spent it on clothes.

"I knew something was up when I was putting snaps on my housecoat to make it look like a mandarin collar, because I thought I would look better in a higher collar," he laughs. He was four at the time. "I knew I was different when I was taking socks and making nice knit outfits for dolls. All that stuff was already there.

My parents didn't want to know about that sort of thing. My father wanted me to quit school when I was ten or eleven, because we had a thriving business. All I could think about was getting out of high school."

Though Ing says he's "sublimated" most of the memories of his youth, some are still close enough to touch. "It's almost stereotypical," he says of his relationship with a close female friend who was his constant companion throughout those painful early years. "A guy who's overdressed and a girl who's *way* overdressed." He laughs warmly at how the memory looks from his current vantage point. "We'd go to Detroit and shop and go to dinner." Years later, the woman died of AIDS. Ing poignantly concedes it was one of the seismic events in the evolution of his career with Fashion Cares. "That's when you turn into a dreamer," he says softly. "My God, when I look at fashion here in Toronto, I wonder how many little kids there were who were just like me, dreamers through public school and high school, who then went into this business with whatever they were dreaming about."

After high school, Ing attended York University and studied film. In 1983, he'd just been laid off his job at Sotheby's when his sister asked him to help out with a fashion show she was producing at Hart House for the Chinese Canadian National Council. Like many a future fashion princeling before him, Ing began his career on his knees. Literally.

"I'd never been to a fashion show before this one, so at the first fashion show I was ever involved with, I was taping shoes backstage, which is just about as low on the totem pole as you can get." He was accidentally kicked in the face by the models as they pranced out onto the runway, something rather hard to imagine happening twenty-one years later. "I was fascinated by the whole thing," he recalls. "The main thing was the designers — Alfred Sung, Winston Kong, Simon Chang, Benny Sung. I said to my sister, 'We could have done this better!'" Someone must have been listening, because Ing promptly found himself producing a fashion show at the National Arts Centre in Ottawa. "I went from taping shoes to producing fashion shows almost immediately," he marvels.

In 1986, Steven Levy, of the Festival of Canadian Fashion, saw him working on a show for designer Vivian Shyu and told Ing he liked his style. Levy invited him to come and work for the Festival. By then, Ing was ready to put his sporadic film work aside, and concentrate on fashion. "Suddenly I was producing twenty-six shows in five days at the Metro Toronto Convention Centre. They were big shows, too. At that time, we had audiences of between two and five thousand people. It was a good experience, because they were huge, theatrical shows that lent themselves to learning how to handle Fashion Cares, which came up in 1987."

By the mid-eighties, the AIDS epidemic had become the spectre haunting the midnight pillow of urban gay men everywhere and the public's initial response was predictably harsh and hysterical when Fashion Cares started.

"There's a huge difference between the eighteen year old that came to Fashion Cares in 1987 and the one who comes in 2003," Ing says sagely. "The 1987 version was hit, as I was, with the immediacy, the horror, and the fear of it. A lot of our reactions were based on fear. It was more emotional at that time. I think it's still emotional, but what a really savvy eighteen year old knows now is that there are forty-two million infected people, and that's something to intellectualize: that this is a disease that has claimed people all over the planet. There's an awareness that it's a global problem more than a local one," he says of the response of young volunteers, "but it's no less of a problem to them. I really admire kids who come in here and say, 'I really want to do something about AIDS.'"

Ing began working freelance with MAC in 1986. The company's edgy, sexy approach to personal style dovetailed neatly with Ing's own work. "I've always been known for theatricality," he says lightly. "I've never been known for straight, clean shows. That was always for other people. I got the more whacked-out stuff. And the best of the whacked-out stuff was the MAC show. That's where I met

Frank Toscan and Frank Angelo." He worked freelance for them between 1987 and 1994, balancing his commercial work with the various Fashion Cares projects.

"I knew that if Fashion Cares was going to keep going, it needed an infusion of cash," he admits, "because there was no steady sponsor who could put money into the production. When we started Fashion Cares in 1987, you couldn't get a sponsor to come near it." He cites the AIDS stigma as the primary source of reluctance. "It was the AIDS thing for sure," he confirms. "In 1987, even ACT was only a few years old." They raised $40,000 in the first year. "You'd get donations and you made money through ticket sales and auctions."

When MAC signed on in 1994, other sponsors realized that it was safe to do the same.

"I went to MAC in '94 to ask Frank if he would become more involved with Fashion Cares and he agreed," Ing says. "At the same time, he asked me what I was doing. I told him I was working in film and fashion, and he said, 'Why don't you work for me?' And that's how I came to MAC."

"We're a very practical society, unfortunately, by nature," Jeanne Beker says, speaking of Canada. "Glamour doesn't usually play a part in that equation. It seems like a hedonistic luxury in many ways. We really don't feel we deserve it, or that we can be very good at it, or that we have the money to support it. Happily, Phillip has found himself in a situation with MAC where there are the funds to exercise his vision."

"I do feel that it's my baby," Ing says with evident satisfaction. "It's a baby I share with thousands of people."

As Fashion Cares sweeps into the new century, Ing revels in its growth and relishes the enduring affection people seem to have for it, even today. Perhaps more so today.

"It's been an amazing evolution for an event," he muses. "I do events for a living, worldwide, and I can count on one hand the number of events that have hit an anniversary of fifteen years and above, and we're one of them. It still has great energy, and it's had great luck, not to mention huge support from the community. You can't say that of a lot of events — they usually peter out and die a natural death. Fashion Cares keeps going. It has a core following, then it attracts new people all the time. Fashion is rooted in new blood and every five years there's an influx of new talent. New designers want to be part of it and models' careers usually run between ages eighteen to twenty-five. So every five years, you have new people. You're never reliant on the same creativity. There's always fresh blood."

And fashion is a haunted landscape in 2003. No other creative field has sustained so many terrible losses in the war against AIDS. The ghosts of the beautiful and the talented crowd the edge of the runway — young dreamers like Ing was at a comparable age, all of them cut down at the dawn of their careers. If their clapping and cheering can no longer be heard above the din of the festive living, Fashion Cares exists as a sort of medium through which their spirit can speak, and not be forgotten. Ing hasn't forgotten, though some might have.

"I think it's easy at Fashion Cares to forget that we're doing a fundraiser and underneath all of this fun, fancy, and frivolity, there's a very serious cause that we're trying to do something about," Ing says soberly. "I think you do have to remind everybody. Half the guys who work with us are under twenty-five and sometimes you have to tell them, 'This may be one of the first commitments you're making to a *cause*.' It goes right past some people, but sometimes it has a profound effect on others.

"You have to keep making that statement over and over again," he says fiercely, suddenly sounding more like a general than the anointed producer of Toronto's most glittering, *fabulous* fashion extravaganza. "We've been saying it for seventeen years. And until the fight is over, we have to keep pounding away at it."

The Full Paige: A Portrait of Peter Paige

2001

HERE'S SOMETHING YOU DIDN'T know about Peter Paige: he's a sugar junkie. Gummy Bears, Sweet Tarts, Rockets, you name it. Following a Zone-approved lunch of broiled salmon on winter greens at Café California, a restaurant on Toronto's gay strip, Church St., which stands in for Pittsburgh's Liberty St. on *Queer As Folk*, the twenty-seven-year-old actor laid waste to the candy departments of two convenience stores in search of sweet adrenaline. The accumulated booty is spread out on the couch between us in his short-term rental apartment near downtown.

"It burns right through you," Paige offers with the guileless logic of the natural mesomorph. Before lunch, he'd spent a couple of hours at the gym. Arriving at the restaurant, kinetic and flush-faced from his workout, dressed in jeans and a bulky blue sweater, he'd sat in a window seat and polished off his meal, oblivious to the covert attention he was attracting from the other patrons, gay and straight, who, with typical Canadian reserve, were far too polite to officially notice.

For Paige, his incognizance might just be a matter of celebrity being too new, coupled with the fact that he has been isolated in Toronto, away from the viewing frenzy, for the duration of filming.

Trips home to L.A. and his boyfriend, an actor, have been few and far between. L.A. would be an expensive weekend retreat even if he didn't hate to fly. He misses his boyfriend and he misses his best friend. He misses his godchildren, Morgan and Charlotte. Mostly, though, he misses the California sun.

"I feel like I've been on a submarine for nine months," he says lightly, looking out the window of his apartment at the pewter Canadian winter sky streaked with freezing rain. "I'm looking forward to a little bit of shore leave."

In person, Paige is surprisingly broad-shouldered and sinewy. He's handsome, his face wide and frank, and there is a solid Midwestern masculinity underlying his demeanour and delivery that stands in sharp contrast to Emmett, the willowy confection he plays on *Queer As Folk*.

Although Paige had heard of the British show upon which the American version is based, it wasn't until a casting director friend showed him the British show, and told him that Showtime had acquired the American rights, that Paige called his manager to make sure he was in on the ground floor when auditions began.

"I read the script and was alternately thrilled and horrified by it," Page says, remembering his initial response. "I was totally captivated by the writing, but there was a part of me that asked, 'Are we really going to tell people this? Are we really going to tell these stories?'" He wasn't the only one with trepidations about the possibility of his landing the role of Emmett. "My manager, who is openly gay and very supportive of me being openly gay and very supportive of me playing both gay and straight roles, called me up the day before I went into my final audition for this and said, 'I don't think you should do it.'" Paige asked him why. "He said, 'The level of sexuality in this piece is such that I don't think I'm going to be able to [find you mainstream parts] after this.' I said, 'Well, that's a really valid concern. Let me think about it.' So I thought about it."

Ultimately, the character proved irresistible to Paige, and the thought of someone else playing Emmett was more than he could bear. "I don't think I could have lived with that," he says. "I knew I had something to offer this project and I'd rather risk it. And if the gods of Hollywood dictate that this is it for me, so be it. I'll move on to other pastures. I wasn't going to turn this one down out of fear."

Nothing in Peter Paige's liberal upbringing would naturally predispose him to that type of fear. Born in Connecticut, his parents divorced when he was two. He lived and travelled with his mother until he was eleven. "My mother worked at a feminist bookstore," he says. "I don't remember what it was called. I always called it 'Uterus Rising.' I used to sleep in a Babe Didrikson T-shirt. I was surrounded by funky bisexual women who all changed their names to reflect their African roots. At the age of six, I would go out with them and engage in conversations." As a child, Paige was most comfortable among adults; an exposure to his mother's world laid the groundwork for an awareness of his own possibilities. "It gave me a sense that there was something out there for me," he remembers.

At eleven, already intent on being an actor, he moved in with his father. He attended an arts high school in Raleigh, North Carolina, graduated magna cum laude from Boston University's School of Theater Arts, then lived in New York and Portland, Oregon, before settling in Los Angeles.

"I came up through a rigorous, classical theatre training program," Paige says. "I was basically bred to do something that barely exists in the United States today, which is regional repertory theatre. For instance, Hamlet on Thursday, a servant on Friday, a dirty street whore in the Saturday matinee. That's what I was taught how to do. I take issue with the idea that actors have to be who they're playing."

The private lives of the actors on *Queer As Folk* have been the subject of endless speculation in the press and, to a lesser degree, among fans. Although Paige receives a modest amount of fan mail, as one of two openly gay actors on the show he has been spared questions about the propriety — or the mechanics — of straight actors playing gay characters. [Author's note: at the time this piece was first published, actor Randy Harrison was the only other openly gay *Queer As Folk* star; in 2002, new cast member Robert Gant came out in *The Advocate*, bringing the total number to three.]

"I find the idea that straight actors playing gay roles is somehow exotic offensive in the same way that I find the notion that I, as a gay actor, might not be able to play straight characters after this show offensive," Paige sighs. "The fuel to the fire is that the show actually has sexual energy to it. Not only are these actors playing gay guys, they're playing gay guys who actually have sex. They are called upon to invest in the emotional lives of the characters, and they're called upon to actually touch bodies with another man."

The cast of *Queer As Folk* is uncommonly close, one result of the producers having plucked a group of relative unknowns out of their L.A. turf and dropped them down in Toronto, Canada, with a week to get to know each other. Paige's earlier reference to "nine months on a submarine" is curiously apt given the circumstances.

When the show debuted last fall, the media machine went into overdrive. Most of the cast members expressed delight at being part of *Queer As Folk*, the likes of which had never been seen on television (the British version was designed as a miniseries, unlike the American version which is designed to be episodic), and the straight actors, almost to a one, seemed perplexed that anyone would question "how it felt" to kiss another man in a drama. The exception to the rule was Toronto actor Chris Potter, who plays Dr. Dave, the love interest of Hal Sparks's character, Michael. In the November 2000 issue of *Newsweek*, Potter told journalist Marc Peyser, "Soon as they say cut, you spit. You want to go to a strip bar or touch the makeup girls. You feel dirty. It's a tough job."

The quote hit many gay men like a surprise punch in the solar plexus. In sharp contrast to the joyous, celebratory mood of most media coverage, Potter's remark was like a reminder that even after the greatest party there's always a mess to clean up.

"I think it was said in a more lighthearted spirit than it was taken," Paige says diplomatically of his co-star, "but it's hard to get a joke across in print, ever, unless someone writes 'joking' in parentheses right beside it. I don't think it shows Chris at his best, his most open, or his most evolved. It's not my favourite thing anyone's ever said, nor do I think it's the most damaging thing anyone's every said." And then, more frankly, "Even if that was his experience of [kissing a man], whatever. He's entitled to his experience of it. I just wish he'd kept that remark to himself. I think it could be construed as hurtful, and I certainly think it was dangerous considering part of the intended audience of the show."

But, Paige points out, there seemed to be an element of baiting to Peyser's query. "There is something about the question, 'What's it like to kiss a guy?' that is innately homophobic. What does it matter? You'd never in a million years ask an actor who was doing an interracial relationship what it was like to kiss a black person."

Potter's perspectives notwithstanding, the culture on the set has been an embracing, if occasionally wondering, one. A film set can resemble a high-tech construction site at times, and a blue-collar ethos more often than not carries the day. Paige allows that although there was some initial trepidation among the crew, it dissolved quickly.

"It comes back to the notion of living out of the closet," Paige explains. "One of the grips came up to me one day and said, 'Before I started to work on the show, I was completely homophobic. But seeing this every day and getting to know you as a person has changed that. I was completely wrong.' And what the fuck *else* do you need? That's what I'm after. That's what I'm about. That's what's important to me."

The phone rings several times during the course of the afternoon and, at least twice, it's Paige's friend and co-star, Scott Lowell, who plays Ted, Emmett's emotionally repressed sidekick. The two actors have formed a close friendship over the course of the last nine months. Paige has nothing but praise for Lowell, and Lowell characterizes Paige as "wonderful to work with" and "very giving, very alive." He proposes that Ted and Emmett are unofficially "the new Odd Couple," referring to the fact that although between the two of them, they represent opposite ends of the same "gay Everyman" spectrum, the actors share more in common than they differ.

"You need to remember that our off-screen personalities are quite different from our onscreen ones," Lowell cautions. "Peter is not as flamboyant as Emmett, nor am I as conservative as Ted is. We do share a similar sensibility. Peter has been great for me in terms of calling me on my shit and vice versa. We're both really good at listening. Early on, those talks were dealing with the show and our roles, and then we became better friends and that led into our personal lives. I don't know what I would have done up here without him."

The question of who Peter Paige is — indeed, who Emmett is, and where the two meet — rides shotgun with the question of whether or not the show is "good for the gays," or whether *Queer As Folk*'s television portrayal of drug-taking, sport-fucking, flamboyant club-puppies paints a negative picture of gay life and one that doesn't accurately represent gay people.

"What I think the show portrays is flawed, human, fully sexualized gay people, which is something we've never seen before on television. So hell, yes, I think it's good for the community!" Paige says hotly. "I'm always drawn to edgy, interesting, controversial stuff. I knew this would be heated. I knew it would be dangerous. I knew it would piss people off in every direction. I understand people being uncomfortable with some of it. I get uncomfortable sometimes. Sometimes I read a script and say, 'Oh my God, I can't believe I'm doing this.' Or, 'Boy, this does not show this character in his or her best light.' But," he continues, "I also knew it was human and true. If I thought for one moment that this was slanderous, or dishonest, or denigrating to the community as a whole, I wouldn't be involved with it in a million years. I can't tell you the number of sophomoric gay independent films I've read for, written by gay people, that I find absolutely detrimental to the gay community, if only because of the patronizing fucking tone they take."

Gale Harold's portrayal of the handsome, predatory Brian is one end of the lightning rod; Peter Paige's superbly nelly Emmett is the other. Both extremes antagonize gay viewers who dislike the characterizations, but in a subculture that holds "butchness" up as an ideal virtue, Emmett's effeminacy grates on some gay men, sending others into deliriums of joy.

"I pray to God that people are relating to Emmett," Paige says, "and that men who are effeminate see a champion in Emmett. I love the fact that he's effeminate and not self-loathing." He recalls a family photograph taken of him as a child, with arms akimbo, wrists on wide hips — an awkward, girlish pose that made him wince for years every time he saw it. "I think that it's when I made my peace with that person that I became a man. In owning the part of me that can be feminine, that was girly, that is sensitive, that cries at romantic comedies and Hallmark commercials. I like to think I'm a masculine guy, but I still can't throw a ball to save my fucking life. In owning it, I came into my power as a man."

And yet, he does worry, sometimes, that his portrayal will make an indelible impression in the minds of industry insiders, perhaps making it difficult for some of them to think of casting him in different roles. Unlike the public, who are more prepared to be seduced by an actor's breakout performance, producers can be famously incurious.

"I wrestle with it," says Paige honestly, even as he and his manager begin to shift through the raft of movie offers that have started to cross the transom since *Queer As Folk* catapulted him into the public's consciousness. "It's a fear of mine," Paige continues. "I've been an actor since I was six years old, and I've never wanted to do anything else. I don't want Emmett to be the only character I get to play. That having been said, I wasn't willing to go into the closet, or create some bullshit PR smokescreen to prevent that from happening. I mean," he adds, "here I am playing this big queen and I've never felt more masculine or empowered. It's ironic."

Scott Lowell is less concerned about his buddy's prospects, though no less aware of what Paige has risked by playing it the way he has. "I really don't worry about Peter Paige or Randy Harrison," he laughs. "They have the strength to prove themselves. The amount of bravery it takes in this day and age to be out in this business is unfortunate, though."

"I've been a good boy my whole life," Paige says. "The main thing was always to be pleasant, to be kind, to make nice. To play by the rules. Well, one day that stopped serving me. It took me a long time to realize that I had my own rules and those were the ones I needed to live by. I needed to figure out what I valued. When I did, that's when my career began."

∞∞∞

HERE'S SOMETHING ELSE YOU didn't know about Peter Paige: he can do handstand pushups, feet against the wall, arms extended, palms flat on the floor, pumping the muscles of his chest and shoulders for a photograph as adeptly as any Calvin Klein model. He is shirtless, his muscular alabaster torso rising from a pair of trashy Lip Service black leather pants selected by the stylist. The makeup artist has smoothed and buffed the skin of his face, highlighting the wide planes of his cheekbones. He looks like a star today and there's no candy in sight. The sunlight streams through the dirty industrial glass of the studio windows. Back in front of the camera, Paige, half-turns and smiles. Photographer Chris Chapman's strobe flashes once, then again.

"It's very flattering," says Paige, in response to a question about how he deals with his new, higher profile. For years, he went out dancing to get cruised, to be noticed. Now, the experience is double-edged. "It's an incredibly vulnerable feeling as well," he adds. "They have a lot of information about who I am and what

I do and I literally have no idea who they are, so it's a very uneven playing field."

Episode 9 of *Queer As Folk* opened with Emmett naked in front of the computer, engaging in cybersex. Paige asked his mother to "tune in two minutes late" for that episode. He imagines her response to his new fame is a complicated one. Although both of his parents were supportive of him when he came out, the differences between being an ordinary out gay man and an openly gay actor playing a controversial gay character, occasionally in the buff, are worth noting.

"There are likely various elements to it," he muses, speculating on his mother's take. "There is seeing your son's success, seeing your son get semi-famous, seeing your son become a poster boy for alternative sexuality and other things that parents and kids aren't supposed to feel comfortable talking about. She's expressed real pride in my candour and in my lack of apology."

How it will affect his primary relationship, the one he shares with his boyfriend, is as yet untested. The two have spent more time apart than Paige considers healthy. "Of course it puts stress on the relationship," he says softly. "I think the notion that any two people can be apart for nine months and not have it be a challenge is absurd."

And for Paige, the as yet undefended border is the line of demarcation not between who he was then and is now, but who — and what — he is *perceived* to be now.

"When I was in the final stages of auditions," Paige says, "a friend of mine went out with my boyfriend and me, and she asked him, 'So what do you think about the fact that your boyfriend is about to become a gay icon?' And I was like, 'That's absurd.' But he said, 'I don't know. It's a tricky thing.' We've not spent a lot of time out together in public since this happened, because we haven't been together very much. Just over Christmas and the odd weekend here or there. But I know he has concerns about what that experience will be like, what it will be like for us to go out to dinner and not have it be what it was. I don't know how he couldn't. I do. It's not jealousy, as much as it's fear of the unknown. How it's going to impact our life together and how it's going to impact his life."

Chapman is ready for another costume change, and Paige effortlessly and unselfconsciously shucks his outfit, donning another. Chapman asks him to try something new this time, jumping. In front of the backdrop, Paige will leap and turn. The camera will catch him in midair, caught between earth and sky, smiling dazzlingly.

"I've never played one role this long," Paige says, before heading over to Chapman and the modest beginning of his own posterity. "I'm ready to get back to the world of my life. And yes, I'm a little scared. I hope my life is essentially the same."

Gale Force: A Portrait of Gale Harold
2002

THE TALL, SLENDER MAN locking his bicycle outside the resolutely unpretentious Toronto restaurant designated for our interview is wearing a fedora tilted down over his eyes in a way that suggests a desire for great distance, as though a veil of inviolability had been drawn about him like an invisible cloak. On anyone else, the hat might seem like a bohemian affectation. Worn this late-fall afternoon by actor Gale Harold, for whom anonymity — or inviolability for that matter — has become a rare commodity in the almost two years since his character, Brian Kinney, the gay white shark of Showtime's *Queer As Folk*, seared himself into gay consciousness and pop culture, the tilted brim of the hat is as declarative as the visor on a steel helmet.

If he could mark off more territory, for instance, by never having to do another celebrity profile, with the journalist's necessary excavation of his private life in order to satisfy the public's immense curiosity about the actor who breathed life into Brian Kinney, he wouldn't.

Questions about what it's like to be a straight man playing gay, or what it feels like to make love to another man in the nude in front of cameras, or what it feels like to be so *handsome*, or what it feels like to be so *famous*, exasperate him beyond distraction, as well they might. In what other context but *Queer As Folk* would a journalist be able to keep a straight face while asking a thirty-two-year-old man, a professional actor at that, what his mom and dad think about him engaging in male-on-male sex in front of millions of people every week?

And if *Queer As Folk* had faded away into the elephant's grave-yard of long-lost cable television shows, instead of exploding into a cultural phenomenon that even its detractors can quote, chapter and verse, Gale Harold might have faded away with it and nobody would ask any of these impertinent questions. But it didn't.

Inside the restaurant, the waiter has brought him a cup of tea and we have ordered lunch

"How could I *not* be ambivalent?" Harold says in response to a pointed query about his deeply equivocal relationship with his new fame (he'll very reluctantly, and with some dry humour, accede to being a "semi junior league star.") "If being famous means that you get to work on great projects all the time, with great people, then I'm not all that ambivalent. My idea of fame may include that. But," he says with some distaste, "it doesn't necessarily include ... *fame*."

Harold reluctantly acknowledges that television culture, with its immediacy and spurious intimacy, is the reason why people think they know him and want to know more. But he doesn't like it, or trust its motivation. "I'm grateful for the attention," he says, softening for a moment, "because it validates that I'm doing something." Even as he says this, Harold acknowledges that it sounds like something hundreds of overexposed celebrities have already said.

"There's a genuine human impulse to want to know more about people you're interested in, for whatever reason. But that impulse has been manipulated by an industry — a bad industry — to sustain itself. It can be tweaked by publicists and studios. It didn't develop as a benevolent machine to provide more pleasure to people. It developed as a tool to sustain itself."

"Gale has very strong opinions, and he's very political," says *Queer As Folk*'s executive producer, Ron Cowen, with no small measure of pride. "Sometimes I think he's the smartest person I've ever met. I know a lot of smart, well-educated, well-read people. But there's something about Gale where it takes a leap, from education, or keen intelligence, to some other place. Genius is a cheap word, especially in Hollywood. But he's *really* smart."

Gale Harold, it seems, has always been asking questions. He was born in Decatur, Georgia, in 1969, to an engineer father and a mother who sold real estate. He is the third generation of his family to carry the name Gale Harold. His parents were devout Pentecostals and his childhood was a classic Southern mélange of church, school, and sports.

"There were so many little things about my childhood that were Southern," he says, "and so many that were suburban American. There was a dairy farm behind my house at one point."

Harold manifested an early affinity for soccer ("the beautiful game," he sighs wistfully). As he moved towards adolescence, however, he began to question the carved-in-stone tenets of both all-American jock culture, and religion.

"I burned out very rapidly on what you refer to as *jocks*," he says. Harold dislikes the word, feeling it has negative connotations. "I couldn't really handle that state of mind. I don't know what it's like to be a girl in team sports, but definitely for a guy in the States, there are so many flag-waving impulses forced upon you. Excellence in sports is a good way to keep you moving in the direction of allegiance to your school and your country."

Although he didn't have the terminology available to him at the time, young Gale was able to observe the homophobia tightly woven into the shining fabric of his suburban world, both on the playing fields of Southwest Dekalb Highschool, and in his parents' church. He is careful not to dwell on the subject of religion out of respect for his mother, who is still Pentecostal. (His father left the church several years ago.)

"I started to lose all interest [in religion] at around fifteen, around the time I got my driver's licence," Harold remembers. "I knew it was bullshit, you know? The choir director was gay. The assistant choir director was gay. Most of the men in the choir were gay. It was obvious. And these were people I talked to and grew up knowing. These were my friends and my parents' friends and members of the church. And they're up there, singing and clapping their hands, then they sit down and some ogre walks up and starts saying something that is basically potentially fatal under the wrong circumstances. And we know how fast those circumstances can shift and become dangerous.

"I think [today] it's probably gotten easier and easier for people to deal with," he muses, "but it's still a monumental achievement for some people to say, 'You're gay, can we talk?' They're so scared, because they don't know what it means about them, about God. But that's happening more now than ever before." Harold suggests it might be generational. Even so, he says, "I wouldn't want to be caught in the wrong place at the wrong time, even now."

Like on the playing field, where Harold was once forbidden to play soccer because his hair was too long. The explanation was that it made him look unmasculine. The same impulse that kept suspected faggots outside the golden perimeter of high-school acceptance kept jocks in their place — with short hair. Further-more, "because he took my side, our goalkeeper wasn't allowed to play either." Harold sighs. "When you're a kid, you instinctively know when someone's blowing smoke up your ass. You react to it, or you don't."

Atlanta, even then, was a culturally mixed city. The best record stores were in gay neighbourhoods and Harold and his close friends would often find themselves rifling through the stacks in those establishments. "You'd look up and you'd realize, 'Oh, this is the deal,'" he shrugs, remembering his nascent awareness of a larger gay presence.

Closer to home, he had friends he says he knew were gay. But it wasn't discussed. "Say I'm fifteen years old," he suggests, remembering. "And I know you're gay. And you know I know. We never actually talk about it because you never bring it up and I don't feel like invading whatever that might be. We're not going to feel compelled to go there. I never had one of those moments when someone came out to me as a confidant," he says. "The acknowledgement was already strong enough. It wasn't like they needed me to tell them that I knew."

After high school, Harold won a soccer scholarship to American University, but dropped out after his first year and moved to San Francisco, attending the San Francisco Art Institute.

"In high school, I was attracted to plays as literature," he says. Years later, being "a totally different person than I was at sixteen," he isn't sure of the exact moment the seeds of his subsequent career were planted, but he developed an interest in acting during his early years in San Francisco. In addition to his studies, Harold worked a series of low-paying jobs that seemed tailor-made for a young man searching.

"I was waiting tables, taking out the trash, painting houses. A bunch of menial shit," he says cheerfully. As time passed, though, his lack of concrete direction began to take its toll. "I wasn't looking [for a direction] and life had started getting beyond the point of enjoyment, you know?" With adulthood setting in, Harold began to think about where his talents and passions lay. When a friend asked him to appear in a movie (which, in the end, was never made), his interest was piqued.

He'd been struggling in San Francisco. The city had grown expensive and Harold was working in a job he disliked, debating whether or not to leave a relationship. When the building in which he was living was sold and turned into a parking garage, he realized he was at a threshold of sorts.

"I knew at some point I was going to have to do *something*, whether it was moving to Los Angeles, or whatever." Feeling in a rut, he left for L.A. in 1997. "I'd met a teacher there I was intrigued by and I took a week-long workshop."

The craft of acting struck Harold as somehow immediate and visceral in a way that two-dimensional, or visual, media didn't. "I had some friends there who were really good to me and helped me out with jobs and places to stay. They helped me get on my feet."

Waiting tables, going to acting classes, he studied "to the exclusion of everything else, for a solid year and a half." He had been planning to move to New York when he acquired a manager, who'd seen him in a play and thought he had something special. For a year, Harold made the actor's boot camp round of auditions, but nothing clicked. At one point, he asked his manager to stop sending him out for television work, sure that there was nothing for him in that medium.

Meanwhile, across town, Daniel Lipman and Rob Cowen, the Emmy-award winning writers of the groundbreaking AIDS drama *An Early Frost* and the long-running drama series *Sisters*, had acquired the American rights to the gay-themed British drama series, *Queer As Folk*. They had already cast actors Scott Lowell, Peter Paige, Hal Sparks, and Randy Harrison as a group of gay friends whose intertwined lives would form the basis for the American version of the story. The casting had been nightmarish for Lipman and Cowen, due to the reluctance on the part of agents to send their clients in to read for the parts in the show. The part of Brian Kinney was particularly contentious.

"Here's a gay man, very sexual, very masculine, not the kind of gay character people are used to seeing," says Lipman. If he were a straight male character, fucking every woman in sight, he'd be a hero. So this was not like the other roles and that was part of the difficulty."

"It was an extremely distressing experience trying to cast Brian, because of what we discovered to be the massive amount of homophobia [in Hollywood]," says Cowen. There are still traces of the pain clearly evident in his voice. "We were so shocked, and so upset, because we went into this thinking that in the years since *An*

Early Frost things had changed. And what we had discovered was that things hadn't changed one iota."

Late on a Friday afternoon, with a meeting scheduled for the following Monday at 8:30 a.m. with the Showtime executives, ostensibly to introduce their cast, Lipman and Cowen still didn't have their Brian Kinney. There were two more actors to read for the part and at the last minute one of them had dropped out.

"It was a test of faith and, by Friday at 5:00 p.m, faith was running out," Lipman says ruefully. At 5:45 p.m., their casting director called. "She said, 'Come on over right now, he's here!' We raced over to the office." The casting director ushered in one last actor. "In walks Gale Harold," Lipman remembers, "and we're looking at him, and he's reading the scene, and Ron and I are looking at each other and, it's like, 'Is he fucking fabulous?'"

"He fell out of the sky," Cowen breathes. "There's truly no other explanation."

Lipman asked Harold to be at the Showtime offices in Westwood at 8:00 a.m. on Monday morning. "He lit up a cigarette and, very like Brian, he said, 'I'm with this repertory company and we have to strike a set on Sunday night and I don't think I can make it.' And we're thinking, *Is he for real? Who says that? We've been in Hollywood too long.* What do you say to that?" Lipman laughs, shaking his head in disbelief. He pressed a copy of the script into Harold's arms and asked him to read it and call them at home the next day.

"I was standing in the kitchen," Cowen remembers, "and the phone rang and a voice said, 'Hi, this is Brian Kinney.'"

"What helped me recover," says Cowen, describing the aftermath of the casting disaster averted in the eleventh hour, an experience that clearly devastated him, both as a filmmaker and as a gay man, "was that Gale was brave enough to take the part. It was the same way with Aidan Quinn [who was one of the few actors willing to consider *An Early Frost* in which he starred as a gay man with

AIDS]. You need the one actor who is not afraid and who is very politically committed to what he's doing. In a way, that was the emotional salvation."

"There was an attraction," Harold concedes, when asked if the chance to play a sexual hunter-gatherer like Brian Kinney — as far from the neutered tabby cat 'gay upstairs neighbour' character as possible — appealed to him. "Another attraction was that it was an interesting story. It wasn't *West Hollywood 90210*, which I would never have been called in for. I'm not that 'type.'"

Harold's initial take was that the character would best be played as "a cross between Lou Reed and Oscar Wilde, with a gold tooth, and go completely over the top with it. Now we know that I can't do that," he says mischievously, "though I still think that's how it should be done. It would be a lot dirtier. But he's not allowed to be that." Nor does he buy into the notion that Brian is a pure predator. "You have to like your character, because if you don't, no one else will either. And if the point of the show is to create a character that nobody likes and everybody hates, that would be the way to go. Make him a predator. But I *liked* Stuart [the character upon whom Brian is based]! I liked the guy."

The thought that he might be typecast playing a gay man never occurred to him when he considered whether or not to take the role. He had asked an actor friend, a gay man, whether he should accept the part or not, not because of Brian's sexual orientation, but because of the show's merit. His friend urged him to do it. *If you want to be an actor*, his friend told him, *then act.* On the heels of that, Harold realized that he had come to a critical watershed in his life, on the threshold of turning thirty.

"There was the creative impulse and the chance to do something," he says honestly, "but there was also $1400 worth of parking tickets and back registration on my truck." Owing money to friends and back rent to landlords, the pragmatist in Harold realized that it was time to grow up. "I'd been through the 'hangdog-barely-making-it' thing over and over again. Your options run out." Looking back today, he says he realizes "the only difference between me now and me then, aside from the experience I've gained working on the show, is that I have money. That I'm able to support myself and pay off my student loans. And the ability to make things right with people over time. That becomes a really important thing as you turn thirty."

The biggest challenge to face Gale Harold since *Queer As Folk*, it seems, has been speculation. And perception. Not, as one might suspect, speculations about his sexual orientation, and the effect it might have on his future. He dismisses that out of hand.

"If someone doesn't want to work with me because I'm playing a gay character, I don't want to work with them," he says coolly. "They can fuck off."

"Gale is totally cool, and secure enough not to be threatened by anything," adds Ron Cowen. "He knows who he is. That makes him more than an actor — it makes him a very fine human being."

The next evening at the studio, Harold and I sit down for one more brief talk before he goes back to work. Harold is still polite and patient, but we are both aware of the fact that the interview is nearing its end, and although Harold is too courteous to show it, he's clearly relieved at the prospect of not having to answer many more questions.

The nudity and the sex with other men is a question that comes up constantly in the media, and from fans, so it's not an entirely illogical one to ask here. The question people never seem to manage to ask, though they want to, is *How on earth do you manage it*? The man who likely rocked straight middle America off the Richter scale in the first episode of *Queer As Folk*, when Brian coldly instructed Randy Harrison's teenage character, Justin, to rim him is matter of fact about the mechanics of onscreen sex.

"We have a really good crew," he says casually. "Between the actors and the cooperation of the producers, we've been able to establish a protocol for the show, where every sex scene has a 'sex meeting.' The director has a shot list of what he wants. It not only demystifies it, but it's like a rehearsal for scenes that aren't rehearsed.

If you know what you're going to do, and why, when you're actually there doing it, you can. You're not thinking, 'What the fuck is going on? Where's the camera? Why are we rolling again? Why am I doing *this* again?' You don't have to deal with it. You understand the scene."

Harold is amused by the response his involvement in the show elicits in some straight viewers. "I've had middle-aged men come up to me, on a shoot-the-breeze level, and bring up the show. The responses range from, 'My wife loves the show!' to 'I loved the show, it's funny as hell!'" Women beg him to tell them that he's straight. Gay men love or loathe Brian Kinney, and Harold is the occasional recipient of the runoff. At a Toronto Film Festival party recently, he passed a group of men he didn't know and, quite naturally, didn't stop to speak to them. As he passed, he heard an expletive fired his way.

"But you can't even acknowledge that as a negative response, really," Harold says philosophically. Friends fax him items pulled off the net, comments that he allegedly made in interviews, "basically putting me in line with other heterosexual actors and their comments."

His family, for their part, seems to have taken their son's nascent fame and newfound profile in remarkably sanguine stride.

"Some of them were shocked," Harold muses, "just by the fact that I had a job. I just let the information come out [bit by bit], so that by the time they actually realized I was on a television show with a budget and that I was getting paid and flying first-class in airplanes, they were, like, 'Jesus, that's beyond anything we've ever considered.'"

The key to understanding what Gale Harold will allow us to understand about him is likely not going to be found in this interview, or in any of the other interviews he's granted since becoming the hyphenated entity known as "Brian-On-*Queer-As-Folk*." It might instead be found by examining where he went while on summer hiatus, before the new season began shooting.

Rather than heading off to L.A. to capitalize on his Brian Kinney status, Gale Harold packed up and headed off-Broadway to the tiny SoHo Playhouse on Vandam and Sixth, in New York, to appear with George Morfogen in a low-budget production of Austin Pendleton's AIDS drama, *Uncle Bob*. The stage was his first love and he had arranged a summer tryst.

His personal publicity from *Queer As Folk* followed him to New York like a wasp in a car on a long road trip as he tried to prepare for his stage role.

"I haven't, no," he says when I ask him if he's ever woken up and asked himself what in the world he thought he was doing, taking on a role as potentially defining as Brian Kinney. "I've woken up after seeing *this*," he says, brandishing a page from a high fashion magazine featuring him sulking elegantly for the camera, "and asked myself what I thought I was doing. Or seeing my cover for *Metrosource*, which was *such* a cheese dish, and said 'What the *fuck* am I doing? I'm supposed to be working on a play!'"

To his credit, Harold acknowledges, Brian Kinney helped open the door for him there, too.

"To be honest," he says, "the profile of [*Queer As Folk*] was one of the reasons I had an introduction to the project." And yet, he admits, "It was very distracting. It was a blessing and curse. I wish it had just been the director and I."

A publicist stops by to see how the interview is going thus far. Gale Harold smiles with brilliant courtesy and, at that moment, my heart goes out to him. I'm very sure there's one place he wants to be and that is back at work on the set. Acting and being with other actors. Working. He's right, interviews can be an enormous cheese dish.

"If anyone can crack the publicity nut and figure out how to not come across hammy and contrived," he sighs, with honestly reluctant resignation, "I'd love to talk to them."

Drew Harris and
the Oracle of Colour
2000

PICTURE IT, IF YOU can; and if you can't, look at these paintings and imagine.

This is what raw feeling would look like if it were interpreted in blood and smoke, in bold flashes of sun-struck ochre, murderous eruptions of vermilion, Mercurochrome, and iniquitous, annihilating black. These paintings elucidate the difference between Feeling and its more accessible first cousin, Emotion. Where Emotion is often incoherent and prone to self-celebration of the basest and most pedestrian variety, Feeling is the marrow at the heart of the species. The universe may need precious little of us, or care even less, but this ability to Feel is what links us to it. Feeling is the insensate white noise at the nexus of the human race's history.

In every society, at every time, the trajectory of childhood to adulthood is fraught with a series of rituals and quests geared to controlling or limiting the expression of strong feeling, a process generally held to be an essential component of maturity. A child might scream and cry till it gets its own way, but such behaviour would be more than unseemly in an adolescent. Where an adolescent might rage, weep, and challenge authority at every turn, a raging adult, whatever the source of his rage, is rarely welcome in his own society. Writing in *The New Yorker* in 1957, the legendary poetry critic Louise Bogan made the following observations: "Innocence and violence are terrible things," she writes. "The severe rituals imposed on adolescents in practically every tribe known to anthropology insist on two basic dicta: grow up and calm down. In maturity, it is necessary, mankind has discovered, to suppress outbursts of strong emotion — joy, rage, grief — that may, in their irrationality, disturb the general peace. The Greeks came to fear those who threw themselves against the will of the gods. The grave choruses of the tragedies continually warn, caution, and seek to make reasonable the man or woman in the throes of whatever overweening passion; the gods are sure to punish such pride. Yet it is true, and always has been, that innocence of heart and violence of feeling are necessary to any kind of superior achievement; the arts cannot exist without them."

For Drew Harris, not losing the ability to articulate passion may have been his most important battle in the war between a society's distrust of expressed passionate feeling, and its desperate need to see, and feel, that passion articulated. The word *oracle* has two meanings. It refers to both the prophet and the prophecy itself. The function of the artist is to be an oracle, an interpreter of dreams and nightmares, both collective and personal. The abstract artist, especially one as committed to truth-telling as Drew Harris, finds himself doubly-burdened, relying, as he must, on the viewer's ability to interpret his interpretations, his oracles. The stories he is telling are not all pretty, nor are they flattering, nor are they particularly optimistic. In a perfumed and sanitized society that likes to believe that the universe is as neatly ordered as a golf course, and that would willingly squint to see that lie, Drew Harris offers a less comforting, if ultimately more honest, perspective. His stories are all there to be read or felt, etched in vivid tints, and available to anyone with the inner stillness needed to interpret them. His palette and brush strokes vibrate with the searing vision of his own world view, focused and distilled through a prism of pure keening.

Harris has spent a great deal of time in Asia, where he is held in high esteem by a public that has always understood his work and never shied away from it. In the Balinese tradition, the word *taksu* can be understood to refer to the private, spiritual connection between an individual and a work of art. It can be understood to honour the purity of that connection. The stories these paintings have told me are mine, and they are private. This is what *taksu* has meant to me in the art of Drew Harris. What it will mean to you is also private, as it should be.

He has been my friend for many years, but I am not an art critic, and my understanding of his work is based on the purest personal impact. I know a few things about him, though, and his life. I know, for instance, that last year he lost his beloved mother in a terrible accident and that it devastated him. She was his finest critic and his most ardent supporter. I watched him crawl from that emotional wreckage with a strength I deeply admire. I know that he is in love with a woman possessed of incandescent beauty, intelligence, and compassion in equal measures; and that she is his lifeblood, the place he goes to lay his head and dream, the place where he can be the protected as well as the protector. I know that he is a father and that he loves his son in the way we all wish we had been loved by our fathers.

I know that all of these things are in his work, and I might have known that even if I didn't know Drew Harris. I know, because in the still place in my own heart and mind these paintings have whispered these, and other stories to me. I have sung and danced and wept with them, and in a significant way, they have reminded me what it feels like to Feel and how an artist can speak volumes without uttering a word. An artist is an oracle of colour, linking every person who sees his work through the impact of that work and whatever stories the viewer invites the artist to tell to his own heart and mind.

Now, picture it if you can; and if you can't, look at these paintings and imagine.

MIRRORS

Other Men's Sons
2001

THE ROAD IS DRY and steady for the first quarter of the ride, and the rental car grips the blacktop surely as we sweep along the highways radiating outwards from downtown Calgary, Alberta, towards less well-charted regions and, ultimately, Bragg Creek, where our son, Shaw, is to be married in an outdoor ceremony in the woods.

Brian, my partner of eighteen years, is driving. He's a physician now, but he worked part-time as a car jockey during one of his undergraduate years, and he isn't afraid of a lot, which is sexy as hell. Brian is a masterful driver, and I've always been a sucker for a masterful driver.

As a teenager growing up in Ottawa, Ontario, in the late-seventies, before I ever dreamed of a world like the one in which I find myself today — driving with my partner to our son's wedding — all of the boys I had crushes on had their driver's licences before I had mine, and the sight of a man's hands on the wheel of a car that is being driven with confidence and skill is a potent aphrodisiac, even today. It is one of the quintessential masculine archetypes. I'm only half-joking when I say that I first fell in love with Brian in an underground parking lot in the summer of 1984 when we started dating. One morning, he manoeuvred his car out of an intolerably disorganized clutter of selfishly parked vehicles in the garage beneath his apartment building on Dundonald Street on the edge of Toronto's gay ghetto with a surgeon's skill. Even though the car was so old the floor had been worn away in some spots, I realized, as we drove uphill out of the parking lot, blinking in the bright July sunshine, that all of my dreams of marriage, home, and family — everything that I had been taught I had forfeited in order to live openly as a gay man — could theoretically come true with this man. He'd know how to fix things, how to get things done, and I would joyfully ride shotgun on our adventures. Brian and I were married at the Metropolitan Community Church a year and a month later, and our marriage — never not called a marriage by us, our families, and the people who love us — has been an adventure. In life, as in cars, I have often ridden shotgun, and Brian has too.

ooooo

THE NOTION OF NON-BIOLOGICAL family eluded me as a young gay man in the early 1980s, and gay marriage — called such — was virtually non-existent in the world into which I came out.

The idea of *mentorship* between an older man and a younger one — another man's son — has classical roots that have been excavated relentlessly by historians, gay and straight alike, though there was usually a sexual component to these *Athenian friendships* that challenged the notion that they were merely para-familial alternatives to the traditional father-son relationship. These relationships have existed as long as recorded history in various guises, with various outcomes. They were never intended to be non-sexual "chosen family," especially not historically, where the notion of "family" carried with it the weight of legacy and inheritance of land and other property. Likewise, committed long-term gay couples have always existed, their apparent scarcity likely having more to do with the fact that they often live their lives away from the bar and club circuit that attracts a young man coming out.

When I was nineteen, I craved the attention of older men, not necessarily sexually, although I often appreciated their skilled sexual authority, and indeed often found them attractive lovers. What I desired most was the protective neutrality of an older, wiser man who could act *in loco parentis* in matters of the new world that had opened up in front of me. The ideal would have been a happy gay couple who would revel in my youth, listen to me, indulge me, take me seriously as a burgeoning adult, and never breach that perimeter that would make us sexual partners in any capacity. I needed to finish growing up. Although there are many young men who burst forth from the restricting confines of their suburban upbringing gasping for air and eager to escape into the life-giving oxygen of their new lives as gay men, I didn't hate the life I had come from, and I never felt the desperation. I loved my parents, liked my home very much, and didn't want to reinvent myself as a snapping, fan-dancing bird-of-paradise as much as I wanted to reorganize the life I had to include a boyfriend, eventually a marriage to said boyfriend, and some sort of family life. If those ideas seem hopelessly bourgeois and suburban from the vantage point of the thirty-nine-year-old man that I am today, I say *so be it*. Among the many gifts of incipient middle age is the ability to finally accept and embrace the boy I was, and make peace with how he formed and met the man I eventually became.

In those days, it seemed, the notion of a gay man aspiring to *marriage* and *a family* were met with derision: at best there was some version of a patronizing "How sweet, dear."

At worst, there was a scorching diatribe about *middle-class values* being the very thing that gay liberation was designed to overthrow that fell just short of calling anyone with such low aspirations a traitor to his brothers-and-sisters-in-arms — indeed, a *bad queer.*

When Brian and I were married at the Metropolitan Community Church on August 24, 1985, we still managed to gather seventy open-minded guests. If we received three toasters as wedding gifts, it was merely because the notion of *gay marriage* hadn't yet caught on among retailers who, nearly two decades later, routinely register same-sex marriage gift lists. In 2001, the staid *New York Times*, that inviolable, last-word bastion of social propriety, began to feature photographs of just-married gay couples alongside their heterosexual counterparts in their wedding listings. With that seismic social shift, the remaining barriers appear to be legal ones.

In 1985, however, Brian and I were merely a young couple starting out on an adventure. I was twenty-two, he was thirty-five, and I had no doubt in my mind that my aspirations lay in the direction of someday having a family of our own, one way or another. How long that would take, or what form it would take, wasn't something I could have ever dreamed. Between the two of us, there haven't been many dull moments. Nothing we have done together has been wasted time. Everything returns to the earth of our years, and is reborn there, manifesting itself in a new and dazzling incarnation.

ooooo

AND HERE WE ARE — a long-married gay couple and two straight men, all dressed to the nines, careening through the rapidly greying Calgary afternoon light, towards a wedding in the woods. In the back seat sits a handsome Tom Cruise-look-alike actor who flew in from Toronto the night before. He had been asked twice for an autograph by awestruck heartland tourists on his flight to Alberta. Both times, he insisted he was not Tom Cruise, and both times his interlocutors almost believed him. Next to him is an Italian-Canadian male model with a sinewy soccer player's body, sloe eyes, and paper-cut cheekbones. Both men are stunning, and straight. Brian and I are neither. We make a motley foursome, and to the naked eye, any number of conclusions about the nature of our various relationships might seem plausible. All of them would likely be incorrect.

The sweet prairie air, dry as champagne, has dropped a degree or two, chilling the currents that rush past the open car window. The four of us in the car, Easterners all, are torn between the desire to inhale the inebriating white-blue chill of it and the more steadying impulse to roll the window up and switch the heater on. Being from Ontario, and not risk takers by nature, we roll the window up. The car speeds forward, and the four of us talk the way people who don't know each other but who share an abiding love for an individual we all have in common, do. The road sings beneath us. The distant mountains, ever-present sentinels, rise majestically to the west of the city into the pure wide sky. There is a rough, undeniable beauty to the terrain surrounding Calgary. Its charm, occasionally elusive to non-residents, seems genetically written into the marrow of its natives. This is the place that has shaped Shaw, and his roots are here in this rich mountain earth.

The edges I love in him, the strengths, the roughness, the tenderness — Shaw's psychic soul-branches of granite and sunlight and cold, clear air and water — have all drawn sustenance from this place.

When someone you love loves a place, you try to love it too.

"Brian, do you know where we are?" I ask him, hating that my voice sounds querulous. "These roads all look the same to me. Where the hell is this place?"

Impossibly, snow has begun to fall from the May sky, and strong winds are buffeting the sides of the rental car. Brian smiles reassuringly into the rear-view mirror.

"Don't worry," he says. "I've got it covered."

"You always say that," I reply peevishly, automatically, telegraphing, in the Morse code of the long-married, that I am worried about being late, or getting lost, or losing our place in Shaw's life. "Don't get us lost."

"We have an excellent map. It's easy to follow," Brian telegraphs back.

Don't worry, it's all going to be fine. I love you. Shaw loves you. Relax.

Brian and I met Adrienne, Shaw's bride, in Toronto the previous year, shortly after they had become engaged, and we heartily approved of the match, as behooved future parents-in-law. We love our boy, and in a way that parents in every time, place, and culture will recognize, there is a heart-deep connection, a sense of rightness, when you know your offspring has met the person who completes them, and who will keep them safe.

Aesthetically, they make a stunning couple. Shaw is tall and handsome, broad shouldered and strapping, a Nordic blue-eyed, blond-haired natural athlete, an ex-international model currently doing the neophyte actor's boot camp round of classes and auditions. Adrienne, is a beautiful woman of Polish extraction — tall, slim, intensely feminine, dark haired and dark eyed, with a melodic speaking voice that manages to be silvery and warm at the same time. She is multifaceted, at once a completely contemporary young woman with a blue-chip education and a promising career, and an elegant anachronism — which I like — a supportive spouse who loves the idea of being a wife and, someday, a mother. I appreciate that in her. I'm old-fashioned that way, and the thought of holding Shaw's children in my arms some day isn't without profound appeal.

Best of all, though, from where Brian and I stand, she loves Shaw very much. He is less of a mystery to her than he is to a lot of people.

Like me, Shaw can be passionate and emotional, sometimes to a fault, traits that are most often associated with creative types, and which have been known to drive more traditionally balanced individuals to distraction. Shaw and I are proud of these traits, yet we are both aware and wary of the effect they have on the world around us.

Adrienne, on the other hand, is as creative as Shaw, but there is a levelness to her that perfectly complements and focuses his headstrong passion through a prism of common sense. It's precisely the same emotional dynamic that Brian and I share. History repeats itself in the second generation. Our family is solid, and in some ways it's very traditional, belying the fact that Brian and I are a gay couple, and Shaw is not related to us by birth, blood, or legal adoption.

This is a story about a non-traditional family, and one of the most intense and important relationships in the lives of three men.

ooooo

I MET SHAW AT the gym on an ordinary summer night in 1994.

In retrospect, it seems like such an urban gay cliché — *Oh, yes, I met Shaw at the gym!* — but denying the inevitability of clichés doesn't make their occurrence any less inevitable.

I had showered and packed up my belongings and proceeded to the front desk. An exceptionally handsome young blond man dressed in a high-fashion suit was leaning up against the counter. His own gym bag was casually slung over one powerful shoulder, and his hair was damp from the shower.

In one of my previous professional incarnations, I was a model scout for a razzle-dazzle Toronto model agency with international affiliations. The model magnate John Casablancas, president of the Elite agency (which is to modelling what Donald Trump's organization is to commercial real estate) once told me that I had an excellent "eye" — that extrasensory ability to judge the alchemic blend of skin, hair, eyes, and bone structure that separates the model from the merely beautiful woman. The agency would send me to malls and local beauty pageants to scout for girls, and then I would convince their parents that they should let them join the agency's roster of young flesh. The agency owner knew that I was gay, and although I never knew this for a fact, I always suspected that I was useful to him as a non-sexual *eunuch*, or *harem-keeper* figure to the girls. I resigned after one such scouting expedition to a "model competition" in some godforsaken rural Ontario hinterland where I watched the complete and utter emotional devastation of one very pretty girl of fourteen who didn't win the competition.

As I watched her father lead her out of the mall, glaring balefully at the judges' table as his daughter wept over the wreckage of her dreams, I thought to myself, *No young girl should care this much about this shit, or have her self-worth defined by it.*

I knew that many of them did, and if their dreams were going to be shattered, I didn't want any further part of the shattering, for karmic reasons as well as a personal aesthetic dislike for feeling like a beauty pimp. I was never sent to scout young men, likely because the agency suspected that my own personal tastes and desires as a gay man would make me less than objective in selecting male models. What constitutes *model material* rarely dovetails with notions of conventional handsomeness.

Except in some cases. For instance, the young man leaning up against the counter. My immediate response was: *Supermodel in the making, doesn't even know it.* But I had long retired from model scouting and was too much of a Wasp to proffer career advice of that sort to a stranger. Although I wouldn't say that I am inured to beauty in men — far from it in fact — I have little practical, hands-on use for it.

A compliment from me such as *Nice suit!* or *Your dog is so cute!* is likely to mean just that — a comment on attractive apparel or an adorable *canis familiaris*. It's not an invitation to discard said suit and head to the bedroom to fuck, with the dog tied up outside.

"Nice suit," I said to the dazzling young man leaning up against the counter. "Dolce and Gabbana?"

"Nope," he drawled, a huge smile breaking across his face like a wave. "Le Chateau."

I expressed good-natured urban-gay-male embarrassment at not having been able to spot a knockoff, and noted flatteringly that he made it look expensive. He replied modestly, graciously. We looked into each other's face, and I, at least, knew that my life was about to change.

Shaw and I struck up a conversation which, by silent mutual consent, stretched out for nearly two hours as we left the gym and walked the streets of the city under the watchful umber eye of a heavy August moon. The night air was pregnant with the promise of rain and the polyphony of summer night city sounds that swirled gently around us as we talked. Our conversation flowed naturally, in the same way that people on airplanes tell strangers whom they'll never meet again private things about their marriages, their families, their jobs, and the minutiae of their real lives.

Shaw knew I was gay in the same way that I'd known he was straight, instantly and without verbal reference. He was twenty, and he had just moved to Toronto from Alberta. He had left his home in Invermere, a small mountain town on the British Columbia side of the Alberta-British Columbia border. He had parents and a sister. He was a skier. He'd moved to Calgary to pursue a modelling and acting career, which pleased his family precious little. Acknowledging the limited possibilities in Calgary, he'd hopped a plane to Toronto to try his luck in Canada's media centre. He had just joined a top model agency in the city, one of the exclusive ones near the pinnacle of the Canadian modelling industry. I confess that I was privately, smugly, delighted not to have lost my fabled "eye," though I remained relieved not to have opened our conversation with something lame-ass like, *Has anyone ever told you that you should model?* Even in the pantheon of sad pick-up lines, that one rates a notch below *Nice suit!* and I was as happy to have retained my dignity as I was to have retained my "eye."

Shaw told me about a problem he was having with his agent. I offered him my opinion based on my past work in the industry and my personal knowledge of the agent in question. It seemed to me that the problem was easily resolved by confronting the agent head-on with the issue, which was far from an insurmountable one. I was profoundly touched at how he listened, and by how grateful he seemed for the advice. He told me that he found Toronto vast and more than a little cold. I agreed with him, and told him that I hoped we would see each other again, and that I could introduce him to my partner, Brian. He seemed to like that idea.

I thought, *My God, this kid needs a home cooked meal in a real home, and some serious warmth, in the very worst way.*

Shaw gave me the name of the restaurant on Queen St. where he worked. I knew it well. I gave him our number and told him to call anytime. As he loped down Yonge St. I watched his broad shoulders disappear around a corner and felt the oddest pang of loss.

When I walked in through the front door at home, I said to Brian, "I just met the most incredible young man."

Brian smiled and said something loving and non-committal about bringing home strays, and how my parents ought to have let me have more pets when I was a child.

Shaw didn't call, which seemed perfectly normal and very much the way of the world. Unlike a rogue sexual collision where the trick takes your number and says he'll call, but doesn't, Shaw's silence simply framed the purity of our encounter. It was as though our walk through the city was a stone cast into a pool of August moonlight, which had then closed over us leaving no ripple to mar the surface. I silently wished him well, and marvelled at what intimacies can spring from chance encounters, even in a city which keeps as few secrets from me as Toronto does.

Six weeks later, I was doing a book-signing at Word On The Street, the annual independent Toronto book fair that occupies several outdoor blocks of Queen St. After the signing, I felt hungry. I wandered along the street till I found myself outside a pizzeria. I looked up at the sign, and recognized it. I walked inside, and was greeted by Shaw with an enormous smile and a reserve-shattering hug.

"I lost your number," he told me sheepishly, shuffling his weight from one foot to another. He looked adorable doing it, and I tried very hard to keep a straight face.

"I've heard that one before," I said archly, though I couldn't hide my delight or, for that matter, the fact that I believed him. In the afternoon light streaming in through the restaurant's windows, Shaw looked younger and healthier and even more coltish.

"No, really!" he said indignantly, but with a smile that could melt steel. "I really *did* lose it."

After re-exchanging numbers, we arranged to meet up in a few days for dinner.

I introduced him to Brian, who was similarly taken with the young Albertan and his sweetness. In short order, Shaw became a staple of our life together. Our home became one of his favourite places to be, and to our immense joy he began to think of it as his home as well. There was a spare room in the basement where he often stayed over. In time, he met our friends. If they thought there was something odd about a barefoot Adonis roaming Michael and Brian's house, doing martial arts exercises shirtless on the patio, they kept it to themselves. Shaw spent long evenings with us in front of the fireplace just talking. His willingness to be vulnerable inspired an answering response in me, and our bond grew at a stunning rate. Here was a man, not a boy, who looked at Brian and me and saw only goodness and wholesomeness. I sometimes noticed him, out of the corner of my eye, gazing at us as though he was searching, trying to place something he couldn't quite identify. I soon realized that I often watched him the same way. It was as though both of us were holding two complementary pieces to a jigsaw puzzle that neither of us could see. At no time was there anything remotely resembling a sexual *frisson*, which would have been more than unnatural, even if Shaw wasn't as enthusiastically and athletically heterosexual as he was. The currency of our relation was becoming para-familial. It became apparent to all of us that there was something growing between us that was unlike anything we'd ever experienced before. For a heterosexual twenty year old from a relatively unsophisticated part of the world, he accepted my and Brian's relationship as effortlessly as he would a heterosexual marriage.

That first Christmas, the city celebrated under a mantle of heavy snow. Shaw spent the holidays with Brian and me by the light of our own Christmas tree instead of returning home to his parents' home in Invermere. They weren't pleased. His absence at Christmas appealed to them rather less than the notion that he was working as a model in Toronto at all. It wasn't the sort of career they envisaged for their son by any stretch, though they tried to be supportive.

Furthermore, they couldn't fathom what he was doing spending "all his time" with a gay couple, which perplexed and troubled them both, especially his mother.

Shaw loved his parents very much, but he was a fiercely independent young man, with a young man's strength, and he was on his own path. In time, this would lead to intense periods of discomfort for everyone involved, but that first Christmas there was only love and the blossoming of a profound and dramatic friendship that would evolve into something more. Shaw lived with us, on and off, for the first two years of our friendship, interrupted once by a modelling trip to Milan. We kept in touch during that year away with letters and the odd, very expensive phone call. I kept a photograph of him on the mantle in our living room, and another in a silver frame on my night stand. He sent us photographs of his work, and tear sheets from magazines. I noted that he was getting very thin. He assured me that he was very healthy, and, somehow was still "too big" for Milan, which prompted an acerbic observation from me about how Milanese fashion designers ought to dispense with male models all together and just design using twelve-year-old girls as their male models. Still, he managed to work for most of the top men's magazines in Italy. He did one memorable campaign for Coca-Cola in Belgium; inexplicably, in the photograph, he is looking up at a coronet of popsicles encircling his head like a laurel. In the Flemish text of the advertisement, apparently, wanting a Coca-Cola made him "cool." I've promised myself that someday I will take it to a Flemish-speaking interpreter for a translation. The concept behind the advertisement struck me as completely ludicrous, and yet it is one of my favourite pictures of Shaw. His smile is beautiful. Unlike his severe high-fashion photographs, in that absurd Coca-Cola photo, he looks like himself. When he came home after his year in Milan, I met him at the airport. We clung tightly to each other in the terminal. If anyone stared, neither of us noticed, nor cared.

"I missed you guys more than anyone else," Shaw said, tears streaming from his eyes. "You're my family now, what can I say?"

"We missed you too, Shaw," I murmured, my own voice as full as my eyes. "You're our family too."

And that was that. Shortly after his return from Milan, I interviewed him for an article I was writing about male models and the gay male cult of beauty. His observations as a straight man working in the fashion industry in Europe were both useful and perceptive.

Shaw soon established himself at an apartment near our house, and was present for all our special occasions: our anniversary, various birthdays, Father's Day *and* Mother's Day. The artist James Huctwith painted Shaw's portrait in oils for me as a Christmas gift. I hung it on the red lacquered living-room wall next to the chair where I had my early morning coffee.

Here are some snapshots if you'd like to see them: Shaw helping Brian string Christmas lights along the edge of the roof of our house, then calling me outside to witness them being switched on. Shaw shovelling the snow, or cutting the grass without being asked; me bringing him out a glass of lemonade, or a bottle of water. Shaw inviting friends and girlfriends over for Sunday dinner, paying particular attention to whether or not they were showing Brian and me the correct level of respect. Shaw playing his ubiquitous, omnipresent acoustic guitar in his room in the basement while I bustled about upstairs or wrote in my study, the music drifting up through the air vents, never a distraction, always a comforting and peaceful reminder of his presence. Shaw with a cold, or the flu, moved back into his room in the basement, under pain of censure, where he could be taken care of properly, filled full of chicken soup and cold medicine. Shaw practising his lines and audition pieces in our living room while I "held the book" on him, working with him to shape the words in ways that would catch the attention of the directors to whom he would offer his talent.

When he won a part in a big-screen thriller, we celebrated together. When the film came out, I sat in the darkened theatre with him and his friends, watching the screen and realizing, with disappointment, that his part had been significantly cut in the editing process of the film. I could sense his disappointment, but Shaw was and is a stoic. And yet, at one point, the soundtrack recorded his unique, bellowing laugh. The sound of it soared above the other voices in the scene, clear as music. There, in the darkness of the multiplex, I began to laugh myself. It was an automatic reaction to Shaw's joy, a reflex I have never lost.

As the years passed, every new shared experience — the hours of talking; the mutual care when the other was sick, or sad, or needing anything at all; the automatic factoring of the other's presence into every important decision, present and future — further sealed us as a family.

What did Shaw *see* in us? It's a fair question, and one that has been asked many times already. It might be more germane to ask what he *responded* to in us; the answer might come more accurately from that vantage point. I know that, especially at twenty, he responded as much to my intuitive, nurturing tenderness — traditionally maternal traits — as he did to Brian's traditionally paternal warmth, practicality, and steadiness. But if there was a model based upon more traditional gender-based stereotypes, it wasn't deliberate or artificial, and, as time passed, it would become a source of humour among the three of us. When asked, we merely shrugged, and referred to ourselves as a family. In time, we would spend less time helping other people understand what we meant by the word. It was enough that *we* did.

When, in 1996, it seemed as though Brian and I were headed for a divorce, Shaw was inconsolable. When we reunited, precariously bypassing what would have been the biggest mistake of our lives, no one was happier than Shaw, except maybe Brian and me.

It isn't as though Shaw and I never fought, however — far from it. I've already said that we were fiercely alike. Shaw was as irritated by my occasional inflexibility as I was by his occasional flights into fantasy. In retrospect, it's ironic that both of us were processing our own parenting models even as we fought to assert the right of this new familial relationship to exist. When I became exasperated at Shaw's dreaminess, he heard the voice of all the adults he knew growing up who belittled his dreams and urged him to "grow up" and "be practical." The irony of the situation is that in Shaw's occasional moony woolgathering I saw and heard myself at his age, and younger. The wounding, fragility-shattering voice I heard issuing from my own mouth — which always shamed me later — was the condescending voice of the parents and teachers and smug adults who had taught me to hate those traits in myself — to see them as impractical, unmasculine, and inhibiting to my growth. It took me decades to unlearn those messages — to learn to separate genuine concern for a young person's well-being from the self-destruction that was second nature to me by the time I was Shaw's age — and I was determined not to visit them on him. It caused us both pain when I failed, however benign my intent.

Christmas remained a special holiday in our family — that is those Christmases he didn't spend with his biological family, who, as it happened, never completely thawed towards Brian and me during the near-decade of our association, prior to the wedding.

I use the term *biological family* for his family with supreme respect, but also as a very deliberate qualifier.

Shaw now had *two* families.

He and Brian and I were forming a unit unlike any we'd ever encountered. Early in my relationship with Brian, I had desperately wanted children of our own. It was something he had never wanted. I came to realize that this particular dream of mine had fallen on barren ground. Indeed it felt as though I were tempting the gods somehow, with my greed. My cup was already fuller than that of many straight couples I knew. In Brian and me, Shaw had found two para-parental figures who understood and supported him exactly as he was. As incongruous as the situation may have seemed to outsiders, given our relatively narrow age difference — Shaw was in his early twenties and I was in my mid-thirties — it made sense to both of us. For Brian's part, their age difference was such that Shaw could actually *be* his son, and on the occasions when that relationship was supposed, neither of them ever corrected the assumption.

Shaw's biological parents were salt-of-the-earth practical, and while they were supportive of anything their son wanted to do, it was the sort of support that came at a price for everyone involved. Having a male model as a son would have been a lot more comforting to them if modelling was a salaried position with health insurance and a pension. They wanted security for their son, and this desire regularly came smashing up against his creative ambition and the transient nature of a career as a model and actor. Furthermore, while I don't believe that Shaw's parents were specifically homophobic, I do believe that they were *profoundly* disturbed by the notion that their son seemed to be happiest in the company of an established gay couple, who were rapidly taking on all the aspects of parents without having had any of the responsibility and heartache of having actually raised him. There were frequent, painful exchanges with them on the telephone. Although he tried to shield Brian and me from most of them, he occasionally wound up in tears, sobbing in frustration, and in anger for us.

One Christmas Day in particular, when Shaw's family knew he was spending the holiday with us, he waited all day for them to call. The phone didn't ring all day. It sat on the kitchen counter like a mute declaration of disapproval. Late that night, when *he* eventually called *them*, it became apparent that they had deliberately not called him at our house. Shaw's hurt at this realization was heart-rending. After so many years, it's one of the clearest memories of him I have: weeping in my arms, wondering why his parents couldn't see Brian and me as he did. For my part, I held him close, grateful that he couldn't see the fury directed at his parents in my own eyes.

On those rare occasions that he went home to Invermere to visit "The Biologicals" (as I nicknamed them), he always seemed a little disoriented for the first couple of days after he returned. He was prone to surliness on occasion, and I sometimes heard an undertone in his voice that I neither recognized nor liked. It all seemed to vanish within twenty-four hours, like a virus, then he was himself again.

Once, when his mother came to Toronto to visit him, Shaw desperately wanted the two of us to meet. She delayed the encounter as long as she possibly could, until he cornered her and insisted. On the designated afternoon when Shaw finally brought his mother to our house, the tension was palpable. The scene would have been very funny if it had happened to someone on television, or in a movie. She never once relaxed her posture, and she never allowed the conversation to do anything but skim the surface of the most banal topics. Shaw sweated, and smiled a great deal, trying to initiate a dialogue between his mother and I. She stayed less than twenty minutes. As she left, she turned to me with an expression I couldn't decipher and murmured something glacially polite. Thus ended our one brief, frosty meeting. Whatever each of us saw when we looked at the other, it was never discussed, would never be mentioned.

ooooo

SHAW HAD A WONDERFUL girlfriend at the time, a bright, attractive young woman with short dark hair and ivory skin, who worked in fashion. For a few years she was also a staple in our lives. When Shaw decided to propose to her, I took him to Tiffany's on Bloor St., and introduced him to a jeweller friend of mine, who helped him pick out a stunning diamond solitaire. On the night Shaw proposed to her, Brian and I called the restaurant and ordered a bottle of Dom Pérignon to be delivered to their table after his proposal. Luckily, she accepted. They came to our house after dinner, whereupon we drank more champagne and toasted the couple, wishing them a long and happy life together. When the relationship ended a year later, Brian and I were bereft. Worse, it appeared to us that Shaw had left his fiancée for an old girlfriend, Adrienne, whom she claimed he loved, and had "never gotten over." As much as we wrestled with the realization that it was *his* life, and *his* choice, we couldn't help feeling that he had behaved shoddily towards a woman whom both Brian and I had come to love, and we were profoundly disappointed in him. It would be a long time before Brian and I saw Shaw's side of the matter. At that moment, all we had was anger. We categorically refused to meet his new/old girlfriend. The effect on him was punishing, exactly as, on some level, I intended it to be. After weeks of silence, Shaw called and pleaded with me to please give the new girl a chance at least.

"She's the woman I love," Shaw said plaintively. "I want you to know her. Can't you please give her a chance? It's so important to me that you and Brian know her. We're leaving Toronto and moving back out west to Vancouver, and I can't stand to do that without healing this."

"All right, Shaw," I said. "Let's meet for lunch at Café California. I'm not promising anything, but I'll meet her."

Adrienne brought a bouquet of daisies, bright, singing yellow, wrapped in dark green paper, which she presented to me at lunch. She had a beautiful smile, full of warmth and goodness. Most importantly, her palpable love for Shaw was like a tidal wave of heat that crashed over me, thawing me instantly. In the face of that much obvious devotion to someone I loved as much as I loved Shaw, there was quite simply nothing to say. Shaw excused himself and went to the restroom. To this day, I'm not sure it wasn't a deliberate gesture to give Adrienne and I a few moments alone, without him.

"Welcome to the family," I said to Adrienne. "And congratulations on your engagement." Instinctively, I reached across the table and laid my hand over hers. "Take care of my baby, would you?"

"I will," she said tenderly. Wordless communication passed through us like a shade. "I promise. Thank *you* for taking such good care of him. He loves you both more than he can say, you know."

"Oh, he says it pretty well," I said softly. "He always *has* said it. I just haven't always listened."

They closed up his apartment two weeks later and moved into our house for the last few days — Shaw's pet ferret and Adrienne's cats in tow — before flying to Vancouver to set up their fresh new life together.

After they left, I walked around the very empty house several times, hearing echoes for the very first time. I felt Shaw's absence like a lengthening shadow, felt the chill of it, missed him from a very deep place.

ooooo

SHAW CALLED US MONTHS later to tell us that he and Adrienne were getting married the following May. When he told us the ceremony would be in Calgary, in order to be closer to his parents — who expected it — and family friends from Invermere, we felt a familiar sense of anger and betrayal mixed in with the fierce, possessive love. *Would this never end?* We told him that we were thrilled for him, but that the prospect of sharing his wedding day with his parents — the source of so much pain and distress to the relationship between the three of us for nearly ten years — on their own turf, would be impossible. Shaw was disconsolate.

Late one night, Adrienne called me and told me how hurt he was by our refusal to attend the wedding.

"I know how you feel, and I know why," she said thoughtfully. "I know how they've behaved towards you and Brian. There's no excuse for it, any of it. And I think Shaw knows it too, in his head. But in his heart, he doesn't understand at all. He thinks of you as his parents as well, and he can't bear the thought of you both not being there."

"Why didn't he think of that before?" I asked her bitterly. "Of all the places for this to happen, couldn't it happen in a neutral place? Why not Vancouver? Why does it have to be on *their* turf?" I raged. "Why couldn't you get married here? What about all of

the *crap* they've put us through. He *knows* this! It's a miracle we
have a relationship with him *at all* given what they've done over the
years."

I ran a home movie in my head of all the little snubs — the
ignored Christmas cards and notes; the curt demands that Shaw be
put on the telephone once The Biologicals realized that they had no
choice but to call our house sometimes if they wanted to speak to
their son; the opprobrium we never actually physically *heard*, but
which darkened Shaw's face on the phone after he spoke with his
parents, and left him remote and shattered for hours and days afterwards; the ways we had been made to feel like opportunists, and
interlopers, and *faggots*.

"Michael, I *know* that," Adrienne said simply. "I know *all* of
those things. But you need to know this. You need to know how he
feels. Shaw is your family — all three of you think of him as your
son — and this is how he is feeling. What you do with this is up to
you, but this is how Shaw is experiencing this. I just wanted to
make sure you knew."

"Thank you, Adrienne," I said. "I don't know what we're going
to do, but I appreciate you calling. Give him our love, would you?"

It was late-evening, and Brian was working out at the gym. I
took a cab there, and met him as he was leaving the locker room.
On the ride home, I broached the subject of Adrienne's phone call
with him.

"You know I feel *exactly* the same way you do about this
wedding in Calgary," I said. "I don't want to go either, but it's going
to change a lot of things for a long time if we don't go. It's going to
hurt him, and he'll never forget it. Whatever else happens, we will
always have boycotted his wedding." I added pointedly, "It's the
sort of thing I would have expected *his* parents to do if you and I
had been hosting the wedding here in Toronto. I'm not sure that's
something that anyone gets over, least of all someone like Shaw."

"I know," Brian said. "I've been thinking the same thing. We
should likely go."

The next day, I telephoned Shaw and told him we were coming to his wedding in Calgary, if the invitation was still open.

"Can you at least find us a decent hotel to crawl away to if it all gets too horrible with your family and all those dreadful inbred friends of yours from Invermere?" I teased him. "Someplace civilized, with a good bar?"

"Are you *kidding* me?" Shaw shouted. In my mind's eye, I could see his exact facial expression, the specific smile. "*Of course* I can!" His joy was as clear as our knowledge that we had made the right decision; indeed, the only decision possible in a family guided by the principles that we ourselves had enshrined, a family that functioned, that was real. "I'll find you a *great* hotel!"

ooooo

SHAW MET US AT the airport in Calgary the day before his wedding looking like death on a stick. My hands flew theatrically to my throat. I think I may have actually screamed, *My baby!* or I may have just felt like I had. It was the day after Shaw's bachelor party, and he'd made rather merry the night before. I know Shaw's face well, and it was obvious that he was balancing his desire to meet us at the airport with the exigencies of an Olympian hangover. His eyes were scrunched up little sulphur pits in the broad planes of his face. His skin was stretched tightly across his high cheekbones like tanned hide on a rack. My baby looked like a beautiful cactus, parched dry and anhydrous as a noontime desert. He was bruised where he'd been playing paintball with his cowboy buddies from Invermere, the closest of whom had come up to Calgary for the wedding. They were all presumably sleeping off their own hangovers, but our boy was a trooper and he wanted to welcome us to Calgary in person. I immediately touched his face, which was hot and dry, and clucked my tongue disapprovingly against the roof of my mouth.

"Shaw, your *skin*," I muttered as I bought him a litre bottle of Evian water from the little airport shop and insisted he drink some of it immediately. "How much did you *drink* last night? Wait, never

mind. I don't want to know. Just drink." I made a mental note that
there were Advil in my tote bag, and another to make sure he took
some immediately when we got to the hotel. I love him dearly, but
sometimes I swear he doesn't have the survival instincts God gave
a mallard duck in autumn.

He hugged me, whispering in my ear, "Thank God someone is
finally here to boss me around and take care of me, *Mom*."

Disengaging, he effortlessly lifted our two heaviest suitcases, one
under each arm, and loaded them into the car. We climbed in and
drove off towards the city. Calgary unrolled before us in the late
afternoon light. Somehow the city struck me as raw and unfinished
from the windows of the car, but there was an undeniable freshness
to the air and a beckoning grandeur to the mountains in the nearby
distance. We checked into the hotel which, like everything I'd seen
so far in the city, was expansive.

We were a long way from home. This was the undisputed domain
of The Biologicals.

"Welcome to Calgary," said the bellman. He pronounced it
Calgree. "This is the hotel where they invented the Bloody Caesar,
you know. Folks like to know that when they come here. It's a
little piece of history," he added, winking.

Up in our room, the three of us had a drink — gin and tonic
for me, beer for Brian, three Advil and another litre of water for
Shaw, which he drank *in toto*, practically at gunpoint, while I watched
intently to make sure he finished it. I scowled at him over the rim
of my glass of gin.

When I was satisfied that he had rehydrated, we sent him off
with one of his very butch friends to attend to some last-minute
wedding crisis having to do with chairs, or rain.

"Brian, let's go for a walk," I said. "I need to find a Holt Renfrew.
There are a couple of things I forgot to pack."

"Why do you need to go to Holt Renfrew?" he asked suspiciously.
"Can't you just pick whatever it is up in the drugstore down in the
lobby?"

I knew the tone of voice well. It wasn't that Brian particularly disliked the notion of heading to Canada's most expensive department store, it's just that he didn't see why something that I "forgot to pack" had to come from its luxurious stock.

I tend to think of Holt's as something of an embassy of civilization and luxury in whatever metropolitan Canadian outpost I find myself when I'm away from Toronto. The stock is high-end and the standards are inflexible. I wasn't about to tell him that Shaw's skin had made me think of how much better I would feel facing The Biologicals tomorrow at the wedding after an Estée Lauder face pack and a bath, or make a Waspish comment about how I wasn't likely to find what I was looking for in the *hotel drugstore*. Likely knowing that quizzing me about it would engender a less convivial response than simply acceding to my wishes, he companionably grabbed his jacket and followed me out of the hotel, and down a few blocks of downtown Calgary.

As a thirty-nine-year-old gay man who has lived in cities for most of his adult life, I'm not fazed by skin care counters or intimidated by the salesladies who stand behind them. I dress well, and I always assume that the person dispensing the product either knows I'm gay or doesn't care. It's one of the many lovely advantages of not living in a small town and I take it for granted.

"I'd like the Estée Lauder So Clean deep pore mask for all skin types, please," I said crisply, pointing to the counter behind her. "The pale green one, there. Yes, that one. The one that smells like flowers."

I handed her my American Express card, and slyly perused a rack of Gucci sunglasses at the next aisle, thinking about how bright the sun would be the next day at the wedding, and how Gucci would likely pay more attention to uv protection than a cheaper brand. The woman rang up my purchase, and packed it up in one of the comfortingly familiar little Holt's bags. As she handed it to me, she smiled encouragingly at me and convivially patted my hand.

"You know, dear," she said. "Your wife is so lucky that you can just walk in here and know what she wants and just buy it for her.

You'd be amazed at how many men are too embarrassed to do it. She's a lucky lady. You have a *nice evening*!"

I stood still for a moment, waiting for the room to stop spinning, wondering if there was any way I had just been mistaken for a straight man on an errand for "the little woman." I wasn't wearing Dockers.

Brian was in the midst of a jovial conversation with a very handsome, well-dressed — and, to my mind — obviously gay, salesman at the Hermès tie counter. I approached them with my dainty little Holt's bag containing my pale green Estée Lauder So Clean deep pore mask.

"All done?" asked Brian innocently.

"Oh yes," I replied. "You wouldn't *believe* what just happened to me," I began, looking at Brian and the salesman with a conspiratorial smile, a prelude to a dishy chuckle at having been mistaken for straight by the hopelessly unsophisticated, if adorable, Estée Lauder saleswoman.

"I was just talkin' to your buddy here," said the salesman in a voice that would have made the Marlboro Man sound like Britney Spears. He indicated Brian with a shake of his expensively coiffed head. The salesman clearly hadn't thought I was going to finish my sentence. "There are some great new clubs in Calgree for you two fellas to take your ladies to while you're here."

"What do you say, *Mike*?" said Brian with a wink, putting his life in my hands by using in public a diminutive of my name that I only ever allow either friends from my very distant childhood — or very new, straight male acquaintances — to use. He elbowed me jockishly in the ribs. "Shall we take the gals out dancing tonight?"

I smiled brilliantly at Brian, who was grinning from ear to ear, and at the young man behind the Hermès counter, who really had very nice teeth as well as a fantastic haircut and a fantastic ass. No wonder my gaydar had been scrambled. *What a waste*, I thought.

With lethal courtesy I said, "Gee, *Bri*," — a name he loathes, one which makes me think of Nascar, and Greg Norman poly-blend golf clothing, one which I never, ever, ever call him — "I'm *damn tired*, dude. I think I'll crack a brew back at the hotel and watch what's left of the game before I crash. I don't care what the hell you do, though, buddy. Knock yourself out."

Later, at dinner in the hotel restaurant, it happened again.

"This is a romantic restaurant, all right," said the waiter with justifiable pride, in response to a gushing remark I'd made about the beautiful wood panelling, the intimate booths, and the roseate light from the candles dancing on the walls. I had, in fact, been thinking that it was indeed a romantic spot, and how long it had been since Brian and I'd had a fine dinner in a strange city. Indeed, for the first time all day, I had a sense that the wedding tomorrow was going to work out just fine. We were the only male pair in the restaurant, which was sparsely populated with heterosexual couples.

"Couples *love* this restaurant," crooned the waiter, beaming down at us.

At last, I thought. I twirled my wedding band reflexively with my thumb.

The waiter blanched, as though he had just made an extraordinary *faux pas*. "Not that I thought *you two* was *a couple* or nothing," he said apologetically.

He dropped his spoon on the table, flustered. He glanced fearfully over his shoulder at the ancient *maitresse d'* with the blue Elsa Lanchester hairstyle who was gnawing a prissy little gold pencil between her jagged yellow molars, and scowling down at a list of reservations. I had privately told Brian I thought she looked like a harridan, and was likely a tyrant to work for. The waiter, an older man, was clearly terrified of her.

Speechless, I looked at Brian, who signalled *No* with his eyes. His intention was clear: *Don't make it worse for the poor guy. He's already in fear of his job. Don't confuse him and make it worse. There's a time to be political and a time to be kind. This is the second instance.*

"Don't worry, I didn't think you thought we were a couple," I said to him in a calming voice. At least I didn't have to lie. It wasn't my proudest moment as a gay man by far, but the "greater good" seemed worth sacrificing this one time for the frightened old man serving our table. If he was straight — and it seemed likely he was, though after my misfiring gaydar incident at Holt's I wouldn't want to take that notion to the bank — then the chance of embarrassing him further by pointing out the homophobia of his comment, made inadvertently to a gay couple, didn't seem worth it, especially given the presence of the Marcel-waved barracuda at the hostess desk. "It's fine. Take it easy. No harm done."

"Thanks, guys," he said, relieved. "Hey, can I get you guys a drink? How about a Bloody Caesar? They invented them right here in this hotel," he said, regaining his equilibrium. "Did you know that? You guys should come back with your wives."

As he went off to make our Caesars, I turned to Brian. "We're in the fucking Twilight Zone here, Brian. You *do* know that, don't you?"

∞∞∞∞∞

THE SNOW ON THE road had become blinding, and Brian was steering carefully. Conversation in the car had slowed and muted, and we were all deep in our various thoughts about Shaw and the wedding. Suddenly, a dark shape launched itself from the foliage on the right side of the road and rocketed out in front of our car.

"Watch out!" someone shouted, as Brian swerved and hit a patch of black ice. For a moment, the boulders on either side of the road appeared to collide and became terribly visible from the car windows. My hand flew to my mouth and my body went rigid. The tires screamed in protest against the asphalt as Brian spun the steering wheel in order to avoid hitting whatever it was that had bisected the road in front of us. He struggled to right the car, which careened wildly across the slick surface of a second patch of black ice.

It may or may not be true that your entire life flashes before you at the moment of your impending death, but I can say for sure that the ignominious thought of dying in a rental car crash on the way to a wedding outside of Calgary, Alberta — birthplace of the Bloody Caesar — after everything it took to get there wasn't remotely appealing.

"What the *fuck* was that?" I shrieked, more relieved than I cared to admit. Behind me, I heard the others uttering similar relief, and someone thanked Brian for his quick response. I craned my neck backwards in time to see a large brown moose glare sullenly at our car before lumbering off into the underbrush like a disgruntled rural Alberta local whose inflexibly entitled daily routine has been egregiously compromised by stupid tourists from Ontario. Which, in a way, it exactly had been.

"It's a moose," the model said, running his long, elegant fingers through his thick, glossy hair. "A fucking *moose* in the road."

"Well, this is moose country," the actor emoted thoughtfully. "I guess this is where they are."

We all concurred that this was, indeed, where they were.

Gritting my teeth, I silently asked myself again why Shaw couldn't have had a nice, simple, elegant wedding in Vancouver at some plummy yacht club or other, or at a nice hotel, instead of subjecting us to this Shackletonian trek across the Alberta tundra that was, by the second, beginning to resemble a lost episode of *Adventures in Rainbow Country*.

The explosion was as loud as a gunshot, and I once again reflexively grabbed the dashboard and screamed. When Brian again grabbed the steering wheel as the car swerved, and the two beauties in the back seat manfully suppressed their terror with virile grunts, full-on *déjà vu* set in. *Déjà vu* was supposed to be difficult to place, however. This was five minutes after the moose, and half an hour after the blizzard began to sheet down from the bright blue spring sky, so the events — Shaw's Saharan hangover, the incidents at Holt Renfrew and the restaurant, the May blizzard, the moose, and now this fresh new horror, whatever if would prove to be — had acquired a certain linear quality that caused me to wonder whether we were deliberately ignoring warning signs from God.

Brian pulled over to the side of the road and stopped the car. We all exited the vehicle and went to examine the damage. The front left tire had blown dramatically, the rubber hanging in tatters. As we stood there with our hands in our pockets, the model sprang into action. He removed his suit jacket and opened the trunk. With his mouth set in a grim line, and without further ado, he withdrew the car jack. He hunkered down and began the process of replacing the tire while we watched, feeling alternately relieved and impotent in that way men usually do when one of them is doing something unpleasant, but paradigmatically male, while his fellows stand uselessly by.

We turned at the sound of tires on gravel on the shoulder of the road behind us. Two vehicles pulled up and stopped. The door of one of them opened, and Shaw's father exited. It was my first view of him, and I was struck by how ordinary he looked. He had likely been very handsome at one point in his life, but now looked primarily dignified and capable. I don't know what I expected, but I rather suspect I thought that he'd look more like the towering ogre of my imagination than this very ordinary father-of-the-groom standing before me. I noted that he and I were dressed identically: navy blazer with gold buttons, and grey flannels.

We shook hands crisply, smiles gleaming, as I thought, *Do you have any idea how much you've haunted my life, and the life of my family, including your son?* We introduced ourselves politely and made four-sentence conversation about the weather and the blown tire.

"You guys havin' some trouble?" Shaw's father asked, glancing down at the car towards safer and more familiar conversational discourse.

"Nope, everything's under control," said the model tensely, barely looking up. He gave the jack another couple of pumps.

"You need a hand there?" Shaw's father asked again, as though doubting that one of Shaw's glamorous male-model colleagues would be able to change the tire without the help of a man not in the fashion industry. The model continued to work on the tire. It was either a trick of the light on the snow, or else he grew a little paler. His handsome jaw clenched, and his mouth set in an even firmer line. He might strut down European fashion runways, or vault athletically across the pages of the Holt Renfrew catalogue with the best of them, but he was also an Italian-Canadian male. Members of his ethnic culture aren't known for their lack of pride at excelling within fairly rigid gender role expectations, especially the men. He didn't need help with the tire, nor did he welcome the suggestion that he might. He spoke in a voice that had dropped an octave, and left no room at all for debate.

"Nope, seriously," the model said, looking up at Shaw's father. "I have it under control. *Really*."

He stood up, lifting the damaged tire with one hand, and walked around to the trunk of the car. He opened the hatch door and tossed the tire inside, slamming the door shut. The sequence of gestures couldn't have been more primal if they had been two generations of stags, each pawing the snow, kicking up dirt, antlers lowered.

Straight men, I thought. *For the love of God.*

"Shall we be on our way?" I suggested brightly, and we were.

ooooo

WE FOLLOWED SHAW'S FATHER'S vehicle for several more miles, a largely silent ride by then. The four of us were lost in our thoughts again. When we reached the edge of Bragg Creek, we saw a small caravan of other cars anchored next to the frosted hills bordering the forest. The snow now fell like a heavy lace curtain, thick and isolating.

Shaw's mother stood with his aunts beside their cars. When she saw me, she smiled warmly and walked over to me with open arms. Perversely, I wondered if it was the occasion of Shaw's wedding — if nothing else, proof-positive in his mother and father's minds that he was as red-blooded and heterosexual as any other "real man," in spite of our malign influence — that was responsible for this new warmth. Inexplicably, she kissed me on the cheek. I embraced her in return. She was prettier and much younger-looking than I remembered. Suddenly, unbidden, the chastening thought came to me that the passing years and my own accumulated antipathy for this woman might have simply blurred my memory of her.

One of her sisters, Shaw's aunt, was a striking, elegantly dressed woman who worked in the arts in New York. She was cultured and articulate and I was instantly drawn to her. She was the first icon of Shaw's background to whom I could completely relate. As she and I spoke, I observed the similarities between her and Shaw's mother, my supposed nemesis. My perception of her began to expand incrementally. How easy, I realized, for people, gay or straight, to cultivate and nurture negative, stereotypical images of each other from a distance. How often did the stereotypes survive in person? True, Brian and I had been egregiously slighted numerous times by Shaw's parents, but seeing them in person — perhaps for the first time without my own prejudices coming into play — I began to wonder how *we* must have looked to *them* in *their* minds, thousands of miles away across the country, sheltering their son and occupying such a prominent place in his life.

Maybe it was just time for reconciliation and forgiveness, perhaps the ultimate wedding gift to a young man whose life had been so marked by our discord. If Shaw was our family, then they must somehow be our family as well. More importantly, they were *his* family. That in itself made them something worth honouring, no matter what it took.

Whatever Shaw was to us, he was another man's son as well as ours.

All of us trudged along the path to the place the wedding would occur. The falling snow had soaked everyone's wedding best in a way that was completely bonding, and too vastly absurd to support bitter, hidden wedding day agendas.

There in a clearing stood Shaw and his best man, surrounded by his oldest friends from Invermere, and family friends from Calgary. The officiant stood in front of him, going over the last minute details of the service. He touched Shaw lightly on the shoulder and asked him if he was ready. Shaw answered in the affirmative. He turned and smiled at Brian and me, his eyes shining with a brilliance I had never seen before.

In truth, he looked like a man on his wedding day. A *man*, not a *boy*. He and Adrienne had arrived at this point without the help or guidance of his parents, or of Brian and me. In every sense of the word, this was *his day*.

Shaw's face, always expressive, was a kaleidoscope of emotions: joy, terror, pride, awareness, yearning. Mostly though, it was lit with a love so primal and joyous that I felt it would melt the snow and ice all around us, drowning us all in a wash of warmth and spring — me, Brian, his parents, and anyone else who needed to be touched by it.

So this is it, I thought in wonderment. *This is how it happens*.

The haunting opening strains of Enya's "Only Time" drifted through the stark, snow-flowered trees as Adrienne walked across the clearing towards her groom to exchange their vows.

As they spoke, and then were declared man and wife, the sun broke through the low clouds, lighting the snow and the velvet green of the forest like phosphorus. The clouds were seized by the warming spring wind and whipped to pillows of meringue.

In the distance the sun skipped across the newly revealed mountaintops that in turn laid their vastness and limitless possibility before all of us.

Later, back at the caravan of cars, we all drank champagne and toasted Shaw and Adrienne as the snow and ice turned to clear water that ran from the trees like vertical rivers, and the air smelled of snow, and alpine flowers, and fresh sunlight.

ooooo

A LATE FRIEND OF mine, a wise, older gay male writer from Massachusetts who taught me a great deal about not only letters but life, often talked and wrote about the time-honoured role played by New England "bachelor uncles" in the lives of families, particularly families that counted young people among their number. In his case, though, he wasn't just talking about his own blood kin. He was talking about the role of older gay men in the lives of younger men. Though not remotely averse to the charms of young, supple flesh and muscle, he was referring to something rarer, and even perhaps more exalted than the mere roles of sexual initiator and initiated. He was talking about family in the truest sense: of love, caring, teaching, protection, and nurturing.

There is a rich contemporary tradition of gay men in extended families. Historically denied our own children, we have "nieces" and "nephews," whom we cherish and love in a way that belongs to us — and them — alone. These children grow up, become men and women, and never forget our soft and caring touch. Although many gays and lesbians are now adopting, or having their own children through more traditional means, there will always be those of us who make our own families our own way. Among the powers with which gay men and lesbians have been endowed is the ability to make a family where before there had only been a chain of unconnected strangers. Whether we forged this power as a defence against a world that would deny us a place at the many family tables that are our birthright, or whether wielding it is merely one of the many gifts that makes us a special people, ultimately matters less than the fact that we *have* that power.

I'm thirty-nine as I write this, and although I am not yet what I would think of as an "older man," I have become increasingly aware of my own aging, and even the outer edge of my own mortality. I meet more and more young men — other men's sons, not mine — whom I must reluctantly acknowledge as adults. I say "reluctantly" only out of personal vanity. Admitting that adult men, even young ones, could be my sons means acknowledging my own aging. To transition from the place in my heart and mind where *I myself* am the one who is forever the young one — and those younger than I am, for all intents and purposes, children — to the place where actual *adults* who are younger than me will look up to me as an older man, a fellow adult, but still something alien to them, is disorienting. I'm not sure I like it, but somewhere inside this treacherous awareness is something attractive. I sense something there that rings with the prospect of immense dignity.

The possibility of forever being able to celebrate the ineffable sweetness of young men without demanding anything from it in return other than to allow it to explode like sunlight on dark water all around me, strikes me as somehow marvellously empowering.

In the meantime — and for always, no matter who comes later — I have Shaw.

ooooo

LATER, AT THE WEDDING reception, Brian smoked a joint with Shaw's father, in itself a slightly hallucinogenic image. I sat for a long time chatting with his mother and sister as though we were meeting for the first time at a marvellous party and liked each other immensely. At that moment at least, the preceding years melted away. Or, more accurately, they were panned like a riverbed for gold. The useless, muddy silt was sifted, rinsed, and combed through in order to best excavate the gilded nuggets buried there. Whether or not this new warmth between Shaw's family and Brian and me would last was a matter of conjecture. At that moment, though, I couldn't have cared less.

And then Shaw stood up in front of his friends and family — our judges, imagined or otherwise — and made his speech.

"Michael and Brian are a gay couple, and they were there for me when I first moved to Toronto and there wasn't anyone else," he said, voice breaking slightly. Pausing, he continued, his voice trembling, yet somehow also ringing and strong. "They loved me, and they believed in me. There was nothing in it for them. They took me into their home and they made me part of their lives. We became a family, whatever anyone might think of that." He paused again. "No two people besides Mum and Dad could have taken better care of me, or been more like parents to me than Michael and Brian were and are. I'm glad they're here today, and I'm so grateful they're in my life." Shaw's blue eyes scanned the crowd till he located me sitting next to his sister, who squeezed my hand. He smiled and said, "I love you guys *so much.*"

ooooo

IN A LIFE ALREADY full of blessings, I will always have a wonderful memory. Shaw's speech, yes — a powerful affirmation in public, as effective in its way as a thousand angry political speeches about the importance of gay rights.

But also this memory — a more private one: how the argentite sky smelled of rain and birch; the reassuring solidity of Brian's hand in mine; the sight of our beautiful son, his tears of joy flowing with the melting snow in a forest clearing at Bragg Creek as his bride walked towards him through the trees like a sylvan wraith. My own heart engulfed by answering, connective joy — nearly too much love to bear — and all of the accumulated memories, too precious to enumerate here, which led us to that moment.

And mostly this: the sure knowledge that at the hour of my passing, the greatest personal triumph of my life will have been the ability to love, and to be loved in return. To have made a family in a world that doesn't want me to.

$\mathcal{O}$ur Libraries, Ourselves

GLBT Round Table of the American Library Association Stonewall Book Awards, Keynote Address Speech, Monday, June 23

2003

LADIES AND GENTLEMEN, ON behalf of your Canadian colleagues and friends, welcome to our great country, and our beautiful city of Toronto. Thank you for braving the CNN images of SARS, our monstrous attempt to undermine American virtue with our recently relaxed marijuana laws, and mostly our attack on morality, decency, and family values as manifested in our recently having become the third country in the world to grant full marriage to gay and lesbian couples.

It feels very good to be in the company of so many gay and lesbian visitors this morning. Of late, I've found myself facing increasingly hostile heterosexual visitors, all of whom seem to have one question about the gay marriage issue. They all want to know why we have to call them *marriages*. Why, they all ask, don't we find something *else* to call them? I generally try to reason with them. I explain to them, with the legendary politeness for which Canadians are justifiably famous, that we *like* the word *marriage* and suggest that perhaps, if *they* have a problem with *us* having that word at our disposal, perhaps they should try *opposite sex civil unions* and see if they like how is sounds.

They find that rather less than helpful.

The word continues to be the problem, and although *they* see it as a problem, I do not. I believe that words matter, that they should mean what they're supposed to mean. I'm a writer, not a diplomat, so when logic and truth fails, I'm reluctant to start manipulating language in order to lie effectively. Fiction writing has been jokingly described as lying for effect; journalism has often been accused of lying for sensation. Surely though, all jokes aside, dishonesty is the hallmark of bad writing. I've always been delighted by the fact the May Sarton, a writer whose work gave me much personal nourishment in my early years, yet whose autobiographical writing occasionally stretched the fabric of truth to near-breaking points, once said that "the more honest and personal a writer's work is, the more universal it is." What she meant was, if you're willing to expose yourself in print, chances are there are more readers than not who will relate to what you're saying. I don't think there has ever existed a writer who hasn't faced the blank page, or screen, wondering who in the world is possibly going to care about some personal pain, fear, joy, or foible that would seem only to belong to the person writing it down. It's always a delight, then, when someone says, "I know exactly what you meant when you wrote that."

Politics was never a particular interest of mine. I am, however, preoccupied with truth telling. I believe it's the highest attainment for any writer, no matter what medium or genre he or she works in. Truth telling usually begins with words, and if it doesn't *begin* with words, then words certainly crown and wreath the truth, holding it up to the light so that future generations might have some lodestar by which to guide them away from the mistakes their fathers' and mothers' generation made, and to allow them a useful and constructive reverence for the great personalities of our times and their achievements. Ultimately, to me, that is the only sort of immortality a writer ought to aspire to. We are given the gift of oracy. Our talent and our power is to be able to give an account of the times in which we live.

I stand before you today, by way of a fortuitous series of events that began when I was born into a family of book lovers. I grew up in a world of books, and they have always been my greatest passion. I never completely trust anyone who doesn't have a decent-sized library. It makes me wonder what makes them tick and none of the alternatives I come up with are very palatable. I grew up in a family that celebrated the written word of nearly every type, and reading, no matter what, was better than not reading. My paternal grandfather, Chelsea Lavern Rowe, was one of the founders of the Canadian Literature Society. In fact both sets of grandparents — the disparate Rowe and Hardt clans, my mother's people — were book collectors. Before she married my father, my mother was a genteel Yankee schoolteacher who had studied at Bread Loaf with Robert Frost. Books are in our blood. All the houses in which I lived as a child had very full libraries. My mother taught me to read at an absurdly early age and she read to me constantly, as did my father. I was conversant with Dickens, Stevenson, and Kipling at the same time many of my friends were reluctantly being dragged through Dick and Jane stories. I was read fairy tales as well as the classics, and this is where I diverged into the beginnings of what would become my own fairly gothic tastes.

I was far less interested in happy endings than I was in stories that took a dark turn. The original Brothers Grimm stories would be unrecognizable to a generation raised on the Disney version of what they actually wrote — a world of trolls, blood, murder, mayhem, and dark witchcraft. I am haunted to this day by the image of an ogress mother-in-law roaming the lightless corridors of her ancient stone castle, hungrily scenting the dusty air for the blood-scent of her own grandchildren, a scene from one of the Brothers Grimm's darkest tales, "The Mother-in-Law." In Charles Perrault's *Bluebeard*, first published in 1697, the young wife's discovery of a locked room full of her dismembered predecessors is a classic horror story moment, and one that was imprinted on my young mind in the pages of an illustrated book of children's stories.

I'm sure that both critics and fans of the *Queer Fear* horror anthologies I've edited as an adult would either deplore or celebrate this early literary grounding — a matter of taste, to be sure.

My first brush with state-sanctioned censorship occurred when I was nine. I wanted to check out Bram Stoker's *Dracula* from the local library. The librarian in charge, a hatchet-faced blue-rinsed Cerberus of the old school, likely thought she was acting *in loco parentis* when she refused to allow me to do so, citing my age and the fact that it was an "adult book."

My mother was furious. She packed me up in the car and drove to the library to confront the librarian in person. Upon discovering that the library had closed for the day, she drove me downtown to a branch of W.H. Smith and bought me a paperback copy of the novel.

"Read to your heart's content, and don't let anyone ever tell you what you can and cannot read," my mother said.

That one negative occurrence didn't dampen my love for the library of my childhood, however. What a world I discovered there. A world of silence and golden light, a world where books were available to anyone who wanted to read them, whenever you wanted to. I was exhilarated by the power of the written word to whisk me away from the mundane mechanics of my own life and into other, more exciting ones.

I'm sure that even then, prepubescent but with the beginnings of an uneasy awareness of the fact that I was different, I knew instinctively that I might find answers to the increasing mystery of my difference in the pages of books. I looked desperately for stories of boys like me: boys who played with dolls instead of trucks; who were soft and gentle, who cried easily and laughed too readily; who preferred the company of girls to the rough, knee-scraping fraternity of boys, with their shouts and smells and crude language.

I never found those stories, though I found others. Everyone but me, it seemed, had a life reflected in books. My difference, my aloneness, was a brand on my heart. But I took comfort in the stories of other kids with problems, problems they overcame. The protagonists in the novels of Paul Zindel and Lois Duncan became as real to me as the people I knew outside the pages of the books and infinitely better company. Surely, I thought, someday I will find someone to love me, in the same way that the characters in these books ultimately did.

As I grew into adolescence, the libraries of the various prep schools I attended became a physical sanctuary as well as an imaginative one. The silent, hallowed halls became a place where no one could shout *faggot* or *queer* in hoarse, cracking, cruel voices. The church-like serenity of the stacks, with that familiar, soothing scent of paper and dust, was a refuge where I could find comfort and peace.

I was fortunate to survive my teen years. Many gay and lesbian teenagers do not. When the pain of bullying becomes a torture beyond endurance and when the sense of being completely alien to everything they've been taught to believe becomes more than they can bear, they take their own lives. They die believing that they will never find a place for themselves in the world, and that there is no one in the world like them. For me, when the pressure of being perpetually at odds with everything around me moved me to the edge of finding a permanent end to the pain of living, I read.

And in those silent, fragrant rooms, I began to write, on my own, privately, in secret, my own stories. In the same way that reading opened a world of possibilities to me, writing allowed me to marshal my sanity, record how I felt, and why. On the page, it all made more sense. I still couldn't find my own life reflected in the pages of books, but at least I had it on paper in front of me.

I grew up, moved out, and started to live. I met a wonderful man when I was twenty-one. We got married in 1985 — not legally, yet, but no less real for that small impediment — and we made a life together. He supported me in my desire to become a writer, and rejoiced in my successes.

In 1992, the summer I was twenty-nine, I went to Harvard Summer School to take a writing program there. I met a writer and anthologist named John Preston in Portland, Maine, that summer, and we became friends. In addition to being the most celebrated gay pornographer of his — or any other — day, John was a journalist, essayist, and expert compiler of anthologies.

He had a passion for documenting the lives of gays and lesbians. He relished the role of community scribe and elder, and saw it as a sacred responsibility to write our history down, so that our youth would know we were here, and that the forces of repression and intolerance that would deny gay men and lesbians our basic dignity would never be able to silence us. The books would speak for us when we were not able to speak for ourselves. Later that year, John took me under his wing as a mentor. As his protégé, I was in an illustrious line of descent of literary mentorship. John had been a protégé of Samuel Steward, who had, in turn, been a protégé of Gertrude Stein.

I am fortunate to have been a working journalist and essayist for most of my adult life, most recently for *The Advocate* and other gay magazines. As a journalist, I have been privileged to be allowed to record some part of our history as gay and lesbian people. I am both humbled and exalted by the number of our brothers and sisters who have let me into their lives and allowed me to record them, to write them down.

Of late, I have begun to write more and more fiction, and I'm finding that I understand what Gore Vidal meant when he said — and I'm paraphrasing slightly — "You can only really tell the truth about people you know in fiction."

The person I know best is myself.

Last summer, I wrote a very long short story about a little boy who is bullied to the point of suicide for being what he — and others — suspect is his dawning awareness of his homosexuality. It's a ghost story, though not in the usual sense. I wrote it for teenagers, and it was published in a small jewel of an young adult anthology called *Be Very Afraid*, edited by Edo van Belkom.

The story is called, "The Night Is Yours Alone," and in my heart

I dedicated it to the little boy I was and to all the boyish girls and girlish boys whose life is made a living hell, every day, by a cruel and intolerant world. It has a happy ending and nothing in my career to date has made me as happy as knowing that it is available in libraries across Canada and the United States. Perhaps someday some little boy will be driven the way I was to find sanctuary in his school library, and he'll find that book. Perhaps he'll turn to my story and read that, although the nights may belong to him alone, at least for now, they wouldn't always be so lonely. And he'll realize that he is not only deserving of love and dignity, but will find it, too.

Librarians and gay and lesbian writers are front-line soldiers in the battle — not only for gay rights, but gay lives. I am proud to be a *gay writer* and not just *a writer who happens to be gay*. I claim that title with pride and in the name of writers like Paul Monette and John Preston, who wore it like a badge and dared anyone to tell them that we are not a beautiful and proud people.

The space that is created when gay writers write the stories of our lives, and librarians buy them and make them available to our young people, is the garden where not only tolerance, but understanding, love, friendship, and bridges, spring up.

In closing, although the notion of *legacy* is far too ostentatious for me to experience comfortably, I have recently allowed myself the luxury of imagining *a body of work*.

If I had my wish, as of this morning, my body of work would record that I lived honestly and intensely, and used the gifts God gave me to give a voice to gay and lesbian people whose stories might otherwise vanish into the darkness of history instead of forming a brightly woven tapestry of light by which future generations of our precious, beautiful young people can see that they are not alone — indeed that they were never alone.

Let them see that generations before them — indeed before *us* — found the strength to live our lives with dignity, grace, and courage, effecting change and redressing injustices through actions, deeds, and, ultimately, our literature, which succeeds us.

From This Day Forward
2003

ON SUNDAY, JUNE 15, I legally married my partner of nineteen years, Brian McDermid, in a private ceremony at St. Mark's United Church in Scarborough, officiated by the Rev. Alan Hall. It was my second wedding, though unlike some other members of my family, it was to the same person the second time around. This time, I am taking my spouse's last name legally, as a testament of our legal conjoining.

The first one, which occurred on August 24, 1985, at the Metropolitan Community Church, was our real wedding, the anniversary we celebrate. It held all of the truest and most honest ingredients required for a union of two people declared before God: an expressed intent to make a life together, to care for each other through the hardest times, and to celebrate each day with the other as best we both could. As a Christian, I felt it to be important that it take place in a church. The difference was that the state didn't recognize it; and Brian and I spent the years between 1984 (when we met) and 2003 in a committed marriage, with all its attendant sacrifices, and none of its protections or sanctioned benefits.

Eighteen years from the day I took my first wedding vows, my day still begins when I see Brian's sleeping face on the pillow next to mine as I get up to feed Harper, our yellow Lab. Brian goes off to his medical practice and I repair upstairs to my study to write. We both have full lives, with satisfying work and a broad group of friends and extended family, and yet, as saccharine as it may sound to some, the highlight of my day, every day, is the sound of Brian's key in the lock at night and Harper's mad scrabbling on the hardwood floor, as, incoherent and surging with Labrador love, he greets Brian at the door.

These moments, and many more in between, are what we took to the altar on that gold-green summer Sunday afternoon at St. Mark's, the year that Canada decided that Brian and I were full citizens, and entitled to the same rights and dignities as any other Canadian, in every way.

In the past few months, I've been asked many times what the point of a *gay marriage* might be. Anyone who has been married for many years would recognize the thousand threads that are woven together in the fabric of a marriage: the incalculable pride in your spouse's achievements; the helpless, hollow desperation of seeing them in pain, or sick, or troubled, and of not being able to relieve them with a touch or a whispered encouragement; the mornings you look at them and wonder how you could be so lucky as to have found someone who completes you like they do; and the mornings (far less often, one hopes) when you wonder what on earth you were thinking when you agreed to walk down that aisle in the first place. There is a moment at the end of the film *On Golden Pond* when Norman (Henry Fonda) suffers a heart attack. Believing that she is about to lose her husband of fifty-plus years, Ethel (Katherine Hepburn) imagines him lying in his coffin. It's one of the most brilliant moments in Hepburn's film oeuvre, and it always makes me cry when I watch that film. While Ethel's words are reasonable, if poignant, her face tells another story. The titanic grief of losing her husband and partner reflected there in that moment is a vast awfulness that is instantly recognizable to any of us who have made a life with someone. It cuts across lines of gender and sexual orientation. It's a terror that lives in the very heart of what marriage and family means, and it is the acknowledged Faustian bargain you make when you love someone more than you love yourself.

Brian and I have made that bargain, our parents (upon whose example our marriage is based) have made it, and millions of married couples, gay and straight, have made it. That's what marriage costs. I know every line of Brian's hands and face, every variegated timbre of his voice, and I know what every shift of his body means. I feel his pain and his joy and I safeguard his walk through life in every way I can. I would die for him, and I believe I would kill anyone who attempted to take him before his time. I defy any married man or woman to tell me they don't know what I mean.

None of these things seem to occur to the people asking that question. It's as though the idea of love itself was ultimately divided into rigidly segregated categories, and marriage was a "gated community of the heart" whose primary purpose was to keep out the undesirables, which, in this case, means people like Brian and me. The more liberal among them suggest that the word itself is the problem, and if we called our marriages something other than marriages — a "same sex civil union" perhaps, separate but equal in the eyes of the law — it wouldn't be as difficult for society to deal with. None of them seem eager to get the ball rolling, though, by offering to redefine their marriages as "opposite sex civil unions." *Separate but equal* never means "separate but equal," it means separate. No one would think to ask a straight couple why they felt they "needed" to get married (and have it called a marriage) instead of remaining a "committed couple." But our straight friends who elect to bypass the rituals that, for many of them, seem outdated and unnecessarily patriarchal do so with the full knowledge that *any time they change their minds*, the societal marriage machine, with all its attendant rights and responsibilities, is there for them.

They don't need to prove themselves *deserving* of the *special* right to marry the person they love, they just do it. Conversely, straight couples who elect not to marry and still raise families are considered progressive at best, and at worst irresponsible. Prior to the legalization of gay marriage, gay couples in a similar situation were just occupying the space that the legal system in our society has allocated for them, period. Not a legally recognized couple; not a family; just roommates of ten, twenty, thirty, forty, fifty years.

I was raised by parents who were, above all, individuals. My father was a maverick of sorts, whose career began in radio and television and culminated in a distinguished diplomatic career that took our family all over the world. My mother was a progressive American schoolteacher, who gave up her U.S. citizenship as a declarative rejection of American paranoia and bigotry in the McCarthy era of the 1950s. A few years ago, my father suffered her loss. They had been married for over forty years and my father's bereavement was annihilating. Watching him endure it was a foretaste of what I will someday have to endure when I lose Brian, and my father's memories of his and my mother's life and adventures was an oblique injunction to celebrate each day and live deliberately. My mother's detailed, elegantly written obituary tribute in the *National Post* noted that "when one of her sons announced he was living with another man, she threw them a party." That son was me. She loved Brian and never didn't think of him as her son-in-law. My mother would have been proud on June 15, not just of Brian and me, but of her adopted country which, in the same summer that American gays and lesbians were celebrating the end of anti-sodomy laws, was becoming the third country in the world to legalize gay marriage.

And in the United States, while waiting for the laws to change, more and more American gays and lesbians are getting married in Canada. Ironically, the gay couple's decision to marry, to publicly declare their intention to make a life together in spite of daunting odds, gets to the very heart of the meaning of marriage. While the people who would deny gays and lesbians the right to marry wallow in the Punch and Judy brutality of Anne Coulter and Rush Limbaugh, or the sideshow vulgarity of Jennifer Lopez and Ben Affleck's on-again/off-again engagement, or Britney Spears's forty-eight hour nuptials, or *The Bachelorette*, many gay men and lesbians are reaching for the solemnity of publicly-announced vows and sanctity of marriage, claiming it as an inalienable right in the same way that widowhood is borne with such dignity by those who lose their partners to AIDS without society's validation of that widowhood. The ability to live, love, and raise families of our own without the laws that support our straight friends is a reason to be proud, as is our determination not to wait until the laws change to get on with the business of making our marriages. The laws *will* change, because the laws are illogical and cruel and future generations will see them for what they are.

The movement of life is forward, and, as George Bernard Shaw said, "the greatest truths begin as blasphemies." The right of gays and lesbians to marry is in the same line of ideological descent, for instance, as the right of women to vote, the right of Jews to hold public office, and the right of blacks to marry whites — all things that we take for granted today, but which were trumpeted as destructive to society when they were first presented. Allowing your fellow man to live well and prosper in love doesn't cost society anything but goodwill.

My mother would have laughed at anyone who told her that allowing her son the dignity of marriage was destructive to the notion of "family," and would likely have sent them packing with the same blistering tongue-lashing she once gave a missionary who urged her to turn away from her son, and impress upon him that he was going to hell for his "lifestyle."

My mother knew, as I know, that we are no threat to "the family."

We *are* the family. We are sons and daughters, brothers and sisters, and entering a blessed union with the one you love above anyone on this earth is the oldest family ritual in the human race's history.

$\mathcal{M}$y Life as a Girl
2002

I CAME UPON THE photographs of myself as a very young girl in a box in my father's study last January, when I was visiting him in Victoria, British Columbia. They were tucked away in a yellow Kodak envelope, covered with a thick coating of dust, marked "Cuba, 1968."

My father had been posted to the Canadian embassy there in 1968, his second diplomatic posting in what would eventually become a long and illustrious career. Seeing the word "Cuba" written in long-faded black ink in my late mother's elegant scrawl momentarily halted my breath.

Gingerly, I withdrew the photographs from the envelope and stared at my six-year-old self.

In one photo, I am standing on the back of a tricycle being driven with macho determination by my younger brother, Eric. I am wearing a fur-trimmed hat and I am carrying a basket.

In another, I am wearing a cowboy hat over a towel that streams down my back like long hair. I am drinking a glass of milk and looking up at the camera like a natural seductress.

In the third photo, I am standing in our driveway in the bright tropical sunlight wearing an old housedress over my khaki shorts and striped Buster Brown T-shirt. My hair is cut short, like a pixie's.

My features are delicate and slender and I am clutching a plush stuffed dog to my breast as though it were a baby. The expression on my face in this one is so ineffably tender, so sweet, so vulnerable, and so *natural*, that my first impulse was to sweep the child in the photograph into my arms and run off with him

Him, not *her*. I am not now, nor have I ever been female. But I look down at the sweet face in the photograph, and I remember, and I feel like weeping.

∞∞∞

BEFORE I EVER HEARD the expression *gender dysphoria*, or the word *transgender*, I knew that I have been two people in my life: one male, one female.

I've always loved the Native American expression *two-spirited*, which has of late been appropriated by many gay social historians in an earnest drive to document the acceptance of homosexuality by ancient cultures. The problem with this approach is the application of a twentieth-century gay cultural definition, which, in this instance, seeks to claim two-spiritedness as a de facto manifestation of homosexuality as it is currently defined.

The term two-spirited has suggested the presence of both male and female spirits in the body of one man or one woman. This lies in direct contradiction to the contemporary gay masculinist assertion that male homosexuality is its own sexual orientation — uniquely male — and exists without reference to the opposite gender.

The emotional component to this argument is rooted in justifiable rage and frustration at years of gay men being told that their orientation made them less than men, more womanly and, therefore, inferior. For gay men who subscribe to this masculinist ideal, there is little room for allowance of the notion that there might be a female presence in the equation. In fact, the disdain that many gay men manifest towards effeminacy often rivals that of their straight peers. In the "testosterone revolution" of the 1970s, when gay men *en masse* flocked to gyms, cut their hair short, grew moustaches, and dressed to out-butch their own sissy history, in jeans and lumber-jack shirts and leather, a new physical ideal was born and there was little quarter accorded to those gay men who wouldn't (or couldn't) live up to it. In retrospect, there was an edge of hysteria to it that wasn't often discussed in those days.

It is with some relief that I note that today's gay youth, in their enthusiasm for the reclamation of "queer space" have largely aban-doned these strict notions of masculinity and femininity, and many of them look at the aging remnants of this Village People clone era with the same amused frustration that teenagers show to their hope-lessly out-of-date parents. Big muscles and being "straight looking and acting" don't carry the cachet they once did, as twentysome-thing gay men redefine not only the very notion of what queerness can mean, but also notions of beauty, masculinity, and desirability.

∞∞∞

WHEN I WAS A little boy, I looked out at the world through a girl's eyes. It might have been my secret if I thought there was anything special about it, but I never did. There was a little girl in my head and she lived in a secret place behind my eyes. She was as natural and real as anything in my world and I liked who she was, who I was.

I had access to dolls because my parents were modern, evolved people, who felt that they were encouraging my nurturing instincts which would, in the fullness of time, make me a good father. I had access to my mother's dresses and jewellery because she thought I was creative and theatrical. The place behind my eyes where I took these things to play was neither theatrical nor bent on any future thoughts of being a father: it was an effortlessly feminine place where I was just myself.

My gender was as natural and uncomplicated to me as it would have been to any other girl, except in the memorable moments when my parents would point out with exasperation that I was "a B-O-Y, not a G-I-R-L!" and they would always spell it out for me, for emphasis.

I would retort that I didn't want to be a boy and I wouldn't be one. At that age, in my mind, it was still a choice.

I received my first Barbie at Christmas in 1968, after much swooning over the Sears Christmas Wish Book. I wanted a Barbie with long ash-blonde hair, and there was a beautiful one which came dressed in a red fishnet one-piece, perfectly accessorized, and carrying a beach bag. I didn't, however, bat an eyelash when Sears ran out of stock of that particular model and substituted a Twiggy doll instead, with short blonde hair and a mod green-and-blue mini dress, looking remarkably like the eponymous sixties supermodel upon whom it was based. I thought she was beautiful and fear that I would still think so today. The moment was pure magic. The closest I ever came to fratricide was the morning I discovered that, in a fit of malicious pique, my brother had scribbled all over Twiggy's face with a blue ballpoint. My parents were furious with my brother, but there was no particular haste on their part to replace the doll.

One evening when I was about seven, I announced to my father that what I wanted to be when I grew up was a "lady teacher." Like many children, I had developed an all-encompassing aesthetic crush on my teacher, who was dark-haired and pretty and who corrected my homework in pink pencil. Even when she wrote admonitions like *Pay attention!* in the margins, it seemed like a benediction because of the glorious rose-pink of that soft pencil.

My father is a jovial man and deft at wordplay. His rejoinder (which I know he thought was quite witty) was, "Well, Michael, I think that's a wonderful idea. You can be a *lady teacher* all right."

I was euphoric at this endorsement of my career plans and beamed up at him.

My father paused for a couple of beats, then added with a flourish, "You can be a *lady teacher*, and *teach ladies!*"

He broke into explosive laughter at his own joke, oblivious to my devastation as I hit the first major wall of my childhood. My father is not, nor has he ever been, a cruel man, and there is no way he could have known the effect his joke had on me. My life at that age was a smooth, unbroken surface, and there was no turmoil surging beneath for him to see. The internal storm that would erupt years later, threatening to split my sexual psyche in half, was still far out to sea and nowhere in evidence at that point. The serenity of a child's logic can be its own balm. When you *know* you're a girl, and your world view is completely female, you have no reason to question it until someone whose authority is unquestioned calls it into question.

I felt cold dread spread upwards from my belly as I realized that not only was my desire to grow up to be a lady teacher incorrect, it was *so* incorrect that the only response to it was explosive humour at the absurdity. An abyss yawned beneath me. My father's casual obviation of my dream was doubly threatening. Not only was my femininity dismissed, but nothing was offered up in its place. I wouldn't ever be a B-O-Y, that wasn't an option in my mind. I thought of the boys and men I knew: all angles, jutting elbows and skinned knees, loud voices and war games. I shuddered. There was nothing there that I could relate to. No, what I was facing was the annihilation of my entire gender identity. In my mind, I was a girl, or I was nothing. And with that came the first stirrings of what would become a lifelong sense of guilt about not being able to be what everyone else seemed to demand.

As an embassy family, we were accorded two live-in servants: a maid-of-all-work named Berta, and a cook named Maria. The two women loved me in that way that older *latina* women often love very effeminate young boys. To my mother's bemusement, they found me adorable, and, to her chagrin, they spoiled me beyond redemption. Berta and Maria worked hard all day for us, and although we considered them "members of the family," it seems doubtful in retrospect that *they* saw *us* that way. Children know when they're loved, however, and I had no doubt that they loved me. Best of all, they seemed to delight in my girlishness: my propensity for wearing my mother's clothes and shoes, my fondness for dolls, and for playing school, with me as the "lady teacher" with my plush animals and my benighted baby brother as my "class."

On weekends, Berta and Maria would undergo a miraculous metamorphosis: they would transform themselves into *women with boyfriends*. Once they were dressed, they would invite me to their room to witness the finishing touches. The scent of their cheap face powder and lipstick, the flowery sweetness of their heavy perfume, the gardenias they tucked into their hairdos, signalled to me a world of transformative possibilities, as did the exaggerated, cheeky feminine sway of their hips as they high-heeled out of our home into the fragrant Havana night. My mother was beautiful and I loved to watch her get dressed for an evening out with my father, but her restrained Yankee elegance was nothing compared to the overblown, meaty femaleness of the two women. Few modern authors have more beautifully rendered this breed of *latina* than the Chilean-Canadian writer Francisco Ibanez-Carrasco in his luminous novel *Flesh Wounds And Purple Flowers*, where he describes "women who do the cha-cha down the sinuous sidewalk."

I approached Berta and Maria one afternoon with my gender dilemma. I wanted to be a girl and everyone was telling me that I couldn't be one because I was a boy. How was I going to fix this?

They smiled and giggled and told me they had an idea: there was a sawmill not far from the house. They could take me there and the sawmill workers could cut off my penis with the whirling buzzsaw. It might hurt a little, they said, but the solution was definitive.

I thought it was a marvellous idea and joyously began to plan for my trip to the mill.

When Berta and Maria realized that their indulgent joke had gone a little too far, they shushed me, frantically looking over the top of my head into the house to see if my mother had heard them, or heard me screaming with joy as I danced around the patio. They swore me to secrecy. As panic stricken as they were at the thought of their inevitable dismissal, they were likely equally horrified by my enthusiasm for the operation they suggested. To me, it was a matter of no consequence. My penis was simply an obstacle to the world seeing me as I saw myself.

Once again, though, I felt the sting of disappointment as yet another adult held out a carrot, then snatched it away, laughing, and telling me not to be so silly.

Late one afternoon, shortly before we returned to Ottawa in the summer of 1969, my father took a series of photographs of my brother and me on our terrace by the pool to send to my grandparents in the United States.

My father must have been in a good mood, because when I put on my favourite housedress over my clothes, and reached for Randy, my blue plush dog, and cuddled him, he didn't tell me to take off my dress because I was a B-O-Y, not a G-I-R-L. Instead, he kept shooting. In some of the photographs I am laughing, which suggests that we were having fun and I was happy.

In my mind's eye, Randy was my baby and I was his mother and I was beautiful.

The red-gold sunlight sparkled on the blue surface of the swimming pool and played across my face, making my eyes very bright. Standing there in my dress, I lowered my head and smiled shyly, tilted my eyes upwards, and held the plush dog very close. In a way, I was as complete and organic in that transient moment as I have ever been since.

ooooo

A SHIFT BEGAN TO occur internally when we returned from the cloistered world of diplomatic Havana and I began a suburban North American childhood. By eight, I had gradually become aware that I wasn't a girl, at least biologically, though what I actually *was* could be anyone's guess. I had begun to think in terms of a third sex (though that terminology would naturally not have been available to me). I didn't find my body *completely* incongruous, as many transgendered children do, and the trip to the sawmill had been long-since dismissed by me as an unnecessary sacrifice. I had no knowledge of female anatomy and had a vague notion that naked girls were like baby dolls: smooth down below, with a small hole in their bottoms to pee out of. I was perfectly happy with my own willowy, girlish frame, and to me, the difference between me and the other boys was internal, though no less definitive for its invisibility. I was simply a different *type* of girl, and it didn't bother me in the slightest.

I wrote fan letters to David Cassidy, confidently suggesting that he be my boyfriend, even though I was a boy, urging him not to let that come between us and swearing I wouldn't either. I wore the shortest shorts I could and when I stood in direct sunlight I pressed my legs together and made a skirt out of the shadow. I dreamed that I had glorious long auburn hair like a beautiful Crissy doll, or like Brenda Starr, Girl Reporter, whom I planned to become when I grew up. ("A crack reporter in high-fashion clothes!")

My identification with, and jealousy of, other little girls, real little girls, was searing, even annihilating. I played with them at their games when they would have me, learning to skip with a pink rubber skipping rope, playing house and always refusing to be the father, or the husband (I often played the beautiful older sister, because I was larger than my female playmates), which the girls accepted with surprising equanimity, at least until just before puberty. I was green with envy when they came to school with ponytails tied up in brightly coloured wool rope, or when their fathers called them "princess," or the boys treated them as delicate, and different. *I* was delicate and different too, and I wanted to be treated that way.

My childhood after Cuba had become an odd admixture of impressions and contradictions. On one hand, my parents continued to indulge me, out of love, with dolls and tea sets; when I visited my grandparents in western New York, my *hausfrau* German grandmother allowed even encouraged me, to wash the dishes and cook with her, and I became her little confidante. She even bought me my own apron, with a red heart embroidered on the pocket. My grandfather, the World War I veteran, on the other hand, kept his distance and eyed me warily, sensing quite rightly that something queer was afoot in his well-ordered house. Closer to home, things got progressively tenser. My mother's fury one night at the fact that I'd left my Barbies out on the rec-room floor was awe-inspiring. As she shouted about the dolls, and how she had wanted a son, not a daughter, she grew apoplectic with rage. Her face grew red and the tendons in her neck stood out like flushed marble columns. Her anger seemed to me out of sync with the crime at hand — the mess of dolls and doll clothes on the floor — which was relatively minor. It appeared to encompass the Barbies themselves and what they represented — aberrant toys for a boy, and the entire albatross of a childhood of indulgence she might understandably regret as she surveyed her young son, about whom nothing seemed normal. In fairness to my parents, other people's notions of normalcy didn't carry much currency in our family. I had already demonstrated a stunning precocity with writing and art, and I read voraciously, so there was a mental folder open where my parents could place my eccentricities. Even so, my mother was clearly growing tired of my weirdness. That Christmas, I received one more doll. My mother explained to me that this was a gift from my parents, not from Santa, because Santa didn't bring dolls to boys of my age. This was the last one, she assured me, *ever*.

I named the doll Heidi, and cherished her until I turned ten, when I outgrew dolls altogether.

ooooo

BETRAYAL OF YOUR GENDER is a fearsome crime, especially if you are a boy, and it is punishable by any number of cruel chastisements. No one is in a better position to enforce these chastisements than unsupervised children in the harsh arena of the playground and you never forget the first time it happens. Although there is a reluctant space in the social hierarchy of school life accorded to the tomboy, the word *tomgirl* is non-existent. In its place, there are words like *sissy, faggot, girl, gaylord*. When society teaches young boys that they are the elect sex, and that girls are pretty, decorative, desirable trophies, to be hunted and speared, males who betray that divine right face the wrath of their tribe. It may be natural to *fuck* a girl, but God help you if you *act* like one, or wish you *were* one. As Quentin Crisp archly observed in *The Celluloid Closet*, Rob Epstein and Jeffrey Friedman's 1995 documentary on gays in Hollywood, "there's no crime like being a woman."

Young women, in their strawberry-scented quest to fulfill their part of the social bargain with the boys, are as merciless, perhaps even more pitiless, than their hunters. The high, cruel laughter of pre-adolescent girls in the playground, as they tossed their pretty, long hair in the sun, was tattooed into the flesh of my memory at that age, without the benefit of anesthetic.

In 1973, I was eleven. We had moved to Geneva, Switzerland, where my father joined the Canadian Mission to the United Nations. I had been enrolled in the French Lycée section of Collège du Léman, an elite international Swiss private school catering largely to children of the diplomatic corps and the multinational business community, cast-off Hollywood kids whose parents were far too busy to raise them, and the scions of wealthy Iranians, including, it was rumoured, minor royalty. The Iranian boys were usually lean and muscular, adept at soccer and precociously sexual and seductive. The Iranian girls wore makeup and high-fashion as a birthright and with more natural panache than American women twice their age. The American girls were in the early-1970s Maybelline mode: clean straight hair parted in the center, Noxema complexions, with misty blue eye shadow and oversized Bonne Bell Lip Smackers always at the ready inside fringed suede shoulder bags. I thought they were all marvellous looking. The American boys were broad-shouldered jocks, classic boyfriend types in Adidas windbreakers and Levis. A lifelong love of American men, and a companion fetish for them, was likely born at some point in the autumn of 1973.

I arrived at school the first day wearing banana-yellow bell-bottoms, a white short-sleeved turtleneck, and black platform shoes. I had taken to wearing a black Kodak camera bag slung over my shoulder like a purse, in homage to the leggy American girls I'd met that summer. My hair was cut straight across, in bangs, like a china doll. This variation on the bowl cut was common in the early seventies, but with my delicate features, I must have looked precious. What causes me to marvel, from the vantage point of thirty years later, is that I somehow thought I would be invisible and that I looked as incongruous as anyone else.

As I alighted from my mother's car, a girl looked at me, pointed, and nudged her friend. They laughed behind their fingers for a moment, then the first girl asked me if I was the new ambassador's son. Thinking that they were being friendly, I smiled and I told her no, I wasn't. Only later did I discover that the new ambassador's son was developmentally challenged, and that there was nothing benign in her question.

My morning classes that first day were innocuous enough, and when the lunch bell rang, I went out to the schoolyard to eat the lunch my mother had packed. As I sat on a bench in the playground, a group of boys approached. They loomed over me, silhouetted in the sunlight. I squinted up at them, shielding my eyes with my hand.

"Are you a boy or a girl?" the leader asked. He had a rough voice, a definitively male voice, even at eleven. I'd learned that his name was Pedro and he liked to fight.

"I'm a boy," I said indignantly. By then, I had learned the currency of language necessary to survive and to enjoy the privacy of my inner world of unselfconscious femininity. Although I was frequently mistaken for a girl, it was important to assert that I wasn't one.

"You look like a fuckin' girl to me," he rasped. His friends broke out in ugly laughter behind him and shuffled their feet.

Intuitively, I smelled the implied offer of violence and I felt the first answering tendrils of dread stir inside me. I stood up, prepared to conciliate, and was slapped hard across the mouth.

I recoiled, shocked by the pain, and tasted blood in my mouth. I touched my bruised lip and burst into tears, which I learned later in my career as an object of ridicule is almost always a mistake.

"*Awwwwww*," Pedro whined. "Is the little girl gonna *cry*? Is she gonna go and *tell a teacher*? Huh? *Is* she?" There were rafts of catcalls from his friends as I sobbed. I gathered my Kodak camera case up and slung it over my shoulder where it belonged. I faced him and, through my tears, said the first thing that came to my mind.

"If you think I'm a *girl*," I sobbed, "then you *shouldn't have hit me. You don't hit girls.*"

It might not have been the most useful answer, but it stunned the bullies with its perverse logic, and they left me alone after that; at least that particular group did.

Two things happened when I turned twelve, and both marked the end of my childhood, the beginning of my adolescence, and the next stage of my gender evolution in a way that was profound and irrevocable.

The first was meeting Nancy, the girl who would become my de facto big sister. She was the daughter of an American business executive; my mother had met her mother at a meeting of the American Women's Club of Geneva.

My mother had recently fired the live-in *au pair*, when the girl became pregnant by the Sardinian waiter she was dating on weekends. This was likely less of a trauma for the *au pair* than it was for my mother. The fact that we lived in a large villa on a hill in a small town outside of the city had clearly been an ordeal for the young woman, and she was likely well rid of us. I know she suspected that I rummaged through her makeup drawer when she wasn't around, exploring the process by which she became so pretty every morning and alluring beyond mere words when she went out on weekends, and she wasn't wrong.

My parents entertained a great deal and were often out at embassy parties and diplomatic receptions themselves. With no one to watch my brother and I on those evenings, my mother was disadvantaged. She solved this problem by hiring a series of young American girls, the teenage daughters of her friends, to babysit us. They were all very pleasant, but when my favourite graduated from our school and went home to the States for college, I was bereft. And then my mother hired Nancy and my life changed.

From our first meeting, Nancy *got* me. She *understood* me, and whatever she might not have understood, she accepted swiftly and silently. She thought I was adorable and I thought the sun rose and set on her. A night when Nancy came to babysit was better than Christmas, and if she stayed for the weekend, it was beyond anything as pedestrian as bliss. I idolized her. Our talks were all-encompassing and anything she could do, I wanted to learn. She taught me how to knit, how to appreciate tea, how to love music. When she failed to teach me how to play the guitar, she wrote a song for me instead. When she failed to help me understand mathematics, she said it was okay. She gave me gothic novels and saucy stewardess books like *Coffee, Tea, or Me* and *The Fly Girls*. She introduced me to a new writer named Stephen King one evening when she brought over a sophisticated novel that had just been published, about a young high-school outcast who discovered telekinetic powers when she began to menstruate. I immediately identified with the protagonist and felt terribly grown-up when Nancy lent it to me after she was done. I managed to read it from cover to cover before my mother picked it up and declared it "too racy" a book for me.

Nancy taught me how to write poetry, and set me on the path to becoming a writer, even though at that age what I really wanted to be was an actress. She became my role model for what a teenage girl should be, and everything about her was in some way incorporated into my life. My bedroom became a facsimile of hers, and it was a place of refuge where I could write poetry or letters, read her cast-off copies of 'TEEN magazine, or listen to James Taylor, or Carly Simon, or Bread, music she introduced me to.

She took me on the train into Geneva for magical afternoons when the world was just her and me, and anything was possible. We shopped in department stores like Grand Passage, where I bought my own bottles of peach-scented shampoo. We ate at upscale pizzerias like Vedia, or at imitation American hamburger restaurants like Wimpy's. I held her hand crossing the street and together we watched impossibly sophisticated men and women move like lacquered angels through the streets of this most glamorous international city of watches, jewellery, and the tireless nurture of other people's fortunes. We walked and walked, till the blue hour of early dusk, when the mist came in off Lake Geneva and the colours of the great floral clock near the train station grew moody and subdued in the dying light. At the water's edge, the seagulls swooped low over the city, long grey shadows in the brilliant electric rainbow footlights of Geneva's famous *jette d'eau*, the spectacular fountain that explodes out of the lake like an arc of liquid silver, shattering across the night water like a shower of diamonds. I was completely at peace in Nancy's safe, protective embrace, and whatever I was or wasn't, it didn't matter to either of us.

My mother appreciated that when Nancy was around, I was calmer and more even, less prone to inexplicable fits of rage and lashing out. Nancy's mother worried that I was in love her daughter. The thought that I wanted to *be* Nancy never occurred to either of them.

Declaring Nancy my standard of beauty, I began to collect makeup of my own that I kept in a pretty wicker basket on my dresser: American beauty products like the blushing gel Nancy brought back from Cincinnati. I told my mother it was "stage makeup," for practising "my acting" and that I was determined to become a Master of Disguise using it. Generously, if inexplicably, my mother turned a blind eye to my predilection for cosmetics, and I practised applying it in private, in the sanctuary of my bedroom. By thirteen, I was so skilled at painting my face that I could leave the house wearing blush and/or foundation, with no one (including my parents) any the wiser.

I smoothed Nivea cream into my face every night before bed to keep my face smooth, as the fashion magazines urged.

Nancy's favourite perfume was Chantilly, a spicy floral fragrance that I still associate with her, even though she has long since stopped wearing it. She gave me her empty perfume bottles and powder boxes, and they lined my dresser like votive candles at an altar until I got the courage to buy a bottle of Chantilly cologne myself to wear on weekends. In the same way I discovered that pink lipstick was almost undetectable if applied lightly and new, I learned that if cologne was sprayed in the air above my head in a mist I then walked through, the scent was light enough to be a mere suggestion of a bouquet. My use of cosmetics had nothing to do with making myself look different, or pretty, it had to do with taking part in a resolutely feminine ritual, something inflexibly forbidden to boys, a tangible gender barrier and one of the few I could vault. Applying makeup and scent near-invisibly was a powerful symbol. I could nurture the girl inside, yet pass as a boy in the outside world. It was an affirmation of my femaleness that I hadn't previously had available. Like the place I'd taken my dolls and my mother's clothes and jewellery, the limitless landscape behind my eyes was the place I took these new symbols, to enjoy them in a private place where I was simply what I was, and all was right with the world.

Nancy loved me and I loved her. She gave me two precious gifts that I realize in retrospect likely saved me from suicide, an idea that began to occur to me regularly in my early teenage years, when the storm inside me began to turn the skies of my adolescence black and cold and violent.

Nancy was the first person to ever love me unconditionally and nurture and celebrate *everything* about me, including the things that made others cringe, or drew opprobrium from them like lightning. Furthermore, she was the first person in my life who allowed me to use her as a role model. She allowed me to project the fragmented pieces of my shattered and fragmented gender identity onto her, and in the light of her love and acceptance I was able to see, and assemble, them into something I could live with.

The second seismic event in my life occurred one afternoon after gym class, and I remember it like it happened yesterday. In French, gym class was called *le sport*, as though the entire humiliating travesty of being the one no one wanted on the team was a healthy exercise in *mens sana in corpore sano*; as though being the weak one, the one the teacher made climb the rope while everyone else waited with derisive, sadistic impatience, was a jovial lesson in being a good sport; and if I didn't enjoy the fun and healthful *bonhomie* of a class that every other boy in the world looked forward to and thought of as his favourite, well, that was my problem, and another example of my maladaptive strangeness.

We had been playing soccer. The locker room was close and stuffy with the musk of pre-teen boys who hadn't quite made the transition between boyhood and young adulthood, and for whom personal hygiene wasn't always a priority. I remember a cacophony of sound, the raucous, cracking laughter of boys, towels snapping, the gym teacher shouting at us to hurry up and get dressed or there would be hell to pay.

Suddenly, there was the sound of exploding glass and the locker room was plunged into darkness. There was a moment of stunned silence, then someone shouted *What the fuck?* in French, then everyone started to babble. There was nervous laughter as boys fumbled in the darkness with their wet soccer clothes and gym bags. There was the sound of someone's head smacking into a metal locker, an expletive, then more laughter.

I had learned to love the darkness for the peace it represented and I closed my eyes and savoured it, standing still, knowing that any minute someone would replace the overhead bulb and the moment of silent evenness would end.

Two hands, strong hands, grasped the sides of my face in the darkness, insistent yet curiously gentle. I gasped as the hands pulled my face forward and I was kissed, full and hard, on the mouth. The lips were full, and slightly chapped, and I felt the warmth of a tongue tasting the inside of my mouth and I tasted it back. The kiss grew more forceful and I tentatively reached out and touched two naked, muscular arms, and the thick, soft, damp hair of a boy I couldn't see. I leaned forward in answering insistence, feeling a smooth hard chest brush against mine. As I pressed my own lips hard against those of my invisible lover, I felt something like my soul leaving my body, taking flight into the miraculous darkness.

Then I heard a regretful sigh and the lips left mine. The heat of the other boy's body retreated and I was alone, flushed and wide-eyed in the blackness of the locker room.

I winced in the sudden cruel whiteness of the overhead light as it went back on.

Across the room, I saw the janitor climbing down the short step-ladder he'd used to climb up to replace the bulb. Wildly, I looked around me, trying to see who was standing near enough to have been the one who kissed me, but all the boys seemed equidistant and none of them were looking in my direction. No one was look-ing *away* from me either, but all the boys were fully engaged in what they were doing prior to the light going out: showering, snap-ping towels, getting dressed, zipping gym bags, hurrying out of the locker room.

Standing half-naked beside the locker, my body was alive with sensation, and I blushed to experience the unfamiliar fire in my chest, the damp flush of my cheeks, the hardness below the towel. I touched my mouth, feeling the ghost imprint of that vividly male kiss burn my fingers, and I knew that nothing would ever be the same after that moment, absolutely nothing.

ooooo

I SPENT MY TEENAGE years at St. John's Cathedral Boys' School, a macho prep school on the prairies of western Manitoba. The school was intensely physical and rigorous and was run by a lay branch of the Anglican Church of Canada. It was designed to promote what the Victorians called muscular Christianity. My entry into the school was swift and brutal, but the mercy of it was the fact that once I was beaten up a couple of times for being a faggot, I was accorded both space and distance to recoup my energies and figure out a way to not only survive, but thrive.

To do so, I buried the world behind my eyes and the girl who lived there, deep enough to make them both invisible.

I was a formidable wit and a punishing mimic and in a cloistered environment like a boys' school, there is always room (and even grudging admiration) for someone tough enough to endure razzing, especially razzing of the cruelest kind. I made close friends over the next four years, and made a name for myself as the school's writer and dramatist, penning Christmas plays that skewered the teachers without sending up any red flags. In my second year, I met Barney, a dazzling, handsome transfer student from Vancouver, and we became lovers. Barney's tenderness was like yarrow, drawing pain from me and offering a sense of completeness in its stead. His passion and erotic skill, even at sixteen, was extraordinary. We became fast friends as well as lovers and when the curiosity about sex, and the passion, faded away, the friendship remained.

Neither of us considered ourselves gay, of course. Barney had a girlfriend back in Vancouver and I was in a sexual limbo. I didn't want to be gay. The ugliness and perversion of homosexuality had been pounded into me by age seventeen and nothing positive about the evolving gay culture of the late 1970s ever reached me through the barricade of unquestioned homophobia, internal and external, that bordered my world. I recoiled at the photographs of mustachioed East Village clones I saw in *Time* magazine, seeing only disorder and an alien world, scarier and more lonely than the one I was in.

Even when Barney told me about gay porn he had seen, nothing in the man-on-man sex struck me as attractive, erotic, or relevant to my life. On some secret, private level, I still saw a girl in the mirror. I was still waiting to be *someone's girlfriend*, and that was the ideal. The knowledge that I would never be that, that I likely *was* gay, was unbearable, and I pushed it far down into my subconscious.

I was jealous of the girls my buddies picked up at the mall, or the roller rink. In their tight jeans and Farrah Fawcett hair, they seemed the luckiest beings in creation. They had the power to turn the boys I lived with twenty-four hours a day into men I didn't recognize. Men who swaggered, who spoke in low, confident voices, who went to any lengths to appear strong and masculine and dominant, and yet, at the same time, danced attendance to these girls like pleasure slaves. I stood back in awe on Sunday mornings and watched my roommates shave, apply flesh-toned Clearasil, sculpt their hair with The Dry Look, and don clean jeans, or cords, and crisp shirts, unbuttoned to expose chest hair. My own ablutions took far less time, as all I was dressing for was the library, where I would read fashion magazines, or the cinema, where I watched horror movies like *The Fury* and *Halloween*. I wasn't lonely — far from it. I regularly had invitations from school and family friends to spend the weekend with them, but there was much more peace and pleasure to be found in retreating to the place behind my eyes where I had been living since I was a child. Without my friends to reflect myself back to me the way they saw me, I was free to be myself, in private.

Another window to the world opened the summer I was sixteen. I signed with a model agency in my hometown of Ottawa, Ontario, and began what was to be a successful, short career as a teenage male model. The fact that modelling was considered a classically feminine career had definite appeal. There was an irony in my working in a world of beauty, makeup, bright lights, and glamour, while the stylists and the photographers turned me into the clean-cut all-American jock I knew I wasn't. I was usually the youngest male model on the shoot, and the older female models indulged me as I quizzed them about their work, their beauty routines, and their lives. I memorized their stories, and stored them like jewels. Every summer, I would return home to Ottawa, check in with my agency, and make the rounds with my portfolio. All summer, I would shoot catalogues and magazine spreads in Ottawa and Montreal, then return to St. John's in the fall to my other life, and bided my time till graduation.

After graduation, I packed up my portfolio and took off to Paris, ostensibly to model, but mostly to try to make sense of my life. I was nineteen, and my attraction to men had led me to the very logical conclusion that I was gay. I came out, embraced that identity, and began living as a gay man. What little I knew of transsexuality was limited to movie-of-the-week clichés, and the thought of having an operation to become a woman was beyond anything I could conceive of. I had, by then, largely reconciled myself to the duality of my gender and sexual nature. If I was two people — one male, one female — then so be it. I liked them both. I had little knowledge of gay life, but I was convinced that in this new world — free from the prying eyes and demands for accountability of friends and family — I would be allowed to be who I was without apology. All I asked of it was that it allow me to be the person I was inside and allow me to find someone to love, who would in turn love me back. I had sex with a man for the first time when I was in Paris — a man, not a boy — and there was none of the hurried rush and friction that had defined my prep-school encounters. I returned home from Paris in time for Christmas, came out to my oldest friend and moved to Toronto in the New Year. There, I threw myself into the joy of my new freedom. I danced, I visited bathhouses, I dated, I had sex with anyone I wanted, and nearly everyone who wanted me. For the first time in my life I was able to hold men close, to be held. My dual gender wasn't an issue for once and it blended together seamlessly. In 1982, I retired from modelling and entered the University of Toronto with the goal of becoming a writer. I fell in love several times, and had my heart broken just as many times as I fell in love. I published inert love poetry in campus literary journals and journalism that the editors of commercial magazines thought was excellent.

In 1984, at twenty-one, I left school to try to become a real writer. That summer, I met a young physician. He was kind, and handsome, and had the most beautiful speaking voice I have ever heard. I fell irrevocably in love. Fortunately, he fell in love with me as irrevocably and we moved in together. In 1985, we did something unusual for the times: we got married in a church. I told him about my life, about the woman in my head and heart who had been the defining architect of my inner world.

Miraculously, he told me he understood. In loving me, he wasn't just looking *past* my history, he looked *through* it, seeing something beautiful there that I myself had never seen. Where I saw a shattered, fragmented psycho-sexual landscape, he saw a complex and beautiful one, gentle, tender, and loving. He accepted me completely and utterly, and in doing so, freed me to be completely and utterly myself. For the first time, I felt an unfamiliar, exciting, masculine energy move in and take over. I was protected enough by my partner's acceptance of me *as I was* to taste my incumbent masculinity, explore it and, eventually welcome it. There was a powerful allure to the alignment between body and mind, and I gradually came to understand that there had been a man there the whole time, slumbering for years, now stirring and stretching, asserting his rightful place, as though my body had only been a leasehold whose deed belonged to him.

The woman in my head still came and went as she pleased, but now her eyes were not the only eyes though which I saw the world. Some mornings, I woke up and she was there, and she would select my frame of mind as though it were an outfit, discarding moods and perspectives with feminine caprice. Other mornings, I would wake feeling completely male and would assess her row of perfumes and skin creams on the bathroom vanity with something between disorientation and disdain. I loved the power of the man in my head and longed to have him linger, but he never did. She always came back and she treasured the prerogatives of her gender. Nothing was ever thrown away and both of them lived inside me in an uneasy truce.

One night, I was working out at the YMCA in Toronto. At twenty-four, I was out of university and working at a series of low-paying jobs while I concentrated on launching my career as a freelance writer. The pace was hectic, but I was young enough to handle it, and my time at the gym was a wonderful stress reliever. I was proud of my body: my flat stomach, my runner's legs, the breadth of my shoulders, the strength of my arms. After lifting weights, I dove into the swimming pool and began to do laps. The water was cool and blue, and, as it swept over my body, caressing my skin and cooling my flushed muscles, my thoughts began to swirl and surge, and my heart began to pound. Feeling the edge of panic, I swam to the pool deck to catch my breath, and looked up.

A man in his mid-thirties, broad shouldered, hairy, with powerful arms and striated thighs, was doing stretches in preparation for his swim. His body was that of a rugby player, the sort of classic male body built for bursts of strength, brute force, and endurance, rather than decorative beauty. He wore pale blue nylon swim-shorts, functional, not fashionable or decorative, and when he bent, the thin fabric stretched across his powerful buttocks. His thick black hair was damp with sweat and his eyes were dark. His features were indelicate: strong nose, square jaw, defiant chin. If I ever saw masculinity incarnate, it was at this moment. Even though it seems unlikely, given his distance from me, I felt I could *smell* him, and I swooned. What I was looking at was the embodiment of something completely alien to me: his indisputable maleness summoned an answering femaleness in me, a desire to be taken, to be invaded and filled up with his *oppositeness* from me. I craved it. It was something beyond mere sexual attraction, with which I was well-versed. No, this was about archetypes, collision, perfect fit. If there was ever a moment when I felt completely female, it was then.

My body was the wrong body and I believed that I would die if I remained in it.

He dove into the pool and I swam several paces behind him, watching his strong body plow through the blue water. He swam with determination and when he reached the opposite end of the pool, he executed a perfect flip, launching himself off the pool wall and rocketing towards me. As he passed, his leg brushed mine. Impossibly, I had a vivid impression of muscle and hair, of physical strength that surpassed mine, and, it seemed, rightfully so. I imagined him pressing into me, my own flesh yielding to take him in, the impact of our two opposite but complementary sexual realities. As I scissor-kicked, I felt a phantom smoothness between my legs. My own body felt satiny and light and delicate in the water and I stretched languorously in the cool blue. I followed him for a few more laps, then I climbed out of the pool, showered, got dressed, and went home.

I told my partner that I needed to have a sex change, that I was physically not the person I was inside and indeed never had been.

I asked him if he loved me and he said yes. I asked him if he could love me as a woman. He held me and told me that he would always love me and support me, but that he was a gay man, not a straight man, and if I changed my sex, I would be taking the man he was in love with and replacing him with a woman he would *love*, but not be *in love with*.

I wept bitterly, thinking of the years I had spent as a gay man, the way I had finally located the male identity that had eluded me for much of my life, how I treasured it, and at that moment, I hated the woman in my head for this last imperious assault on my psyche.

I thought of my life as a gay man, the way it was growing and evolving, what gifts and yield I had already harvested from it. I thought of the long road to self-acceptance, the way I had begun to love myself as I never could before. I thought of my partner, who was holding me with such assured strength.

I could claim all this as mine, once and for all, or I could change my body to suit the woman who lived in my head, in the place behind my eyes that was as real as anything I could touch, whose need to assert herself had become so real and so insistent and begin again.

I told my partner I wished I was dead. He held me and assured me of how glad he was that I was alive, how much more perfect the world was for my presence in it, and how much he loved me. I thought of the years I believed that love was the exclusive province of the born-blessed, a privilege that others took for granted, and one to which no one as damaged as I was should even dare to aspire. As he held me, I wept against his shoulder, soaking his shirt. I felt a great ripping somewhere deep in the depths of my soul, as though I was being torn in half.

ooooo

THE FACTS OF MY own personal physical history are resolutely unremarkable: I am a forty year old gay man with dark brown hair and blue eyes. My skin is pale, and burns before tanning in a way that is classically English. I've been called handsome and I'm pleased to say that with the exception of smile crinkles around my eyes that I'm rather fond of (and which people tell me make me look friendly), I'm aging well, as the phrase goes. I tend towards largeness, not necessarily in body weight, though I'm not slim, but in the sense of a certain muscular lack of physical delicacy — a breadth of shoulders, a length of stride, of height. I *occupy space* in a way that is archetypically male. I am like my father in many ways and, like him, I can be effortlessly dominant in a way that doesn't always serve me well. I dress conservatively in a way that suits me, I think. There is nothing remotely feminine in my appearance or delivery and no one sees the woman who lived in my head when they look at me.

Frankly, I don't see her anymore myself and I sometimes miss her. She was with me for many good years and I knew her as well as I know myself now. She seems to me now like a beloved, long-dead relative who lives in the warm amber of memory.

I made the defining choice that night when I was twenty-four, and whatever my life could have been if I had altered its physical manifestation, it wouldn't have been better than the life I have now. Perhaps *as good*, but not *better*. My partner and I celebrated our eighteenth wedding anniversary this year. His love is my bulwark and both of us have allowed each other to be the best they can be, and both of us are individuals. As I've said before, my day begins with the sight of his sleeping face on the pillow next to mine and ends with the warmth of his body pressed next to mine in the dark, the sound of his soft breathing, his arm protectively thrown across my back. We're thought of by our friends as a model *couple*, let alone a model *gay* couple. I identify fully and joyously as a gay man, without apology and without ambivalence. I take pleasure in my body, in its strength and its hardness, its capacity to give and receive pleasure, its ability to endure pain when necessary, and its potential to protect me and those I love. I savour the differences between men and women, and occasionally find myself guilty of enjoying the male prerogatives that society has deemed my birthright. I have found comfort and peace in the perfect *click* between the exterior and the interior in a way that I couldn't have dreamed of when I was a young man on the threshold of my own life.

In the summer of 2002, I met two special women, both of whom had been men a million years ago, though in the face of their seamless femininity, I was unable to locate traces of it. They were both beautiful, both kind, both fiercely intelligent. Their strength was Promethean and I was in awe of it. Their life stories moved me beyond measure, and their accomplishment — aligning their bodies to suit their female gender — caused me to marvel. Through meeting them, I was finally able to confront my own most personal and private history and I was able to write it for the first time. I would be proud to believe that had I taken their path, I would have managed it with as much grace as they have. They are *women*, and their transgender is a badge of courage. I respect them too much to claim that title myself. I can't bring myself to compare my ordeal to theirs. Whatever I am, or was, I elect to leave it unnamed and I live in the present now.

At the same time, I dream of a day when all of us — lesbian, gay, transgendered, or anything in between — can take our places fully in the wider society, without reference or apology. A world that encompasses and celebrates *true* difference and diversity strikes me as something worth dreaming of and working for. The notion that the things which make us truly different and special ought to be treasured is wonderful. I dream of that day's eventual arrival and I pray that even if I'm not here to see it, some young person as plural as I was will be loved, and allowed to live as he is, without pressure to be something he isn't and, indeed, could never be. My writing has enabled me to explore many facets of gay life, focusing on the intersection between gay and straight culture, and why it is so terribly, terribly important that we all learn to celebrate what makes us different and unique and perfect, instead of wielding such sharp chisels in the relentless, bloody drive towards conformity.

I sense her presence inside me on certain days, but they're rare. She's a lady, after all, and would never impose herself in any obdurate way.

I feel her tenderness when I comfort a crying child, or a frightened dog. I feel a sense of proud, primal identification in the presence of certain women who embody the highest attainment of their gender, strong women who see no conflict between power and nurturing, women anyone would be proud to be. I feel her coquettish shade pass through me when I am in the company of a particularly handsome young man, or a twinge when I see a young mother whispering sweetness in the ear of her rapt infant, or a grandmother surrounded by adoring grandchildren, content in the knowledge that she will leave this earth well-seeded, and that she will live on in the eyes of her descendants. I remember her history when I catch the odd scent of Chantilly perfume, or the cool evening dampness of lake mist that reminds me of Geneva on a rainy afternoon. In those vertiginous moments, I gather up the discordant facets of my character, anoint them, and call them beautiful. I thank her for that gift of special sight, and call myself blessed.

ooooo

LAST JANUARY, I LEFT my father's home in Victoria and took the ferry back to Vancouver. I tucked the photographs away in my Filofax. I looked at them several times on the long ride. I stared and stared into the eyes of the little boy in the housedress and desperately tried to locate the line of demarcation between where his light went out, where he ceased to be, and where the man I am today began. I felt tears gather briefly as I looked into his sweet face, but I wiped them away lest anyone on the crowded ferry see me and stare.

Men rarely cry. Most of us have forgotten how to. I learned that lesson, as well as many others, a long time ago.

$\mathscr{A}$cknowledgements

THANKS, FIRST AND FOREMOST, to Marc Côté at Cormorant Books, for bringing together this collection of articles and essays, and believing there was a book there, and stories worth telling.

Thanks to my longtime assistant, Lyn Underwood, who has worked with me on all my books since the beginning and has become an indispensable part of my process.

I'm grateful to the magazine and anthology editors who've helped me craft the essays and journalism in this book: Mitchel Raphael at *fab* magazine; Muriel Duncan and Donna Sinclair at *The United Church Observer*; Greg Wharton, who commissioned, "My Life As A Girl," for his anthology *The Love That Dare Not Speak Its Name*; and Richard Labonte, who commissioned "Red Nights: Erotica and the Language of Men's Desire" for *Best Gay Erotica 2004*.

My editors at *The Advocate* — Bruce Steele, Alonso Duralde, John Caldwell, and especially Anne Stockwell — changed the course of my career when I began to write for them in 2000. To be an *Advocate* writer is to be working at the pinnacle of the gay journalism pyramid.

Thanks to Prudence Emery and Stephanie Keating, glamorous and showstopping redheads both (and publicists *par excellence*), for smoothing the process by which many of these interviews occurred, as did David Dodds at Seraphim Films, Jackie Ioachim at Showtime, and Lisa Ghione on the *Queer As Folk* set. Thanks also to *Soldier's Girl* producers Linda Gottlieb and Doro Bachrach, screenwriter Ron Nyswaner, and Calpernia Addams. Thanks to Pat and Wally Kutteles, for spending time with me in Kansas City and reliving painful memories of the events surrounding their son's cruel death in the hope that it might shine more light on the violence done to gay and lesbian soldiers every day in the U.S. military. Their trust of me with their son's story was humbling.

Thanks to my literary posse: Sephera Giron, Katherine Ramsland, Lauren B. Davis, Gemma Files, Sandra Kasturi and Brett Savory, William J. Mann, David Thomas Lord, David Nickle, Mark Wheaton, Michael Thomas Ford, and especially Steven Bereznai.

For their care of my well-being over many afternoons during the writing of this book, I would like to acknowledge Fadil Abdullah, Michael Arruda, Camilo Ballen, Claudia Diaz, David Marques, Hung Nguyen, Oana Gug, Janice Ho, Ali Salam, Ricardo Pascoe, and Rahel Abraha.

I owe a special note of thanks to Brad Niven, whose unfailing support during a very cruel time showed me what true friendship looks like in action, and how rare it actually is. In the same line of descent, sincere appreciation to my friend Eric Advokaat for those dark winter nights hiking the dog trails with Harper and Chelsea. And thanks to my friend Aaron Prothro.

And of course to Barney Ellis-Perry, Christopher Wirth, Nancy and Jay Bowers, Steward Noack, Tony Timpone, Nancy Anne Sakovich, Randy Murphy, Lesley Durnin, Consuelo Jackman and Tim Rostron, Alexandra Schleicher and James Small, Charly Lin, Jenny Griffiths, Michael G. Durrant, Jon Larson, Toni Wheeler, Michael Elliot, and Jean and Don Hutchison.

Likewise to Duncan Jackman, who has never passed up an opportunity to celebrate a friend's success, however small, with his warmth, kindness, and legendary generosity.

255

And to T.P. MacPherson, for reasons well known to both of us.

If this book didn't already have a worthy dedicatee, that distinction would unequivocally belong to Laurie Braun, one of the great passions of my life, and proof to me that the brightest lights can shine in the darkest places.

To my family — the Littles, the Gyles, the Shaws, the Olivers, my father Alan Rowe and his partner, Sarah Doughty, my husband Brian McDermid, and Shaw Madson and Jason Chow — the closet thing Brian and I will ever have to sons — much love.

And lastly, supreme thanks and love to Ron Oliver, for reasons both of us are too old and dignified to relate in public.

$\mathscr{P}$ublishing History

"Walking With the Ghost of Barry Winchell" first appeared in a slightly different form on *Advocate.com* on June 11, 2003; "Murder at Fort Campbell" first appeared in a slightly different form as "Lovers In A Dangerous Time" in *The Advocate*, May 27, 2003; "The Dealer Behind Fashion Cares" first appeared in *fab* magazine, May 22, 2003; "Drew Harris and the Oracle of Colour" appeared as a biographical essay in the Lydon Fine Art catalogue for the *Drew Harris Interpretations* exhibition at Lydon Fine Art Gallery in Chicago in July 2000; "The Full Paige" first appeared in a slightly different form in *The Advocate*, June 19, 2001; "Gale Force" first appeared in a slightly different form in *The Advocate*, February 5, 2002; "Hollywood Darkness: Clive Barker on *Coldheart Canyon*" first appeared in a slightly different form as "Horrors, It's Hollywood!" in *The Advocate*, December 4, 2001; "Eloise on Church St." first appeared as "Look My Darlings, This Is My Daughter" in a slightly different form in *fab* magazine, October 6, 2006; "The Carpenter's Hands" first appeared in a slightly different form as "The Long Road Back To Christianity: An Introduction to *The Highway*" in *The Highway: Reflections of a 21st Century Heretic* by Mark Braun (Philadelphia: Exlibris 2003); "The Reinvention of

Scott Merritt" first appeared in a slightly different form as "Great Scott" in *The Advocate*, August 19, 2003; "Red Nights: Erotica and The Language of Men's Desire" first appeared as the introductory essay to *Best Gay Erotica 2003*, Richard Labonte, ed. (San Francisco: Cleis Press, 2003); "In Praise of Queer Fear" first appeared as the introductory essay to *Queer Fear*, Michael Rowe, ed. (Vancouver: Arsenal Pulp Press, 2001) "Other Men's Sons" is original to this collection; "Our Libraries, Ourselves" is original to this collection; "From This Day Forward" first appeared in a slightly different form as "True and Honest and Finally Legal" in *The United Church Observer*, September 2003, and select paragraphs first appeared in *Hero* magazine in August 2000; "My Life as a Girl" first appeared in *The Love That Dares Not Speak Its Name: Essays on Queer Sexuality and Desire*, Greg Wharton, ed. (Wasaga Beach: Boheme Press, 2003.)